Founding Gods, Inventing Nations

Founding Gods, Inventing Nations

CONQUEST AND CULTURE MYTHS FROM ANTIQUITY TO ISLAM

William F. McCants

PRINCETON UNIVERSITY PRESS
PRINCETON AND OXFORD

Published by Princeton University Press, 41 William Street,
Princeton, New Jersey 08540
In the United Kingdom: Princeton University Press, 6 Oxford Street,
Woodstock, Oxfordshire OX20 1TW
press.princeton.edu

ISBN 978-0-691-15148-9

Library of Congress Cataloging-in-Publication Data

McCants, William Faizi, 1975-
Founding gods, inventing nations : conquest and culture myths from antiquity to Islam / William F. McCants.
p. cm.
Includes bibliographical references and index.
ISBN 978-0-691-15148-9 (hardcover)
1. Middle East—Civilization—Historiography. 2. Middle East—Civilization—Philosophy. 3. Civilization—Philosophy. 4. Mythology, Middle Eastern. 5. Middle East—Intellectual life. 6. Middle East—Colonization. 7. Greeks—Middle East—History. 8. Romans—Middle East—History. 9. Arabs—Middle East—History. 10. Acculturation—Middle East—History. I. Title.
DS57.M434 2012
939'.40072—dc22 2011009295

British Library Cataloging-in-Publication Data is available

This book has been composed in Palatino

Printed on acid-free paper. ∞

Printed in the United States of America

10 9 8 7 6 5 4 3 2 1

FOR MY FATHER,

---

who loves to tell the story of the founding of his nation, Texas

Contents

Acknowledgments

Thanks to Michael Cook, who advised the dissertation that became this book and encouraged me to publish it; to Peter Brown, who helped me develop its Hermetic kernel; and to Patricia Crone, who gave generously of her time and insight and introduced me to classicists with similar interests at a seminar on postcolonial ethnic chauvinism in antiquity. The seminar came too late to incorporate their thoughts into my dissertation, but I have now referenced their published work throughout.

Thanks also to my editor at Princeton University Press, Rob Tempio, for sticking with the project; to Ben Holmes and Dalia Geffen for ironing out the wrinkles; and to Princeton's anonymous reviewers, whose criticisms made the book much better. Any errors that remain are, of course, mine.

I am grateful to my family (Mom, Dad, David, Halleh, Martha, and Sina) and scholarly friends who kept the wind at my back. Of the latter, I want to thank Vahid Brown, Michael Doran, Najam Haider, Thomas Hegghammer, Stephanie Kaplan, Stephen Lambden, Todd Lawson, Afshon Ostovar, Sam Parker, and Farzin Vejdani. A special thanks to Michael Horowitz, who provided very helpful feedback at the last minute.

This book could not have been written without the support of my wife, Casey, and my colleague and friend Sholeh Quinn. With two little daughters, Ariana and Eva Daisy, and a full-time nonacademic job, I had no spare moments to work on the manuscript. Casey, determined that I should publish it, gave me every Sunday as "Book Day." Sholeh, equally determined, showed me how to make the revisions without making a mess. Thank you both from the bottom of my heart.

Founding Gods, Inventing Nations

Introduction

In the ninth century AD, Abū Maʿshar, an Iranian Muslim astronomer from Balkh (in modern-day Afghanistan), wrote that Adam and his grandson Hermes had founded the arts and sciences before the biblical Flood. Fearing that the coming Flood would eradicate "all the arts," Hermes inscribed knowledge of them for posterity in temples he built in Egypt. After the Flood, a second Hermes from Babylon retrieved this knowledge, and, through his student Pythagoras, it passed to the Greeks.[1] Prefacing this account, Abū Maʿshar explained that the Hebrews equated the first Hermes (a god in Greek mythology) with the biblical Enoch; that the Arabs equated him with the mysterious Idrīs mentioned in the Qur'an; and that the Persians equated him with the ancient Iranian king Hōshang and identified Adam with their first man and king, Gayōmart.

Abū Maʿshar's account is heavily indebted to pre-Islamic thought about the origins and transmission of the arts and sciences.[2] But it also reflects the social and intellectual tensions of ninth-century Iraq, the center of an Islamic empire whose Arab founders were losing their political dominance. At that time, scholarly elites with divergent learned traditions were competing for cultural ascendancy. Some of them were oriented toward Mecca and Jerusalem, others toward Persepolis, and still others toward Athens. They, like Abū Maʿshar, wrote about the origins and transmission of the arts and sciences not only out of antiquarian interest but also to tell their contemporary audiences what arts and sciences they should value and who should preserve them. Through their accounts of civilization's origins, they defined themselves and their groups, legitimated their authority, and differentiated their learning from competing traditions and claims. Comparing their accounts synchronically provides a map of early Muslim elites and the tensions between them; comparing them diachronically shows how the identity of these elites changed in response to political and social developments.

To understand what is unique about early Muslim theorizing on the origins

[1] Ibn Juljul, *Ṭabaqāt al-aṭibbā'*, 5–10.

[2] See Van Bladel's *Arabic Hermes* for a thorough discussion of the textual genealogy of Abū Maʿshar's account.

of civilization, it is necessary to compare it to similar periods of intense writing on the subject. The best analogs are the three hundred years following the establishment of Greek and Roman rule over the Near East (respectively 323–30 BC and 31 BC–337 AD),[3] which roughly approximates the three hundred years of prolific writing on civilization's origins following Muḥammad's death and the establishment of the Arab Islamic empire over almost the entire Near East (632–934 AD). All three conquering peoples hailed from the margins of the Near East, and their conquests united separate, complex societies with ancient native traditions of learning and legitimation distinct from those of the conquerors and one another.[4] The status of these traditions and those of the conquerors were worked out textually in the postconquest period through lists and histories of civilizational firsts. What these texts suggest is that the dominant understanding of civilization's origins that emerged three hundred years after each conquest was the product of a complex process of borrowing in which the conquerors took from the conquered and vice versa, and the conquered took from one another. Their reasons for doing so had as much to do with the immediate political and social dilemmas created by empire as they did with the workings of detached antiquarian pursuits.

There is at least one major difference between the three postconquest periods. The Greeks and Romans came to the Near East with a learned high culture, and native elites contested it, adopted it, or did something in between. But the conquering Arabs had no comparable learned culture; consequently, the conquerors and conquered argued over the next three centuries about the content of not only "Islamic" but also "Arab" identity and scholarship. As this book demonstrates, the orientation of early Islamic culture was not fixed toward Arabia, and its content drew as much from pagan learning and mythology as it did from religious scripture. What we know today as Islamic culture is the product of a contested process of self-legitimation in the first three centuries of the Islamic era—a process reflected in the mythmaking of the period and whose protagonists drew heavily on the lore of non-Arab and pagan antiquity.

In all three postconquest periods, etiological speculation clustered around four subjects: divine providence, first inventors, founders of native civilization, and the origins of the sciences. A fifth subject, theories of cultural formation in prehistory (*Kulturentstehungslehre*), was a feature of only pagan Greco-

[3] The periods are not exactly analogous because unlike Alexander's conquest of the Near East, the extension of Roman rule over the region covered less territory and was a gradual process, beginning with the defeat of Asia in 188 BC and its establishment as a Roman province in 133 BC. Seleucid-ruled Syria and Ptolemaic-ruled Aegyptus did not become Roman provinces until the mid- to late first century BC.

[4] Compare this with the Mongol conquests of the Near East in the thirteenth and fourteenth centuries AD, which did not lead to the proliferation of culture myths. The relative homogeneity of Near Eastern elite culture at that time (compared with the three periods treated here) and the conquerors' adoption of it may explain the difference.

Roman society. Other peoples, including many Greeks and Romans, rejected the idea of an ancient, unknowable history and instead explained the origins of culture by attributing it to heroes living at the dawn of recorded events (*Kulturgeschichte*).[5]

The modern terminology used to describe this material and its object of study can be confusing. Folklorists use the term *etiology*, which they apply to any myth about the origins of things (e.g., rituals, rocks, alchemy).[6] A more apt but less used term is *culture myth*, or myths about the origins of the arts and sciences.[7] *Culture heroes* are famous figures who originated them.[8] In this book, I prefer *culture myth* because it is more restrictive than *etiology*, but I use both terms interchangeably to refer to myths about the origins of the arts and sciences of civilization. Similarly, my use of the word *culture* refers to these arts and sciences. This is a more restrictive definition of culture than that employed by anthropologists, which can include all learned thought and behavior.

As for what constitutes "the arts and sciences," it depends on whom one asks. The Sumerians used the term *me* and the ancient Greeks *technai* to refer to everything associated with complex civilization, but they did not define their terms; definitions have to be inferred from usage and can include arts like poetry and pottery as well as sciences like mathematics. The Sophists, who were among the first to think about cultural formation in prehistory, limited *technai* to skills based on knowledge and experience that improved life and embellished it; for them, geometry and astronomy were not included.[9] In the fourth century BC, Plato and Aristotle disagreed with the Sophists' negative valuation of the mathematical sciences, which they classified as *epistēme* (knowledge as such), but concurred that they should be separated from technai (knowledge that serves practical needs), giving us our phrase "arts and sciences." Nevertheless, there was and still is confusion over what disciplines belong to each category.[10] For this book, I define "the arts and sciences" as disciplines that are learned, that alter humanity's relationship with nature, and that are commonly

[5] On the distinction between theories of cultural formation in prehistory and the history of culture, see Zhmud, *Origins*, 48–49, 51, 54. The explanation for why theorizing on prehistory was confined to pagan Greco-Roman authors is in Matthew Goodrum's "Prolegomenon" and "Biblical Anthropology," but he incorrectly singles out the early Church Fathers for rejecting the idea of an ancient, unknowable history. A number of Greek and Roman authors, going back to Hesiod in the eighth century, held the same view.

[6] Childs, "Etiological Tale," 388; Sharon, *Patterns*, 74, 76; Niesiołowski-Spanò, "Two Aetiological Narratives," 369–70.

[7] Spence, *Introduction*, 149; Rüpke, *Religion of the Romans*, 128. *Webster's Revised Unabridged Dictionary* defines a culture myth as "a myth accounting for the discovery of arts and sciences or the advent of a higher civilization, as in the Prometheus myth" (1998).

[8] Spence, *Introduction*, 119; Leeming, *Storytelling*, 130–31; Seal, *Folk Heroes*, 51–53; Bastian and Mitchell, *Native American Mythology*, 83; Hansen, *Classical Mythology*, 141–43; Yang, An, and Turner, *Chinese Mythology*, 261; Espín and Nicholoff, *Introductory Dictionary*, 302.

[9] Zhmud, *Origins*, 46.

[10] Ibid., 14, 20–21; Cuomo, *Technology*, 13, 18.

associated with complex urban societies. The one exception is language, which, although it is a feature of both simple and complex societies, is included here because the Greeks, Romans, and Arabs believed it to be the necessary precursor of complex civilization.

Classicists, biblical scholars, and scholars of the ancient Near East have thought more about culture myths than have Islamicists (academic scholars of Islam). One reason is that the first three groups have long debated the influence of Near Eastern myths, including culture myths, on the Bible.[11] Another is that classicists have been interested in whether antique authors had a concept of progress.[12] More recently, classicists have explored modern postcolonial approaches to understanding the nature of native identity after conquests of the ancient Near East.[13] All of these inquiries involve culture myths. In comparison, there has been little discussion of the notion of progress[14] or postcolonial[15] identity in early Islam,[16] and Islamic culture myths have less relevance to the debate about the Hebrew Bible's date and origin.

Because the study of pre-Islamic culture myths is so well developed compared with the study of early Islamic culture myths, I have foregrounded the former and used it to frame the Islamic material in the following chapters. This framing also reflects my belief that Islamic thinking about the origins of civilization is deeply indebted to antique thought on the subject, both in content and assumptions. Furthermore, Muslim authors were shaped by social and political circumstances that were similar to those confronting Hellenistic- and Roman-

[11] For a good example of how this debate still embroils scholars of ancient, classical, and biblical mythology, see Gmirkin's attempts to justify a late date for the Pentateuch (*Berossus and Genesis*).

[12] For example, Dodds, *Ancient Concept of Progress*; Edelstein, *Idea of Progress*; Guthrie, *In the Beginning*.

[13] See Bohak, "Recent Trends"; Malkin, "Postcolonial Concepts"; Moyer, "Limits of Hellenism"; Barclay, "Empire Writes Back"; and Lyman, "Justin and Hellenism."

[14] The only treatment of the idea of progress in classical Islam of which I am aware is Khalidi's "The Idea of Progress in Classical Islam." His attempt to divide classical Islamic thinking on progress into three periods is undermined by his anachronistic quotations. Thus, he adduces Jāḥiẓ (d. 869 AD) as an example of stage-two optimism about scientific progress, which lasted from 900 to 1100 AD (282). As I will argue in chapter 5, pessimism and optimism about scientific progress were concurrent. To his credit, Khalidi acknowledges that the reality may be more complex and offers his article as a starting point for others (284–85).

[15] As Patricia Crone ("Post-Colonialism," 2) recently observed, scholars of early Islam are not comfortable with the term, which includes the immediate postconquest period. Presumably, it is out of fear of anachronism. That is a shame, since there are a number of historical parallels with classical and modern postcolonialism, and the early Islamic period can enrich the theoretical literature and also benefit from it.

[16] Crone ("Imperial Trauma" and "Post-Colonialism") has analyzed early Arab Muslim anxieties about their fading power but does not look at how the conquered peoples represented themselves. Tavakoli-Targhi ("Contested Memories") has engaged with postcolonial theory, but only to look at the creation of the dominant Muslim discourse about Iranian history. Similarly, Bashear (*Arabs and Others*) looks at how Arabs saw others, not how others represented themselves to Arabs.

era authors and thus share many of their concerns and solutions to intellectual and cultural dilemmas. Finally, by bringing Islamic material into the debates of classicists, I hope to encourage scholarly communities on both sides of the Arab conquests to consider the Mediterranean and Near Eastern patrimony through a wider-angle lens.

The indebtedness of Islamic culture myths to antiquity is not only evidenced by the fact that Islamic culture myths cluster around the same subject areas as pre-Islamic culture myths but also by the fact that there are numerous linkages between the myths themselves. I have organized the chapters around these subject areas, preceded by an introductory chapter on ancient culture myths to set the stage and provide a point of reference.

Thinking about the origins of civilization is as old as written history. Nearly all of ancient Near Eastern mythology that treats the subject depicts the gods or their divine interlocutors as purveyors of civilization's arts, which are wholly beneficial. Greek and Jewish myths are different, perhaps because they are comparatively new (i.e., first millennium BC rather than third or second). Greek myth preserves the Near Eastern model of a beneficent deity, but the deity teaches humans the rudiments of civilization only after another god punishes them by making them toil for their sustenance. Humans later invent ironsmithing, which leads to violence and eventually humanity's demise. Jewish myth is similar to the Greek in that humans acquire culture after a deity punishes them with toiling for their sustenance; however, they acquire culture of their own ingenuity. The deity has nothing to do with it and frowns on their innovations, which eventually lead to the invention of ironsmithing and the destruction of humanity. Ironically, these two pessimistic stories of civilization's origins, written on the margins of the great powers of the Near East, were the primary culture myths of civilizations that came to value human ingenuity.

Although the Qur'an is a "biblical" text in the sense that it draws heavily on the stories of the Bible, the Qur'anic conception of cultural origins is similar to that of the ancient Near Eastern authors: a beneficent sky god, Allah, gives culture—even ironsmithing—to humans. However, this is not a revival of ancient mythology but the confluence of two Hellenistic developments. The first is that of Jews and Christians adopting the Greek Stoics' notion of divine providence, in which God must be the provider of everything. The second development is noncanonical Jewish and Christian scriptures that envision a more positive role for God in the development of civilization. The author of the Qur'an draws on the examples and arguments found in these separate literary traditions to bolster his claim that if humans do not properly worship their ultimate Provider, He will give their possessions to others. This claim may have provided a justification for the Arab conquests of the complex civilizations of the Near East.

The Arabs were politically dominant for only a century following the conquests. As their dominance faded, scholars in Iraq began compiling lists of cultural "firsts" (*awā'il*) attributed to biblical and Arab heroes.[17] Their writing about firsts, an activity I call "protography,"[18] reflects their scholarly interest in the biblical background of the Qur'an and the Arab environs that produced it. Their lists were also an attempt to make sense of a century of religious and cultural innovation and inter-Arab rivalry by grounding it in pre-Islamic tradition. A similar period of innovation and rivalry preceded the creation of Greek protography,[19] suggesting a correlation between cultural competition and the flourishing of protography.

Muslim authors of awā'il lists were initially reluctant to recognize the contribution of ancient foreign civilizations to their culture. Indeed, some authors in the ninth century wrote awā'il lists that studiously ignored foreign influences, emphasizing only the Arab and Abrahamic character of the empire at a time when it was rapidly turning toward Iran. Pre-Islamic Greek and Roman protographical lists, in contrast, almost always included foreign influences, although some authors were no less uneasy about it than their Muslim counterparts. Christian apologists in the Roman era exploited these lists of foreign firsts to

[17] The best bibliographical surveys of awā'il lists are Rosenthal's article on awā'il in the *Encyclopedia of Islam* (2nd ed.) and ʿAbd al-ʿAzīz al-Māniʿ's English introduction to his edition of Ibn Bāṭīsh's (d. 655 AH/1257 AD) *Ghāyat al-wasā'il* (al-Māniʿ, "An Edition of *Ghāyat al-wasā'il*"). For brief treatments of the place of awā'il literature in Islamic historiography, see Noth, *Historical Tradition*, 104–7; Wansbrough, *Sectarian Milieu*, 36; Khalidi, *Historical Thought*, 34; Dziekan, "Origins of Things," 26. See Lang, "Awā'il," for a more extended discussion.

[18] Classicists call this material heurematography, or writing about discoveries. The term is based on the Greek *prōtoi heuretai*, "first discoverers," which is a genre of literature that originated in fourth-century BC Greece. *Heurematography* has the virtue of being more restrictive than *etiology* (myth of origins) and describes a genre of literature that is more self-consciously about civilizational firsts. However, it implies that civilizational firsts should be thought of as discoveries or inventions, which is not always the case; Greek texts often have gods revealing technology to humans. The Arabs, on the other hand, use the less restrictive term *awā'il*, "firsts," for the same type of material. In a nod to the linguistic and textual similarities between the Greco-Roman and Arabic texts, I prefer the term *protography*, or "writing about firsts," which is less expansive than *etiology* but not as restrictive as *heurematography*. I sometimes refer to an instance of protography as a "protograph" or "protographical material."

[19] There have been several good surveys of Greek and Latin etiological literature written in German, the most recent of which is Klaus Thraede's article on inventors ("Erfinder II"). There has also been one attempt to link this literature with Arabic awā'il lists in an 1867 article by Richard Gosche, "Das Kitāb al-awā'il." Later awā'il lists, whether scattered throughout chronologies and biographies or compiled into lists, are almost always drawn from works written in the first three centuries. For good examples of awā'il digests, see al-Shiblī's (d. 769 AH/1367 AD) *Maḥāsin al-wasā'il fī maʿrifat al-awā'il* and Suyūṭī's (d. 911 AH/1505 AD) *Wasā'il ilā maʿrifat al-awā'il*. The same could be said of medieval European literature on inventors, which consisted basically of catalogs of classical etiological literature (for a good example, see Polydore Vergil's *On Discovery*). In both cases, the respect of later authors for the earlier classical traditions made them more inclined to compile earlier opinions on the origins of culture rather than to posit their own—a sort of closing of the *wasā'il al-awā'il*. There were also social and political reasons why new etiologies were not devised after this period.

demonstrate that Greco-Roman culture was barbarian derived and thus no less foreign than Christianity.

Muslims who wrote lists of Arab cultural achievements were modest in their own way, claiming only parochial firsts for the Arabs. But this could also be exploited by the conquered, as when Iranian authors supplemented lists of underwhelming Arab accomplishments with the universal achievements of ancient Iranian kings, such as their invention of statecraft. Iranians did the same in early postconquest histories of Iranian civilization. Although they wrote them in Arabic and retained the biblical and Qur'anic narrative of events and personalities, they also emphasized the secular achievements of the first Iranian kings.

These native accounts of civilization's origins do not fit neatly into the categories of resistance, assimilation, or hybridity in postcolonial theories of native literature.[20] They neither explicitly challenge the dominant discourse nor merely reproduce and reinforce it. [21] Homi Bhabha's concept of hybridity is a better fit, since the resulting historiographical mix was neither wholly Islamic nor wholly Iranian and thus destabilizing for both. [22] But scholars looking for a hegemonic culture that native authors were resisting, assimilating to, or mixing with may miss the fact that there was no dominant culture. Instead, the cultural orientation of Islamic scholarship was heavily contested, and Iranian authors were just as likely to try to persuade the conquerors to become more like the conquered as they were to adopt their culture. In this, some Iranian histories of civilization written in Arabic are similar to accounts of civilization's origins written in Greek by native elites after the Greek and Roman conquests of the Near East. These earlier native histories sought to correct cultural misunderstandings, teach the foreign rulers to behave like local kings, bolster the author's status as custodian of an ancient culture, and diminish the achievements of other competing civilizations. The early Iranian native histories functioned in the same way. They also became the basis of a national epic, the *Shāhnāmih*, and legitimized the establishment of independent Iranian dynasties, demonstrating the ambiguity of boasting about ancient cultural achievements. Such boasting could be intended to draw the conquerors closer as well as to push them away.

The growing Iranian influence on the Islamic empire led to the translation of Greek scientific texts into Arabic because the Muslim rulers styled themselves as Iranian kings, one of whose functions was to patronize translations of this

[20] There is a growing body of literature that argues for the application of postcolonial theory to the premodern period, particularly in biblical (Seesengood, "Hybridity," 10n3), Hellenistic (Malkin, "Postcolonial Concepts," passim; Barclay, "Rhetoric," 318), and Roman studies (Lyman, "Justin and Hellenism"). There are also dozens of monographs that apply the theory (for example, Vasunia's *Gift of the Nile*).

[21] For the two categories, see Said, *Culture and Imperialism*, 195, and Spivak, "Can the Subaltern Speak?" 296.

[22] Bhabha, *Location of Culture*, 102–22; Barclay, "Empire Writes Back," 317.

sort. Muslim and non-Muslim elites also needed scientific texts for practical purposes, such as the practice of medicine, and for resolving the religious quandaries of the day, which had become acute in cosmopolitan Baghdad.

The translation of these texts led to speculation about the origins of some of the disciplines they described—mainly philosophy, the mathematical sciences, and medicine. In antiquity, such speculation had arisen in periods of intense social and political disruption and centered on the question of the role that the Greeks had played in creating the sciences. First, had the Greeks originated anything of their own or taken it from others? The Greeks certainly originated many sciences, but their tendency to attribute Eastern origins to them encouraged non-Greeks to do the same. Second, could humans develop complex sciences with the unaided human mind? Many believed they could not and instead required divine revelation to get things started.

The same two questions are found in early Islamic histories of science, with advocates on both sides of each question. The solution that won out was that the sciences had come from the biblical prophets, who were more ancient and who had access to revelation. This was the same solution arrived at by some Roman-era Jews and the Church Fathers. But whereas Jews and Christians had advanced this argument primarily to blunt the pagan charge of being cultural traitors, Muslims advanced it to make the sciences safe in the eyes of their coreligionists.

In recounting these culture myths, authors worked out their place in post-conquest society. By describing the origin and transmission of science, they tell us where they stand in relation to that tradition, to their contemporaries who practice it, and to those who detract from it. By writing histories of the cultural exploits of ancient heroes, they tell us how they think of their ethnic origins and how others can join or be excluded from their group. By making lists of beneficial arts and sciences, they encode the ideal cultural genealogy of their societies and provide the knowledge needed to navigate it. By demonstrating how God works in the world, they explain how society should be ordered and who should maintain it. These scholarly activities were at no time more important than after conquest, when the place of the conqueror and the conquered were both unstable and in need of mooring to the ancient past.

Although the primary material surveyed in this book is old, it is hard not to draw parallels to groups and historical processes today, living as we do only a few decades after the end of European rule in large parts of the Near East. I have resisted this temptation until the conclusion—and there treated it only tentatively—so as not to distract from the subject at hand or force it into a framework too shaped by modern concerns. That said, the parallels are striking: conquerors leaving behind languages of scholarship and science in which the conquered articulate their native traditions; the competition over cultural priority; the heightened interest in civilization's origins; and the emergence of a new story of civilization's development that is neither that of the conquerors nor that of the conquered.

Perhaps the parallel that will strike readers most, because of its immediacy, is the similarity between Jews living under Roman rule and Muslims living in the West today. The hostility the Jews faced and the strategies they developed to overcome it while preserving their identity remind one of the hostility Western Muslims currently face and the thin line Muslim elites walk between assimilation and resistance. As this book demonstrates, early Islamic identity was fluid and a product of more than the Arabian desert, which should give pause to both Muslims and non-Muslims who claim Islam is incompatible with modernity and civilization. Indeed, Jews living under Roman rule, who were similarly accused and who had a scripture that took a dim view of civilization, created a form of Judaism—Christianity—that became the religion of their conquerors and laid the foundations of Western civilization.

ONE

Gifts of the Gods: The Origins of Civilization in Ancient Near Eastern and Greek Mythology

The lord, that which is appropriate verily he caused to appear,
The lord whose decisions are unalterable,
Enlil, who brings up the seed of the land from the earth,
Took care to move away heaven from earth,
Took care to move away earth from heaven.
In order to make grow the creature which came forth,
In the "bond of heaven and earth" (Nippur) he stretched out the . . .
He brought the pickax into existence, the "day" came forth,
He *introduced labor*, decreed the fate,
Upon the pickax and basket he directs the "power."
Enlil made his pickax exalted,
His pickax of gold, whose head is of lapis lazuli,
The pickax of his house, of . . . silver and gold,
His pickax whose . . . is of lapis lazuli,
Whose *tooth* is a one-horned ox ascending a large wall.
The lord called up the pickax, decrees its fate,
He set the *kindu*, the holy crown, upon his head,
The head of man he placed in the mould,
Before Enlil *he covers* his land,
Upon his black-headed people he looked steadfastly.
The Anunnaki who stood about him,
He placed *it* as a gift in their hands,
They soothe Enlil with prayer,
They give the pickax to the black-headed people to hold.

—"The Creation of the Pickax"

To Adam (God) said, "Because you have listened to the voice of your wife, and have eaten of the tree of which I commanded you, 'You shall not eat of it,' cursed is the ground because of you; in toil you shall eat of it all the days of your life; thorns and thistles it shall bring forth to you; and you shall eat the plants of the field. In the sweat of your face you shall eat bread till you return to the ground, for out of it you were taken; you are dust, and to dust you shall return."

—Genesis 3:17–19

To see how the Greek, Roman, and Arab conquests of the Near East shaped the conqueror's and conquered's understanding of the origins of civilization, I begin with a survey of the region's ancient mythologies before the conquests: Mesopotamian, Iranian, Egyptian, Greek, and Hebrew (the surviving Hurrian, Hittite, and Canaanite texts do not treat the subject). In Mesopotamian, Iranian, and Egyptian myths, gods create civilization ex nihilo and give it to humans, sometimes through special human or semihuman interlocutors. The arts and sciences they create are almost always beneficial, and their point of origin is usually associated with cities, not with peoples.

Beginning in the early first millennium BC, we see two exceptions to this pattern; these are in the Greek myths of Hesiod, a late-eighth-century BC Greek poet, and in the Hebrew myths of the so-called Yahwist author of the Adam and Eve story in Genesis. In them, humans cope with their fall from divine favor by inventing technology. However, invention is not a good thing, for it leads to the development of metallurgy, iron weapons, violence, and finally the demise of humanity. It is also not created by the gods in cities but by bronze and iron races (*genē* in Hesiod) or by a sinful tribe descended from the first man and woman (according to the Yahwist account). Thus, at the end of the Iron Age and on the eve of the Persian invasions of the Near East and the Ionian peninsula, there was a new conceptual development in Near Eastern and Greek mythology: peoples had created civilization, and it was bad.

The similarity of the two myths is not only due to their common Near Eastern origin (Hesiod's father had emigrated from Cyme, on the coast of modern Turkey).[1] It is also due to the shared perspective of the authors. Both men, separated perhaps by only a century, wrote on the margins of greater Near Eastern powers, and their works reflect the disdain of rural agriculturalists for the violence and urbanization associated with empire building, which was anathema to their ideal of the good life.

The genres of texts surveyed below are heterogeneous because of the ways that culture myths from the different ancient societies survived. Mesopotamian myths survived in poems and medicinal texts inscribed on clay tablets, Egyptian myths in paintings and inscriptions adorning funerary structures and other monuments, and Iranian myths in oral traditions. Because of their antiquity and obscure context, the specific motives of the scribes and authors for recording the texts are not always clear. Since most of the texts resulted from state patronage, one might suppose that their contents benefited the state's interests (e.g., to appear as guardians of tradition, to legitimate themselves as heirs to ancient empires). The myths might also have benefited the scribes or priests who

[1] Nelson and Grene, *God and the Land*, 38. The first epigraph is a third-millennium Sumerian poem taken from Kramer, *Sumerian Mythology*, 51–52. The translation and formatting are his. Ellipses indicate lacunae in the original.

preserved them by connecting them to an ancient tradition and justifying that tradition's importance, thus reinforcing their role as cultural guardians. In some texts written by authors who had lost their state and been conquered by others, as may have been the case with the Yahwist, one can also see evidence of culture myths being used to delegitimize the conquering state. Thus, in addition to providing much of the substance for later culture myths, ancient Near Eastern mythography also prefigures some of the strategies of legitimation and delegitimation that later native authors used after foreign conquests of their land.

Ancient Near Eastern Culture Myths

The dominant way of thinking about cultural transmission among the inhabitants of the ancient Near East was that culture was a gift received directly from the gods in the distant past;[2] for the most part, these cultural bestowals were beneficial. This notion reflected political developments in the Near East in the late fourth and early third millennium BC: as Near Eastern societies reached a level of organization that enabled them to establish the institution of kingship, their mythology followed suit. Thus, in third-millennium Sumerian poetry—the earliest record of Near Eastern mythology—a high god is depicted as the ruler of a city, with lesser gods attending his court; rather than being identical to basic natural forces (as they might have been in earlier mythology),[3] the gods are differentiated from these forces and are responsible for their maintenance, each one taking a separate task.[4] Usually, it was the high god who dispensed culture, just as the earthly king was the source of patronage for the arts and sciences.

The supreme god in Sumerian mythology was Enlil, the sky god. As the chief authority, he was the one by whose leave much culture came into being, either through his permission for others to create it or through his direct intervention. The "Hymn to Enlil" portrays Enlil acting behind the scenes:

> Without (warrant of) the great mountain, Enlil,
> no city could be built,
> no population settled therein,
> no cattlepen built, its sheepfold not set up.
> No king could be raised to office,
> no lord created
> No high priest or high priestess
> designated by the (omen-)kid,

[2] Castellino, "Origins," 93; Van Seters, *Prologue*, 66.
[3] Jacobsen, *Treasures*, 21, 26, 73.
[4] Ibid., 80–84.

> among the troops no general and lieutenant
> could be had.[5]

In "The Creation of the Pickax," quoted at the beginning of this chapter, Enlil has a more direct role. He causes seeds to grow in the earth and gives humans the pickax so they can harvest its fruits.[6]

Another major purveyor of culture in third-millennium Sumerian poetry is the water god Enki. As a water god, Enki not only fertilizes the earth but molds it, giving rise to the depiction of him as an artificer.[7] Sometimes he works with the sky god Enlil to produce culture. Thus, in the myth "Cattle and Grain," the two gods send the sibling gods Lahar and Ashnan to earth. The two gods set up a sheepfold for Lahar, who becomes a shepherd, and they give a plow and yoke to his sister, Ashnan, who becomes a farmer (there is no mention of how this technology is passed on to humans). Although relations between the two godlings are initially amicable, they begin to quarrel after drinking too much wine, which leads each of them to boast of his or her livelihood and denigrate that of the other.[8]

Elsewhere, Enki acts alone. In "Enki and the World Order," he bestows the plow, yoke, pickax, and brick mold on the people of Sumer. He then turns his attention to the construction of dwellings and bestows the *gugun* (a building tool) on humans, sets foundations, and builds houses. After this, he populates the land with animals and plants and builds stables and sheepfolds. Along the way he appoints various gods to oversee these gifts.[9]

Enki's role as a purveyor of civilization is a motif that also appears in the myth "Inanna and Enki: The Transfer of the Arts of Civilization from Eridu to Uruk." In it, Inanna, the queen of heaven and patron goddess of the Sumerian city Uruk, wants to make her city the center of civilization. Therefore, she decides to go to Eridu, Enki's city, and obtain his *me*, the foundations of civilization. Enki provides a banquet for her and, after becoming drunk, gives her over a hundred of these *me*.[10] Although these largely pertain to kingship and cult, he also gives her the *me* of art, music, musical instruments, carpentry, metalworking, the scribal arts, smithcraft, leatherworking, masonry, and basket weaving, all of which she takes to Uruk.[11]

[5] Ibid., 100–101.

[6] Kramer, *Sumerian Mythology*, 51–52; see Jacobsen, *Treasures*, 103.

[7] Jacobsen, *Treasures*, 111.

[8] Kramer, *Sumerian Mythology*, 53–54. This sibling rivalry between a shepherd and an agriculturalist is reminiscent of the story of Cain and Abel. The connection between farming, wine, and drunkenness also recalls the story of Noah (see below).

[9] Ibid., 59–62; see Jacobsen, *Treasures*, 115.

[10] Kramer, *Sumerian Mythology*, 64–66; and see the more recent translation in Kraemer and Maier, *Myths of Enki*, 59–63.

[11] Kramer, *Sumerian Mythology*, 66; Kraemer and Maier, *Myths of Enki*, 62–63.

This final etiology foregrounds a theme that runs throughout a number of these Sumerian creation myths: civilization is intimately associated with the patron deity of a particular city—Enki is the patron god of Eridu, Enlil of Nippur, and Inanna of Uruk. This association between deities, cities, and the creation of culture reflects the political organization of Sumer in the third millennium BC, which was a collection of independent city-states for most of that time.

Although gods were the primary donors of culture in Mesopotamian mythology, they were not the only ones. Seven half-men, half-fish "sages" (*apkallē*, *apkallu* sing.) served the god Ea (called Enki in Sumerian texts) as upholders of the cosmic order and as dispensers of the foundations of civilization (*me*).[12] This latter function is preserved in their names—the third of the apkallē is called Enmedugga ("lord of the good *me*"), the fourth Enmegalamma (lord of the *me* of the land), and the fifth Enmebulugga, which might mean "lord of the *me* of enormous greatness."[13] Their culture-bringer function is also alluded to in several texts. For example, a medical tablet from Ashurbanipal's library claims to record knowledge of salves and bandages written by the apkallē "from before the Flood."[14] The myth titled "Twenty-one Poultices" suggests that they did not originate this knowledge themselves but merely conveyed it from Ea,[15] whom they joined in the abyss after the Flood, according to the *Epic of Erra*.[16]

While pre-Flood culture seems to have largely been the gift of the gods or their messengers in Mesopotamian mythology, its rebirth after the Flood is the work of human hands. In *Gilgamesh*, the human Utnapishtim "restored to their rightful place cult centers which the Flood had ruined."[17] He may have been assisted in this endeavor by the craftsmen he put on board the ark,[18] but we are not told so. We are also not told that he invented anything new; he just remade what he remembered from the antediluvian period, perhaps based on a "tale of times before the Flood" that he brought back with him.[19]

Although Utnapishtim cannot be credited with any sort of creativity, another Sumerian myth, "Enmerkar and the Lord of Aratta" (from the first half of the second millennium), indicates that there was a place for human innovation in Mesopotamian thought. In this story, Enmerkar, the second king of Uruk after the Flood, wants to build a lavish temple for the gods in his city. Since he lacks

[12] Reiner, "Seven Sages," 6, 9–10; Hallo, "Antiquity," 176; Dalley, "Near Eastern Myths," 49–50; Dalley, "Semiramis," 13; Lenzi, "Uruk List."

[13] Kvanvig, *Roots*, 193.

[14] Lenzi, "Uruk List," 149–51.

[15] Lambert, "Poultices"; Greenfield, "Apkallu," 72.

[16] Greenfield, "Seven Pillars," 16.

[17] Dalley, *Myths*, 51.

[18] Ibid., 112.

[19] Ibid., 50. The standard Babylonian redaction of *Gilgamesh* also plays on this buried wisdom motif when it claims to be the hidden record of Gilgamesh's journeys (Michalowski, "Commemoration," 79).

the necessary precious stones and metals, he sends a messenger to the ruler of Aratta, a wealthy city. This messenger runs back and forth relaying messages between the two men. Eventually he tires out. Seeing this, Enmerkar creates a clay tablet and writes his message to the ruler of Aratta. The text explicitly says that this was the origin of writing on clay tablets: "Formerly, the writing of messages on clay was not established."[20] It is best to see this final etiological myth as an exception to the general model of cultural development in Mesopotamian mythology—the etiologies of culture in these myths usually place cultural creation in the hands of the gods, who gave it as a gift to humans either directly or through the apkallē.

To the east of Mesopotamia, records of Iranian lore that can be reliably dated before the Arab conquests (but may be much more recent than the other myths surveyed here)[21] exhibit the same pattern: a god sends down culture or instructs humans in its use. Thus, in the twentieth *fargard*—a section of the Avestan *Vendīdād*, a religious text on how to thwart evil spirits—Zoroaster asks Ahura Mazdā, "Who was he who [was] first of the healers?"[22] Ahura Mazdā answers that it was Thrita (a priest), to whom he had sent down healing plants and to whom Khshathra-Vairya—one of Ahura Mazdā's spiritual companions associated with metal—gave a "source of remedies" (presumably a surgical knife).[23]

A similar pattern of cultural bestowal is found in the story of Yima. In the second fargard of the *Vendīdād*, we learn that Yima was the first mortal man to converse with Ahura Mazdā and learn of the religion of Zoroaster. However, he refuses to be a bearer of Ahura Mazdā's religion and to teach it to others.[24] Ahura Mazdā then asks him to govern the world and cause it to flourish, to which Yima consents. Ahura Mazdā bestows on Yima the "golden seal and a poniard inlaid with gold" as symbols of his sovereignty.[25] After ruling for three hundred years, Yima has to increase the size of the earth, since it is too small to contain all the men and their herds. During the next fifteen hundred years, he does this twice more. Ahura Mazdā then warns Yima that "evil winters" are about to freeze the world and tells him how to build an enclosure (*vara*) from the earth in which specimens of each animal and plant species can be sheltered.[26]

[20] Translation by Black et al., *Electronic Text* (http://etcsl.orinst.ox.ac.uk/cgi-bin/etcsl.cgi; accessed January 2, 2010), lines 500–514. See Michalowski, "Commemoration," 83–84.

[21] The *Vendīdād*, cited below, is probably from the Achaemenid period (ca. 550–330 BC) but preserves much older material (see MacKenzie, "Bundahišn," in *Encyclopedia Iranica*).

[22] Anon., *Vendīdād* 20.1 (in *Zend-Avesta*, pt. 1).

[23] Ibid., 20.3–4. *Fargard* 7.44 lists three kinds of doctors: those who heal with a knife, those who heal with herbs, and those who heal with the "Holy Word."

[24] Ibid., 2.2–3. The *Dēnkard* notes that Yima rejected the religion of Ahura Mazdā because of his "attachment to the religion of the ancients." The *Dēnkard* does remark that he accepted instruction from Ahura Mazdā on "other things to develop, extend, and improve the world thereby" (*Dēnkard*, bk. 8, chap. 44, in West, *Pahlavi Texts*, part 4).

[25] *Vendīdād* 2.4–6.

[26] Ibid., 2.11–38.

As with the story of Thrita, the portrayal of Yima has all the elements of a Near Eastern etiology of culture: a god gives culture to a human, and a catastrophe threatens to eradicate it. There are also some important Iranian elements, such as the bestowal of universal kingship.

In the west, contemporaneous second-millennium Near Eastern myths from Anatolia and Syria yield even less information on the origins of culture. From Anatolia, the Hurrian *Kumarbi Cycle* of songs tells us a great deal about the creation of the gods and their infighting,[27] but says nothing at all about the origins of culture. Hittite mythology is similarly lacking.[28] Canaanite myths found in Ras Shamra in northern Syria tell us a bit more about cultural origins, but there are no clear etiologies of culture.[29] For example, in the *Baal Cycle*, a fourteenth-century BC text, we are not given a cosmogony or anthropogony. We do read that the high god El is the "Creator of Creatures" (his epithet),[30] but we are not told how he created his creatures or provided for their welfare. As for the creation of culture, the smithing god Kothar-wa-Khasis does create material culture: he builds a palace for El and for his rival Baal.[31] He also makes a gold and silver throne, along with a table and ornamental bowls,[32] and he fashions two different double-headed maces for Baal so that he can defeat El's son Yamm.[33] But it is not clear that these passages about Kothar-wa-Khasis are etiologies of material culture, and there is no indication that these items are passed along to humans. In *Aqhat*, another Ras Shamra text of the same period, Kothar-wa-Khasis does fashion something for a human: a bow and arrows for the hero Aqhat. But as with the *Baal Cycle*, this story is not a clear etiology.[34] Although one cannot rule out that future archaeological finds might yield Canaanite culture myths,[35] those that survive focus more on explaining the conflicts between the gods than explaining the origins of civilization.

[27] Pritchard, *Ancient Near Eastern Texts* (hereafter abbreviated as *ANET*), 120–25. For a recent translation, see Hoffner, *Hittite Myths*, 38–61.

[28] See Hoffner's *Hittite Myths* for one of the most recent collections and translations.

[29] Before the discovery of the Ras Shamra texts, the main source for Canaanite mythology was *The Phoenician History* of Philo of Byblos (fl. in the second half of the first century AD). Philo claimed that the book was merely a Greek translation of a Phoenician text authored by Sanchuniathon, a Phoenician who lived before the fall of Troy. In this work, a large number of cultural innovations are attributed to humans; according to Sanchuniathon, these humans were later deified for their accomplishments. As we will see later, the etiologies of culture in Philo's book reflect the concerns of a Hellenized author, not of someone who lived before the fall of Troy. This, along with other clues in the text, casts both its authorship and its periodization into doubt. I will treat the etiologies in this text more fully when we come to discuss Roman-era reworkings of ancient myth.

[30] See *ANET*, 140.

[31] Ibid., 129, 133–35.

[32] Ibid., 132.

[33] Ibid., 131.

[34] Ibid., 151.

[35] Dalley, in "Near Eastern Myths," 59, discusses some hints that Canaanite creation stories may yet be discovered.

In contrast, early Egyptian mythology has several etiologies of culture. However, they are not found in the earliest cosmogonies: the third-millennium *Heliopolitan Cosmogony*, reconstructed from a variety of funerary texts, lacks them, as does the second-millennium cosmogony of Thebes.[36] One of the earliest etiologies of culture is found in the "Instruction for Merikare," a type of "mirror for princes" literature. In this text, dated to around 2000 BC, the pharaoh Akhtoy tells his son Merikare to revere the Egyptian sun god Re. One of the main reasons for this reverence, Merikare's father explains, is Re's creative power and control of the world.

> Well directed are men, the cattle of god. He [Re] made heaven and earth according to their desire, and he repelled the water-monster. He made the breath of life (for) their nostrils. They who have issued from his body are his images. He arises in heaven according to their desire. He made for them plants, animals, fowl, and fish to feed them. He slew his enemies and injured (even) his (own) children because they thought of making rebellion. He makes the light of day according to their desire, and he sails by in order to see them. He has erected a shrine around about them, and when they weep he hears. He made for them rulers (even) in the egg, a supporter to support the back of the disabled. He made for them magic as weapons to ward off what might happen or dreams by night as well as day.[37]

Here we see that Re, the sun god, has made animals and vegetation to feed humans and created the institution of kingship and magic to protect them. As in early Sumerian mythology, the primary purveyor of culture is the head of the pantheon of gods who altruistically provides the basic necessities of human life.[38]

A similar, if more comprehensive, account of cultural origins is found in *The Theology of Memphis*, the only remnant of which is a badly damaged stone inscription copied around 710 BC from a worm-eaten text. In it, the Memphite god Ptah, who was an amalgam of all the gods, creates the world ex nihilo and fashions "all crafts" by speaking some words. He also fashions humans, cities, and shrines in the same manner.[39] In this cosmogony, which some have dated to the second millennium,[40] the chief god not only is responsible for the basic needs of human life, as we find in the other cosmogonies,

[36] See "The Creation of Atum," in *ANET*, 3; and "Thebes as the Place of Creation," in *ANET*, 8.

[37] *ANET*, 417.

[38] However, in a twelfth-century text from Thebes, both humans and gods are said to depend on these basic necessities. In this text, Osiris reminds the high god Re that he (Osiris) made barley, emmer, and cattle to keep the gods alive; his son Horus, therefore, should receive special favor (*ANET*, 16).

[39] Ibid., 5.

[40] The content of the text may be much earlier, but as Junge has argued in "Zur Fehldatierung," on philological grounds, the text is a collection of New Kingdom (sixteenth to eleventh centuries BC) material combined in the Late Period (seventh to fourth centuries BC).

but is also credited with creating all of the crafts. The latter suggests that the myth originated after the earlier, more modest cosmogonies, where cultural creation is not mentioned. The depiction of Ptah as an amalgam of earlier gods also suggests that *The Theology of Memphis* was a later attempt to harmonize various local cosmogonies. However we date this cosmogony, it shares a feature with the other cosmogonies: its etiologies of culture are very unspecific. For example, we are not told in *The Theology of Memphis* what crafts Ptah made, just that he did so.

In the main, Egyptian culture myths are similar to those of Mesopotamia: a god associated with a city creates the arts and sciences ex nihilo and gives them to humans. However, there are two notable exceptions. The first is an exception in the mode of creation. The lunar god Thoth, the representative of the solar god Re, not only gives writing to humans but invents it.[41] Thus, writing came to be called the "script of Thoth," and scribes venerated him as their patron, often calling him the "expert" and "Lord of the Books."[42]

The second is an exception in who creates an art or a science. Egyptians regarded the human Imhotep, a minister to the pharaoh Djoser of the Third Dynasty, as the inventor of the pyramids.[43] Because of his accomplishment, Egyptians came to regard him as a god, the son of Ptah, and believed him to be a founder of medicine.[44] As was done to the Mesopotamian apkallē, later scribes attributed a number of their writings on temple construction and refurbishment to him.[45]

Continuities and Changes: Culture Heroes in Greek Mythology

Some early Greek mythology (i.e., the seventh century BC or earlier) was much the same as Near Eastern mythology with regard to the model of cultural origins: gods, often associated with cities, created the arts and sciences ex nihilo and gave them to humans. For example, in the *Hymn to Aphrodite* (a Homeric hymn composed around 700 BC),[46] Athena, the patron deity of Athens, is praised for teaching craftsmen how to make bronze carriages and chariots and for teaching women domestic handicrafts.

> She was the first to teach the craftsmen of this earth
> how to make carriages and chariots with complex designs for bronze.

[41] Boylan, *Thoth*, 98–100; Derrida, "Plato's Pharmacy," 137n4; Bleeker, *Haothor and Thoth*, 140–41; Senner, *Origins*, 10–11; Zhmud, *Origins*, 33–34.

[42] Boylan, *Thoth*, 99, 100, 103.

[43] Zhmud, *Origins*, 34n50.

[44] Wildung, *Imhotep*; Redford, "Review," 172.

[45] Wildung, *Imhotep*; Redford, "Review," 172–73.

[46] Athanassakis, *Homeric Hymns*, 81.

> And she taught splendid works to soft-skinned maidens
> in their houses, placing skill in each one's mind.[47]

In a later Homeric hymn, the *Hymn to Hephaestus* (probably composed in Athens in the fifth century BC),[48] Athena's tutelage of craftsmen is complemented by that of Hephaestus, the Greek god of smithcraft.

> Sing, O clear-voiced Muse, of Hephaistos renowned for skill,
> who along with gray-eyed Athena taught fine crafts
> to men of this earth; indeed before that time
> they used to live in mountain caves like wild beasts.
> Thanks to Hephaistos, the famous craftsman,
> they learned crafts and easily for the full year
> they lead a carefree existence in their own homes.[49]

Presumably, metallurgy was one of the crafts Athena and Hephaestus teach humans, just as Prometheus teaches humans how to mine metals in Aeschylus's (d. ca. 456 BC) *Prometheus Bound*.[50]

The *Hymn to Hephaestus* is late and some of its elements betray its fifth-century origin (see chapter 3). Nevertheless, its description of Athena and Hephaestus as culture heroes for craftsmen is certainly based on much earlier lore. In addition to the reference in the *Hymn to Aphrodite*, Athena and Hephaestus are mentioned together in *The Odyssey* as patrons of metalworkers.[51]

These etiologies of the crafts parallel early Near Eastern mythology in that the gods give humans culture.[52] But there are also several differences. Although these divine benefactors were sometimes associated with cities, as in Near Eastern mythology, this was not always or exclusively so. Hephaestus was not the patron god of a city, and Athena was the patron god of a number of cities. Moreover, there is a pronounced interest in explaining the origins of metalworking that does not exist in Near Eastern myth, aside from the Hebrew Bible (see below). Admittedly, there is one etiology of smithcraft in the myth titled "Enki and Innana," but it is mentioned only in passing in the midst of a long list of cultural gifts given by the gods. Kothar-wa-Khasis in Ugaritic myth also

[47] Ibid., lines 5.12–15 (43).

[48] Ibid., 89.

[49] Ibid., lines 5.1–7 (56).

[50] Aeschylus, *Prometheus Bound*, lines 501–4, in *Works*.

[51] Homer, *Odyssey* 6.233; see Athanassakis, *Homeric Hymns*, 82, 83. In Athens, smiths held an annual festival in honor of Athena, and one of her common epithets was Ergane, the "work-woman" (Athanassakis, *Homeric Hymns*, 82).

[52] As in Near Eastern culture myths, the Greek gods were usually motivated by altruism. However, there is an example of a selfishly motivated bestowal of culture: the competition between Athena and Poseidon for the affection of the Athenians. Poseidon offers a salty spring and Athena an olive tree (see Agard, "Athens' Choice," 14).

fashions metal objects, but there are no clear etiologies of smithcraft. In contrast, the etiology of smithcraft is the centerpiece of the two hymns cited above.

The origins of smithcraft also preoccupied Hesiod, one of the earliest Greek mythographers (fl. eighth century BC). In his *Theogony*, we learn that humans once lived like gods, not needing to toil for their livelihood. However, this ease was disturbed when Prometheus—the offspring of the Titans and, like them, a god—tricked Zeus into accepting the less desirable half of a sacrificial ox—the bones. Humans ate the other half, thus instituting the practice of sacrifice and setting themselves apart from the gods by becoming meat eaters. As punishment for their insolence, Zeus forced them to toil to provide sustenance for themselves without the use of fire. However, Prometheus took pity on them and stole fire for them from Zeus.[53]

Like Sumerian mythology or the Greek *Hymn to Aphrodite*, Hesiod's myths of human origins depict the gods as giving beneficial culture to humans. However, there are two important differences. First, the cultural gift of fire comes to humans after a god rebels against the chief god and steals it; the chief god wants to withhold it from humans so they will suffer. We do not find these notions in ancient Near Eastern mythology. Gods give the arts and sciences freely, and although there are trickster gods such as Enki who give culture to humans, their trickery and the bestowal of culture are not connected. Several centuries after Hesiod, we do find a somewhat similar story in the Jewish *Book of the Watchers* regarding illicit angel instruction (see chapter 2), but the divine beings who bestow culture are malevolent, and they do so without theft or trickery.

Second, Hesiod sees the history of culture as a devolution in which the human condition worsens with the introduction of more and more technology. Of course, technology (the introduction of fire) does alleviate the initial fallen state of humans after their punishment,[54] but from that point on it has a baneful effect on the human condition. In his *Works and Days*, Hesiod writes of five races; four of them correspond to metals, beginning with gold and ending with Hesiod's age, iron. Each of the successive races is worse than the one before (with the exception of the people living in the heroic age that preceded the Iron Age). Although Hesiod does not specifically discuss technological innovations in his account, he does write that the people of the Bronze Age fashioned bronze and that they destroyed themselves by fighting, suggesting that metalworking was their own invention.[55] The final age, Iron, is also filled with war, toil, and death. Therefore, in contrast to Prometheus's beneficial cultural bestowal in *The Theogony*, the objects wrought by human hands lead to ruin in Hesiod's *Works*

[53] Hesiod, *Theogony*, 535–69; Hesiod, *Works and Days*, 44–50, 108–25, in Evelyn-White, *Hesiod.* Clay (*Cosmos*, 125–26) speculates that humans already had fire before Zeus took it away; Prometheus merely restored it.

[54] Blundell, *Origins*, 18.

[55] Hesiod, *Works and Days*, 150–55.

and Days. Further, metallurgy, violence, and cultural decline are all linked together, a theme that also appears in Genesis.

Culture Heroes as Antiheroes in the Hebrew Bible

The Hebrew Bible begins with a cosmogony that includes an anthropogony, which is followed by an anthropogony without a cosmogony. The cosmogony, which was written by the so-called Priestly author, is perfectly at home in the Near East: a god creates the heavens and the earth, differentiates night from day, fashions the firmament, makes land and sea, and then finally populates the world with plants, animals, and then humans (Gen. 1–2:3).[56] Unlike the sky gods of the Near East and Egypt, however, God does not give humans the basic arts and sciences of civilization.

Information on the cultural development of humans follows in the anthropogony, written by a different author, called the Yahwist by modern scholars because he refers to God as Yahweh. The Yahwist's model of cultural transmission is broadly similar to that found in Near Eastern and Greek mythology: a god gives beneficial culture to humans. However, in the Hebrew Bible beneficial culture is more narrowly conceived as the law and revealed wisdom given to God's chosen mouthpiece, the prophets. Material culture, on the other hand, is almost always a negative development in the Hebrew Bible; it is to be attributed to those who are disobedient to God rather than to God or His elect. The Yahwist, therefore, casts human discovery and invention in a negative light, which makes him intellectually closer to the Greek Hesiod than to mythographers in the Near East.

Like Hesiod, the Yahwist also depicts the genesis of civilization as accompanying the fall of humans from an idyllic state; there is no equivalent to this in other Near Eastern myths. His account of cultural origins begins with a description of a comfortable human existence at the beginning of creation in which two humans, Adam and Eve, live as creatures undifferentiated from nature; hence, they are naked but not ashamed (Gen. 2:25). Although Adam is charged by God with keeping and tilling the garden (Gen. 2:15), there is no sense that he does this to obtain food, which is bountiful (Gen. 2:9); he just picks fruit off the trees (Gen. 2:15).[57] These verses do not constitute an etiology of agriculture, since its origins are explained later, after Adam has been exiled from Paradise.

[56] Similarly, in *Enuma Elish*, a work that probably dates to the second millennium BC but survives in first-millennium tablets, the Babylonian god Marduk (or Bel) separates the waters of heaven and earth, creates dry land, and makes constellations and the moon, mountains and rivers, and finally humans (Dalley, *Myths*, 255–60). For an analysis of the parallels between *Enuma Elish* and Genesis, see Heidel, *Babylonian Genesis*, and Gmirkin, *Berossus and Genesis*, 92–100.

[57] See Kawashima, "Homo Faber," 486–47, for additional commentary.

While in God's good graces, Adam names all of the creatures that God has created (Gen. 2:19–20). The plain sense of the text indicates that this act is the result of Adam's independent creativity and not derived from supernatural knowledge given to him by God.[58] Although this is a cultural achievement of some sort, it is not the creation of human language, which is how this episode was understood in later Jewish tradition. More important, it is not the creation of material culture.

The creation of material culture occurs only after Adam and Eve sin by eating the forbidden fruit of the tree of the knowledge of good and evil. Eating this fruit leads them to differentiate themselves from nature and become aware of their nudity. To cover themselves, they sew together aprons of leaves (Gen. 3:7). Thus, the first material invention of humans, the sewing and wearing of clothes, arises out of shame and the knowledge that their natural state is no longer acceptable.[59] Compare this with a Mesopotamian myth that explores the transition from nature to culture. In *The Epic of Gilgamesh*, Gilgamesh's companion Enkidu is born in the wild and lives like an animal. It is only after he is seduced by a prostitute named Shamhat that he is differentiated from nature and able to participate in city life.[60] In the Old Babylonian version of the story, he puts on clothes "and bec[omes] like any man," a sign of his participation in civilization.[61] Similar to the Yahwist account, clothing is used to differentiate humans from animals; but in *Gilgamesh* it is a sign of progress, whereas in the biblical account it is a sign of decline from an ideal state.

As punishment for their transgression, Adam and Eve are exiled from Eden; but before they leave, God makes "garments of skins" for them (Gen. 3:20). Unlike their garments of leaves, this innovation is not the work of their own hands but is bestowed on them by God. This is one of the few instances in the Hebrew Bible in which God bestows material culture on humans. Like Prometheus's gift

[58] This is certainly the opinion of pre-Christian Jewish authors, who did not regard Adam as a prophet (see Ginzberg, *Legends* 5:83n29 for a list of the sources). Only in the works of Christian authors do we find the claim that Adam derives the names through prophetic knowledge from God (see ibid., n. 30, for some of the early Christian sources). The Christian notion that Adam was a prophet is derived from the Greek translation of Genesis 2:21. In the Hebrew text, God puts Adam into a "deep sleep" (*tardemah*) while extracting his rib in order to make Eve. The Septuagint renders this phrase as "trance" (*ekstasin*). Although one pre-Christian Jewish author, Philo, does write that Adam may have "philosophized" during his trance, he is careful to note that this is not the trance of a prophet who "says nothing of his own, but everything which he says is strange and prompted by someone else" (Philo's *Quis rerum divinarum heres*, 51–52, in *Complete Works*). It is unclear to me why Louis Ginzberg takes the Septuagint translation of Genesis 2:21 and Philo's comments on it as evidence of a pre-Christian Jewish understanding of Adam as a prophet (see Ginzberg, *Legends* 5:83n30; Ginzberg mistakenly cites Genesis 2:20 and section 52 of Philo's *Quis rerum*).

[59] Kawashima, "Homo Faber," 487.

[60] Dalley, *Myths*, 52–56.

[61] Ibid., 138.

of fire, it is meant to soften the punishment of exile issued by a high god (although it is not precisely parallel, since Yahweh's counterpart, Zeus, does not give any culture to humans). Whether or not this is to be taken as an etiology for garments made of animal hide is unclear. Even if it is, this is an isolated instance of God giving material culture to humans. In general, He leaves them to fend for themselves.

Agriculture, the next innovation depicted in Genesis, arises after Adam and Eve are exiled. Before they depart, God curses the ground as punishment for human transgression and tells Adam that he will now have to provide food for himself through farming: "In toil you shall eat of it all the days of your life; thorns and thistles it shall bring forth to you; and you shall eat the plants of the field. In the sweat of your face you shall eat bread till you return to the ground, for out of it you were taken; you are dust, and to dust you shall return" (Gen. 3:17–19).[62]

Now the human differentiation from the natural environment is complete. Whereas clothing arises out of shame once Adam and Eve recognize their separation from nature, Adam now has to bend nature to his will in order to survive, forced to "till the ground from which he was taken" (Gen. 3:23). Significantly, God does not tell Adam how to till the ground; either Adam already knows how to do it from his time in paradise or he discovers it on his own. This negative depiction of agriculture's origins differs markedly from other Near Eastern culture myths, which portray its development in a positive light and conceive a helpful role for the gods, who give humans the tools they need to work the land.

The theme of curtailing the fertility of the earth as punishment for sin appears again in the story of Cain and Abel. Cain, like his father, is a tiller of the ground, and his brother Abel is a shepherd (Gen. 4:2). They both make an offering to God; Cain's is an "offering of the fruit of the ground" (Gen. 4:3), whereas that of Abel is the "firstlings of his flock and of their fat portions" (Gen. 4:4). God accepts Abel's offering but rejects that of Cain. When Cain slays Abel out of jealousy, God tells Cain that the ground will no longer yield food for him. As a consequence, he is forced to spend the rest of his days as an outcast in the land of Nod, which means "wandering" (Gen. 4:12). Adam and Eve are compensated for their loss of Abel by the birth of another son, Seth (Gen. 4:25).

In the absence of an explanation for the rejection of Cain's offering, we might assume that his means of subsistence was of lesser value in God's eyes than that of Abel. However, the Yahwist also notes that the pious Noah was the "first tiller of the soil" after the Flood (Gen. 9:20), so it would probably be wrong to interpret the story as a condemnation of agriculturalism. Instead, the Yahwist has reworked some version of the ancient Sumerian myth "Cattle and Grain" (see

[62] Here and elsewhere I have used the revised standard version (RSV) for translations of the Hebrew Bible.

above) to further illustrate his theme that God punishes human sin by curtailing the means of subsistence from the ground.

Rather than an etiology for nomadism, Cain's punishment was probably meant to explain the origins of an itinerant smithing tribe in the Near East.[63] First, Cain's name (Heb. *qayin*) originally meant "smith."[64] Second, almost all of the cultural developments attributed to his descendants are associated with transient groups who serviced the needs of settled rural farmers.[65] Thus Jabal, the son of Lamech (a great-great-grandson of Enoch, son of Cain), was the "father of those who dwell in tents and have possessions" (Gen. 4:20).[66] Such itinerant peddlers would have sold various commodities, including jewelry and metalwork.[67] Jabal's brother, Jubal, is described as the "father of all those who play the lyre and pipe" (Gen. 4:21), a skill associated with itinerant metalworkers (see below).[68] Tubal-Cain, another son of Lamech by a different wife, was the "forger of all instruments of bronze and iron" (Gen. 4:22). In addition to fashioning weapons or farming implements, this may mean that he is credited with being the first to put a sharp edge on metal weapons[69] or farming implements like the plow.[70]

Because of their specialized knowledge of metallurgy, blacksmiths were viewed with suspicion by the settled, rural population of the Near East (see the discussion in chapter 2). Rather than a vague allusion to ancient Mesopotamian smithing cities, as argued by some scholars,[71] this depiction of Lamech's family was probably an etiology for a transient metalworking tribe in the Near East that was marginalized for its trade.[72] That the Yahwist had a dim view of such a tribe and the cultural achievements associated with it is indicated by his linking

[63] Maccoby, *Sacred Executioner*, 57.

[64] Ibid., 13.

[65] Hiebert, *Landscape*, 41–44. Some scholars have argued that the technology associated with Cain's descendants indicates that they were desert nomads (see, for example, Westermann, *Genesis 1–11*, 324; Gunkel, *Genesis*, 51–52). Others have focused on the city-building activities of Cain or, reading the verse differently, his son Enoch and asserted that the technologies associated with Cain's descendants are urban activities (Castellino, "Origins," 93; Hallo, "Antediluvian Cities," 64–65). The former interpretation seems closer to the mark, since, as Theodore Hiebert explains, the latter reading is based solely on the incidental mention of Cain (or Enoch) as a builder of a city and ignores the general focus on agriculturalism in the rest of the Genesis narrative (Hiebert, *Yahwist's Landscape*, 42).

[66] I have changed the RSV translation of *miqneh* as "cattle" to "possessions" based on Sawyer's suggestion (Sawyer, "Cain," 160).

[67] Ibid. See the references in note 63 of Sawyer's work for other contemporary views regarding the professions of the Cainites.

[68] Ibid., 160.

[69] Ibid., 161.

[70] Hiebert, *Landscape*, 44.

[71] Castellino, "Origins," 93; Hallo, "Antediluvian Cities," 64–65.

[72] Sawyer suggests that it may be a reference to a transient Edomite metalworking community ("Cain," 159–62).

them with the descendants of the sinful, nomadic Cain, not the righteous Seth, whose line is not directly credited with any cultural innovation and who continued farming the "cursed" land (Gen. 5:29). The Yahwist also seems to associate the Cainite innovations, or at least metallurgy, with the violent retributive justice of desert nomads, since the invention of metallurgy is immediately followed by Lamech's boast that he killed a man because of a wound he had received (Gen. 4:23–24).

Ostensibly incongruous with the depiction of Cain's descendants as transient peddlers is the Yahwist's linkage of the genesis of urban life with the line of Cain. We learn that immediately after God condemns Cain to a life of wandering, he builds a city, which he names after his son Enoch (Gen. 4:17). However, the text is unclear at this point and may instead say that it was Enoch who built the city, which he named after his son Irad. Since this name is similar to the name of a major city of Sumerian mythology, Eridu, it may indicate a Mesopotamian origin for this etiology.[73] However, the fact that the founder of urban civilization was either a murderer or the son of a murderer contrasts with the positive Mesopotamian etiologies of city life. When read this way, we can conclude that the Yahwist credited Cain with being the first transient smith and Enoch with being the first builder of a city. These two etiologies are not incompatible, since they represent the perspective of someone who views settled, rural agriculturalism as the ideal lifestyle.[74]

In the Yahwist's account, the Cainite genealogy is followed by a description of the debauchery of human civilization, implying that it was spurred on by the innovations of Cain's descendants (Gen. 6). This displeases God, who decides to wipe out humanity with a flood and start over again with Noah and his family. Unlike the Mesopotamian flood myth in which a god unleashes the deluge to solve a population problem (humans had grown too numerous because the gods had not arranged for them to die), the biblical flood is brought on by social devolution spurred on by cultural development.

As a descendant of the righteous line of Adam, Noah returns to the respectable occupation of his forefathers after the Flood; he is described as the "first tiller of the soil" (Gen. 9:20). Noah, therefore, provides the crucial cultural link to the antediluvian period and starts the story of culture all over again by returning to the occupation of Adam. However, the old family curse revisits Noah when one of his sons, Ham, commits a sin and bequeaths the consequences of that sin to his progeny. According to the story, Noah plants a vineyard after the Flood. (Although this might have been a cultural first, we are not told that; rather, the Yahwist emphasizes that Noah was the first tiller of the soil, not the first vintner, so presumably the husbandry of grapevines was part of the job description.) From these vines, Noah produces wine, which he drinks and then

[73] Hallo, "Antediluvian Cities," 64.
[74] Hiebert, *Landscape*, 42.

becomes inebriated, leaving his naked body exposed. Ham sees his father lying naked and tells his two brothers, who turn away and cover their father. When Noah awakes and hears what his youngest son has done (Gen. 9:24), he curses Canaan, the son of Ham, and condemnes his line to enslavement to the descendents of Shem (i.e., the Israelites).

As with the depiction of Cain's descendants, the innovations associated with the most prominent of Ham's descendants, Nimrod, are cast in a negative light because of the iniquity of their forebear. Nimrod is remembered in Genesis as the "first on earth to be a mighty man" (Gen. 10:8), presumably meaning that he is the first king. The most prominent city he rules is Babel, which had been established in the land of Shinar by men migrating from the East (Gen. 11:2); this seems to be an allusion to Cain wandering east of Eden.[75] Once there, these men make bricks and fire them (Gen. 11:3), saying to each other: "Come, let us build ourselves a city, and a tower with its top in the heavens, and let us make a name for ourselves, lest we be scattered abroad upon the face of the whole earth" (Gen. 11:4). God, who already had a dim view of city building, is annoyed by the linguistic unity that makes larger-scale cooperation, and hence more complex civilization, possible: "They are one people, and they have all one language; and this is only the beginning of what they will do; and nothing that they propose to do will now be impossible for them" (Gen. 11:6). To prevent humans from overstepping their station, he "confuses their language" so that "they may not understand one another's speech" (Gen. 11:7) and then scatters them. Not only is Yahweh's confusion of tongues a further example of the devolutionary picture of cultural history painted by the Yahwist, it is also a defiant stand against cultural evolution and urban civilization.

So far we have seen that the Yahwist attributes the invention of material culture, with the exception of the garments of skins, to wayward humans. By way of contrast, the righteous descendants of Seth and Noah are not credited with any cultural innovations other than the receipt of law from God. Enoch, son of Jared (not to be confused with Enoch, son of Cain), who was to become a major Jewish culture hero in the third and second centuries BC, is only briefly mentioned by the Yahwist and not credited with any innovations. Even when the Priestly author expands the Yahwist's account of Enoch, we learn only that he was the father of Methuselah and walked with divine beings (*hā'ĕlōhīm*) for three hundred years following his son's birth, after which God "took him" (Gen. 5:21–24). Although the Priestly author may have based his depiction of Enoch on a version of the flood hero Enmeduranki of Sumerian mythology, who was credited with giving humans revelatory knowledge and the divinatory techniques he received from the gods,[76] the Priestly author avoided crediting Enoch with any of these revelations.

[75] Ellis, *Yahwist*, 133.
[76] Vanderkam, *Enoch*, 35–45.

The biblical patriarch Abraham, who would become another major culture hero in the second century BC, is not credited with any cultural inventions or revelations by the authors of the Hebrew Bible. In chapter 12 of Genesis, for example, we are not told why God chose Abraham to go to the Promised Land; he is told only to go there and is promised that a great nation will come from him. Before he leaves for the Promised Land, he does not, as in later tradition, reject the idols of his countrymen or gaze upon the stars and intuit monotheism.

In summary, we can observe three general themes in the etiologies of culture found in the Yahwist portion of the Hebrew Bible. First, humans are overwhelmingly responsible for the creation of their own culture. In addition to giving the Israelites guidance and laws, God is explicitly credited with giving humans only one item of material culture in the Hebrew Bible: garments made of skins. This is in marked contrast to early Near Eastern and Greek myths of cultural origins in which the gods bountifully bestow material culture on humans.

Second, the development of material culture is viewed in negative terms. If we leave aside the garments made of skins, the development of material culture is, at best, a punishment for sin; if the sinners repent, like Adam, they will accept their punishment and not sin further or innovate. Thus, Adam's son Seth and his righteous descendants remain farmers and do not invent new things. At worst, a punishment for sin leads to further innovation and more sin, as with Cain's progeny. In both cases, cultural development accompanies further movement away from the idyllic state. Humans are responsible for their misery, and God has done little to ameliorate it. This is similar to Hesiod's depiction of social decline after humans' punishment, a decline that, like the Yahwist, he links with metallurgy, violence, and cultural decline (this theme also appears in one of the earliest Jewish scriptures written after the Babylonian exile, the *Book of the Watchers*—see chapter 2).

Third, the story of civilization's origins in the Hebrew Bible either explicitly or implicitly reverses themes found in Mesopotamian mythology. In Mesopotamian mythology, human kinship with animals is deplored and attainment of the knowledge of the arts of civilization is a good thing; in Genesis, living with animals is good, and knowledge of civilization is the cause and consequence of sin.[77] In Mesopotamian mythology the arts of civilization are a gift of the gods; in Genesis they are a human invention.[78] In Mesopotamian mythology humans attain their full potential when living in cities; in Genesis they reach their lowest point there.[79] The building of Babylon is a great human achievement, but in

[77] Gmirkin, *Berossus and Genesis*, 101–2.

[78] Kawashima, "Homo Faber," 485, 492. Kawashima's assertion that the Yahwist "portrays human achievements in a largely positive light" (499) is very difficult to maintain given the evidence outlined above. He does concede that these achievements "are not free of moral ambiguity," but that does not go far enough.

[79] Hendel, "Mesopotamian Problem," 29.

Genesis it is a sign of hubris.[80] In short, things start badly in Mesopotamian mythology and get better,[81] whereas in Genesis (1:31) they start "very good" and get worse.

As Hendel argues, these reversals indicate that the Yahwist was using historiographical strategies to undermine Babylonian mythology and diminish its greatness, suggesting that he was writing during the Babylonian exile of the Jews.[82] Little wonder, then, that God's community is fully constituted in the Yahwist's account only when its founder, Abraham, leaves Mesopotamia, the land of his birth and the cradle of civilization, and goes to the Promised Land.[83] It is then that the Hebrew Bible adopts a more positive attitude toward urban civilization and human invention—or at least that associated with Israel.[84]

Conclusion

In the texts we have surveyed, gods (sometimes through human or semihuman interlocutors) are the agents of civilization's development, which is portrayed positively and created out of nothing. Of course, there have been a number of departures from this basic model, such as the human king Enmerkar, who invented clay writing tablets in Mesopotamian mythology, or the Egyptian god Thoth, who "invents" writing. But the basic model holds true from Mesopotamia to Greece, from the fourth millennium BC until the early first millennium BC. The two significant departures from this model, the myths of Hesiod and the Yahwist, have later origins and indicate a shift in thinking about cultural origins solely as the work of the gods. Hesiod does adhere to the standard model by making a god the agent of civilization's genesis. But he departs from it by depicting subsequent cultural history as a devolution in which each succeeding generation of humans creates material culture that hastens humanity's decline, particularly metallurgy. The Yahwist eliminates God almost entirely from the creative process, and he makes a stronger connection between human sin and cultural creation, especially metallurgy. Both authors are of one mind in disparaging civilization, portraying it as a consequence of humanity's fall from divine favor. Thus, very early in the history of human civilization, we have examples of its discontents. It is ironic that two men who expressed such disdain for cultural development and its attendant violence should have written works that were to become major parts of the cultural canons of three great empires: those of the Greeks, the Romans, and the Arabs.

[80] Ibid., 29, 32.

[81] Jacobsen, "Eridu Genesis," 529.

[82] Hendel, "Mesopotamian Problem," 24.

[83] Ibid., 34.

[84] Ibid., 33–34.

TWO

The Beneficent Sky God: Cultural History in the Qur'an

> And Azâzêl taught men to make swords, and knives, and shields, and breastplates, and made known to them the metals (of the earth) and the art of working them, and bracelets, and ornaments, and the use of antimony, and the beautifying of the eyelids, and all kinds of costly stones, and all colouring tinctures. And there arose much godlessness, and they committed fornication, and they were led astray, and became corrupt in all their ways.
>
> —*Book of the Watchers*

> And We gave David bounty from Us: "O you mountains, echo God's praises with him, and you birds!" And We softened for him iron: "Fashion wide coats of mail, and measure well the links."— And do ye righteousness, for surely I see the things you do.
>
> —Qur'an 34:10–11

> Like servants on the call of their masters, [bees] go out from the hives, collect what is useful, keep carrying their loads, eagerly make the honeycombs, and imprint their seals and signets on the streams of honey brought in as on a treasure, and they continue to pay this tax or tribute to men as if they were kings. Why, then, you wretch, do you misrepresent the situation and, while enjoying the tribute, revile its Maker, treat wantonly the labors of other creatures, and release the slings of ingratitude at the One who provides these things?
>
> —Theodoret of Cyrus, *On Divine Providence*

> And thy Lord revealed unto the bees, saying: "Make your homes of the mountains, the trees, and of what (men) build. Then eat of all manner of fruit, and follow the ways of your Lord easy to go upon." Then comes there forth out of their bellies a drink of diverse hues wherein is healing for men. Surely in that is a sign for a people who reflect.
>
> —Qur'an 16:68–69

When the Arabs conquered the Near East, they shared with their subjects (mainly Jews and Christians) the notion that civilization had arisen as a consequence of Adam's fall. But in contrast to the Hebrew Bible, the Qur'an portrays the rise of civilization positively and makes God its prime mover, much like the gods of ancient Near Eastern myths. There are at least two reasons for this difference. First, Muḥammad draws on noncanonical biblical scripture and storytelling that link God, angels, and chosen human interlocutors to the development of beneficial arts and sciences.[1] These scriptures and stories were written after Alexander's conquests, and some were meant to justify the use of foreign sciences (mainly Babylonian) and to positively assert the cultural contributions of ancient Hebrews to civilization.

Second, Muḥammad draws on some version of these texts (perhaps oral) to prove his argument that God is the source of all civilization, an argument influenced by late-antique thought on divine providence. He makes this argument to justify either proselytizing among or conquest of non-Muslims, who have forgotten the source of civilization and thus deserve to lose it. So whereas the Yahwist culture myths disparage an empire and its attendant civilization, the Qur'an provides a rationale for establishing a new one.

The Fall of the Angels and the Rise of Enoch: Culture Heroes in Postconquest Jewish Scripture

In the last chapter, we saw that the Hebrew Bible has a negative take on civilization's origins, one that might have been shaped by the Babylonian exile of the Jewish community. The scriptural shift away from these negative culture myths began after the Persians conquered the Babylonians and permitted the Jews to return to Palestine. We see evidence of this shift in the *Book of the Watchers* and the *Astronomical Book*, which later became parts of a larger collection called *1 Enoch* by modern scholars. The texts, which were considered biblical scripture at various times because of their purported authorship by the Enoch who walks with divine beings in Genesis 5, are concerned with the Babylonian legacy of Judaism and the Mesopotamian origins of civilization. Their final form appeared soon after Alexander's conquest of the Near East in the third century BC,[2] suggesting that they were meant to resolve the intellectual and cultural dilemmas of the Hellenistic period as well.

[1] While acknowledging the contentiousness, for both Muslims and some modern scholars, of identifying Muḥammad as the Qur'an's author I will do so for the sake of conciseness. The first epigraph to this chapter is from *1 Enoch* 8.1–2, translated by Charles in his *Apocrypha*, vol. 2 of *Apocrypha and Pseudepigrapha*. The third, by Theodoret of Cyrus, is from Discourse 5.6. And the fourth is a modified translation of Arberry's *The Koran Interpreted*.

[2] The *Book of the Watchers* was probably written in the third century BC and later combined with other writings into what is now called *1* (i.e., the Ethiopic) *Enoch*, preserving a text that was considered scripture by the Jews until the destruction of the Second Temple in the first century AD and by Christians until the time of Augustine in the fourth. For dating this work, see Milik, *Books of Enoch*, 2; Stone, "Enoch," 484; Reed, "Fallen," 1–2. See Reed for the most detailed history of the text's reception (now as a book, *Fallen Angels and the History of Judaism and Christianity*, which I have not had time to compare with her dissertation). The *Astronomical Book* dates to the same period as the *Book of the Watchers* in *1 Enoch*.

In the *Book of the Watchers*, the notion that civilization is a bad thing is retained from Genesis, but there is a shift away from human responsibility for harmful arts and sciences. The *Book of the Watchers* tells the story of wayward angels called the Watchers, who have sex with human women; these women then give birth to giants. The story is an expansion of Genesis 6:2, where the "sons of God" have sex with the "daughters of men," which leads to human corruption and eventually the Flood. However, the *Book of the Watchers* adds a new twist: the angels also contribute to the waywardness of humanity by teaching them various corrupting arts. In *1 Enoch* 7, for example, we learn that the angels teach their wives sorcery, spells, and the cutting of roots and herbs (i.e., drug preparation). In *1 Enoch* 8:3 this list of arcane magical arts is expanded to include various types of divination and the names of the angels who taught them to humans. One angel, Shemihazah, is especially criticized for teaching humans spell binding and root cutting (*1 Enoch* 8:3). The biblical theme of metallurgy as the source of violence and human degradation also appears in *1 Enoch* 8:1–2, where the fallen angel Asael teaches humans how to mine metals and use them to fashion weapons, armor, and jewelry; he also teaches them the use of cosmetics (*1 Enoch* 8:1–2). Consequently, "there was much godlessness upon the earth" (*1 Enoch* 8:2).[3] As in Genesis, the corruption finally leads to the Flood; however, the responsibility has shifted from wayward humans to wayward angels, thus mitigating human responsibility for sin and replacing the Adamic story as an explanation for evil in the world.[4]

The shift from humans to angels as the locus of cultural development is more closely akin to ancient Near Eastern mythology than it is to the Hebrew Bible, since the angels closely resemble gods. Indeed, the original story may have been about rebellious gods whom Jewish authors transformed into angels in order to make the story compatible with Jewish religious sensibilities, a technique also used by the authors of the Hebrew Bible when appropriating the mythology of other nations.[5] But unlike the Near Eastern stories of gods who beneficently give desirable culture to humans, the angels in the *Watchers* story are sinful and teach undesirable culture to humans. In this, the *Book of the Watchers* agrees with the biblical notion that material culture, particularly metallurgy, is detrimental, and that it comes from the wayward; the difference was in the shift of responsibility for cultural transmission from sinful humans to sinful angels.

But what of beneficial culture? For this, we have to look in the *Astronomical Book*, another early work of scripture that was contemporaneous with the *Book of the Watchers* and was later included in *1 Enoch*.[6] This work is an expansion of the enigmatic passages about Enoch in Genesis 5:21–24, where we are told that

[3] Here and in the following quotations from the *Book of the Watchers* and the *Astronomical Book*, I rely on Nickelsburg's translation (Nickelsburg, *Commentary*).

[4] Reed, "Fallen," 79–80.

[5] VanderKam, *Enoch*, 44.

[6] Consult Nickelsburg and the references in note 2 above for dating.

he spent three hundred years walking with divine beings (see chapter 1). In the *Astronomical Book*, these beings are angels, one of whom, the archangel Uriel, gives the righteous Enoch a guided tour of the cosmos. There he tells Enoch to look at the "heavenly tablets, and read what is written on them, and learn every individual (fact)" (81:1). Enoch looks and beholds the "deeds of all men and all the sons of flesh" for all eternity (81:2b). Seven angels then return Enoch to earth and tell him to write down a testament for his son Methuselah containing all that he has seen so that Methuselah might pass it down to his progeny (81:5–10). The rest of the *Astronomical Book* is meant to be this testament wherein Enoch records "revealed" knowledge (82:1a) containing "wisdom" for his posterity (82:2).

Like the *Book of the Watchers*, the *Astronomical Book* assigns the role of cultural purveyor to angels, not humans. But since the angels in the *Astronomical Book* are obedient to God, they are credited with giving beneficial culture to humans. Their revelations of cosmic knowledge to Enoch, which he passes on to humans, are meant to establish Enoch as the premier source of heavenly knowledge; the revelation given to Moses, the primary culture hero of the Hebrew Bible, is now preempted by the celestial revelations in *1 Enoch* given to the antediluvian prophet.[7]

Although the authors of the *Book of the Watchers* and the *Astronomical Book* agreed with the basic outlines of the Yahwist's model of cultural development, they had very different polemical concerns. The Yahwist wanted to denigrate nomadic and urban culture and score points against a local tribe of itinerant tinkers, the Cainites, and against the Babylonians, the descendants of Noah's wayward son, Ham. True culture for him was the religious law given by Yahweh and rural agriculturalism, the closest that fallen man could get to paradise. The authors of the *Book of the Watchers* and the *Astronomical Book*, on the other hand, were more concerned with differentiating between good and bad sciences. Anything that altered the natural state of the world or revealed its secrets without the consent of God was bad; hence, the origin of metallurgy, cosmetics, and spells of all sorts was attributed to bad angels. Conversely, anything that revealed the secrets of the world by God's permission were good; thus, writing, calendars, and lawful knowledge of the future were given to Enoch by good angels. Since many of these things had long been associated with Babylonian society, one suspects that these etiologies were the result of internal Jewish debates over the status of Babylonian sciences after the return from the Babylonian exile in 537 BC.[8] Given the depiction of Enoch,

[7] Nickelsburg, *Commentary*, 52.

[8] Many authors believe that the negative etiologies of culture in the *Book of the Watchers* were meant as a critique of Greek culture (see Graf, "Production," 320; Nickelsburg, *Commentary*, 62; and Suter, "Fallen Angel" 115, 132–33). However, the recasting of Babylonian astronomy in the book indicates that it was written by scribes who were learned in Mesopotamian sciences (see Reed, "Fallen," 101–5). Thus, it seems more reasonable to suppose that this was their main concern in the texts, not Greek culture, which had barely intruded into their lives at the time these texts were redacted.

the main culture hero, as a scribe, it is safe to assume that the authors of these texts were from that class.[9] That their depiction of Enoch's revelatory ascent in the *Astronomical Book* was heavily indebted to Mesopotamian mythology reinforces this line of argument. Enmeduranki and Uanadapa ascend to heaven, as does Enoch. Enmeduranki reads the heavenly tablets, as does Enoch. In contrast, Uanadapa reveals astronomical knowledge, whereas Enoch learns of it in a work shown him by the angels.[10]

The *Book of the Watchers* and the *Astronomical Book* engage very little with Hellenistic thought, perhaps because they were written so soon after Alexander's conquests.[11] Not so with a later retelling of the Genesis story found in the *Book of Jubilees*, a scripture purportedly revealed to Moses by an angel but written in the second century BC either at the beginning of the Maccabee revolt against the Greek rulers of Palestine or in its aftermath. Although the author or authors of the *Book of Jubilees* did not warmly embrace Hellenistic culture, they were clearly influenced by its debates about the origins of culture.[12] Thus, they describe their culture hero Enoch in terms that indicate they were aware of the "grand debate" about cultural priority that raged after Alexander's conquests (see chapter 4).[13] In the *Astronomical Book*, Enoch had been obliquely portrayed as a culture hero, but one is left to infer that he was the "first" to bring various scribal innovations to humanity. But in the *Book of Jubilees*, this is made explicit and suggests an awareness of Greek protography (see chapter 3). He is described as the first to write, the first to organize a calendar, and the first to record a testament (*Jub.* 4:17–18). Although the authors of the *Book of Jubilees* could have been influenced by similar statements in the Hebrew Bible (Noah is the "first tiller of the soil" [Gen. 9:20] and Nimrod is the "first on earth to be a mighty man" [Gen. 10:8]), there was no reason to explicitly name the various firsts of Enoch unless the author was conscious of the etiological polemics of the Hellenistic world;[14] as we saw above, the authors of *1 Enoch* felt no such compulsion even though they were also familiar with such statements in Genesis.

As in the *Astronomical Book*, Enoch is taught the arts and sciences by good angels. But whereas the angels' role was confined to teaching Enoch about the cosmos in *1 Enoch*, in *Jubilees* their instruction includes teaching Adam in the practice of farming (in stark contrast to the Yahwist's negative depiction of the origins of farming). In *Jubilees* 3:15, we learn from Moses's angelic interlocutor that "we gave him [Adam] work and instructed him to do everything."[15] When Adam was exiled from paradise, he continued to till the land just as the angels

[9] Reed believes that these scribes were rivals of the Temple priests (Reed, "Fallen," 90, 91).
[10] See Kvanvig, *Roots*, 607, for a side-by-side comparison. See also VanderKam, *Enoch*, 8.
[11] This second point is made by Reed, "Fallen," 89–90.
[12] VanderKam, *Enoch*, 184.
[13] The "grand debate" is Mendels's terminology (*Land*, 31).
[14] VanderKam makes a similar point (*Enoch*, 181).
[15] Translated by Charles in his *Apocrypha*, vol. 2.

had shown him in paradise (*Jub.* 3:35). Such an account suggests a reevaluation of the negative portrayal of agriculture in the Hebrew Bible and God's abandonment of humans to their own devices. Angels also teach Noah (at God's bidding) every kind of medicine, which he then records in a book and gives to his eldest son, Shem (*Jub.* 10:10–13).

Like *1 Enoch*, *Jubilees* also mentions the Watchers. But whereas the Watchers in *1 Enoch* rebel against heaven and illicitly teach humans secret knowledge, the Watchers in *Jubilees* come to earth at God's behest to teach humans how to be righteous (*Jub.* 4:15); they do not directly give them cultural knowledge. Nevertheless, they are overcome with sexual desire for "the daughters of men," and the offspring of their union propels the world toward greater violence (*Jub.* 7:21–22). The text ultimately blames the angels for this moral lapse, but it arises as a natural consequence of associating with women on account of their seductive beauty (*Jub.* 5:1). Thus, the authors of *Jubilees* change the story of the fallen angels from one of angels corrupting humans to one of humans corrupting angels.[16]

Even though *Jubilees* highlights the beneficial cultural contributions of angels, it does not entirely absolve them of detrimental cultural contributions. After the Flood, Cainan (a son of Arpachshad, who in *Jubilees* 9.4 is given the land of the Chaldeans by his father, Shem, son of Noah) learns writing from his father and later discovers an inscription carved on a rock (*Jub.* 8:2–3). It turns out that the inscription contained knowledge of celestial divination written down by the Watchers before the Flood. Cainan transcribes this knowledge and keeps it a secret (*Jub.* 8:3). We are also told that he sins as a result of learning it, but we are not told what the nature of his sin is (*Jub.* 8:3). Presumably, this is a reference to the science of divination that the Watchers had illicitly given to humanity before the Flood in *1 Enoch*; the fact that Cainan tries to keep it secret further emphasizes its dangerous nature.[17] But here, the authors of *Jubilees* exonerate the Watchers from culpability for directly giving detrimental culture to humans,[18] further emphasizing the point that they desired to absolve angels from sin and creating harmful culture. Since Cainan was believed to be the forefather of the Chaldeans (i.e., Babylonians), his rediscovery of illicit knowledge and his subsequent sinning on account of it was meant to highlight the dangerous nature of Mesopotamian astrology in the eyes of other Jews.[19]

Later noncanonical scriptural retellings of the antediluvian story continued to widen the scope of beneficial arts and sciences revealed by angels to humans. In one striking example, an Armenian translation of the *Book of Adam* (a Jewish or Christian retelling of the life of Adam in circulation by the third century

[16] Hanson, "Rebellion," 229; VanderKam, "Angel," 154–55; Reed, "Fallen," 131–39.

[17] Reed, "Fallen," 135–36. According to Reed, the author of *Jubilees* definitely knew the story of the Watchers.

[18] Reed, "Fallen," 136.

[19] Adler, "Time," 91–92.

AD),[20] we read that Adam received smithing tools and instruction in smithcraft from an angel.

> Due to envy and malice, Adam, who had lived in that garden, had to go out. And he cried, without enjoying food, five days long, until an angel came. And he [the angel] comforted him and gave him tools. And the angel brought him the tools of the forging art, the fire tongs and the hammer and taught him, on the command of God, how they could be tools. As a result, there came afterward among the grandchildren of Adam Tubal, an artisan of iron and copper equipment. And he [Adam] was not as experienced as Tubal.[21]

This is a complete reversal of the Yahwist's story and the *Book of the Watchers*, in which the discovery of metallurgy was associated not with good angels and Adam but with his sinful progeny or bad angels. As the date indicates, the scope of God's involvement with civilization had widened considerably by the time that Rome became Christian.

God's Providence

Paralleling these scriptural developments in which God and His messengers were given a greater role in fostering material civilization, Stoic and Neoplatonic thinking about divine providence had influenced Jews and Christians to further widen the purview of God's interaction with the world.

According to Diogenes Laertius, it was Plato who introduced the terminology of "divine providence" (*theou pronoia*) into Greek thought.[22] In the *Timaeus*, it is the Demiurge, the creator god, who rationally and beneficently orders the world through his divine providence (29d–30c). In the *Laws*, it is the beneficent gods in general who regulate the cosmos, intervene in human affairs, and care for things great and small (10.896e–905d). The Stoics took up the idea but made it part of their materialist philosophy in which a rational universe emanated from a first principle.[23] But whether one thought of the gods as real beings or first principles, providence was closely associated with them by the time of Cicero (d. 43 BC): "As a matter of fact 'providence' is an elliptical expression . . . so when we speak of the world as governed by providence, you must understand the words 'of the gods' and must conceive that

[20] Stone, *History*, 58. De Jonge and Tromp argue that it could be dated as late as 600 AD, but it probably originated between the second and fourth centuries AD (see De Jonge and Tromp, *Life*, 77).

[21] *Book of Adam* 2.1 (translated from Preuschen's *Die Apokryphen Gnostischen Adaschriften*, 24; see Ginzberg, *Legends* 5:83n31).

[22] Diogenes Laertius *Lives* 3.24.

[23] Cicero *De natura deorum* 2.57–59; Dillon, "Providence," 520; Gerson, "God and Greek Philosophy," 166.

the full and complete statement would be 'the world is governed by the providence of the gods.'"[24]

It was a short step for the Jewish exegete Philo (20 BC–50 AD) several decades later to attach the doctrine of divine providence to the single God, Yahweh. Philo devoted a treatise to the subject[25] and discussed the concept elsewhere in his works, notably in *Creation of the World*.[26] In these texts, he draws heavily on Stoic arguments to answer the most difficult objection to the notion of an inherently good and providential God, the existence of evil in the world.[27] Philo rebuts the objection with a cosmological argument, contending that natural phenomena (such as storms) may harm some people (like sailors and farmers) but benefit humanity in general (by watering vegetation). He uses a physical argument to prove that some natural phenomena are the secondary effects of other natural phenomena, such as smoke from fire. Smoke may be harmful, but God can be held accountable only for fire. Philo employs a logical argument to make the case that good things are not known without knowledge of less good things, which are wrongly understood as evil. Finally, he makes an ethical argument that physical evil may actually be a chastisement or deterrent from God to morally train a person.[28] The latter is often used to punish those who have grown neglectful of God because of their attachment to the good things God has provided them.[29] On the other hand, bad things that happen to good people may really be evidence of God working behind the scenes toward a greater good. For example, when Joseph is sold into slavery by his brothers, it is really the working out of God's providence.[30]

Philo's application of Platonic and Stoic arguments for providence to the biblical God was preserved several centuries later by the Church Father Eusebius in his *Evangelical Preparation* and expanded by several later patristic authors, most forcibly by Theodoret of Cyrus (d. 460 AD) in *On Divine Providence*. Theodoret assembled a number of proofs of God's providence—many of them part of the standard repertoire on the topic[31]—to demonstrate that God cares for His subjects. For example, God's providence is indicated by the regularity and maintenance of the heavenly bodies and the alternating seasons, which bring forth crops (Discourse 1).[32] It is further demonstrated by the wind, earth, and sea, which provide human sustenance and means of travel (Discourse 2). It is also proven by the intricate functioning of human organs (Discourse 3).

[24] Cicero *De natura deorum* 2.74; see Frick, *Providence*, 6.

[25] Fragments survive in Eusebius's *Preparation for the Gospel* 7.21.336b–337, 8.14.386–99.

[26] Frick, *Providence*, 1.

[27] Ibid., 140, 144.

[28] Ibid., 145–52.

[29] Philo *On Providence* 2.32–34, in *Complete Works*.

[30] Ibid., 2.36; Frick, *Providence*, 183–84. A similar argument is made in the Qur'an (12:21).

[31] Thomas Halton, introduction to Theodoret's *On Divine Providence*, 4.

[32] Theodoret, *Providence*.

The fourth and fifth discourses of Theodoret's work are particularly germane to the subject of the creation of the arts and sciences. If taken out of context, some passages indicate that humans can invent material culture on their own because of their God-given rationality and physique (particularly their hands). Thus, Theodoret states that humans derived "the art of shipbuilding from the smith's craft, which had already originated through the discovery of the axe, the saw, the adze, and the other tools of carpentry, and also from its older sister, agriculture" (Discourse 4.19). Elsewhere, however, Theodoret makes it clear that man "received a knowledge of all these things from his Maker, and that the Creator implanted in his nature the faculty of invention and of discovering arts" (Discourse 4.23). Such arts include metallurgy, weaving, and medicine (Discourse 4.23, 4.24, 4.28).

Theodoret goes on to argue that humans are not alone in possessing knowledge of the arts and sciences innately. Worms are able to spin yarn, and bees can make geometric shapes in which to store their honey (Discourse 4.26, 5.3–5). That God has enabled animals to possess such knowledge is a further sign of His providence, since humans can learn from their crafts (Discourse 5.11), as fishermen learned how to weave nets from spiders (Discourse 5.15–19).

The purpose of Theodoret's book, disclosed in the final two discourses, is to remove doubts about the possibility and necessity of a physical resurrection and to explain why God was incarnated in Jesus. The resurrection is possible, Theodoret argues in discourse nine, because God is able to do anything. If one accepts that God has created the world, then one can accept that He is able to undertake the less difficult task of resurrecting physical bodies (Discourse 9.34–39). Resurrection is necessary, Theodoret further argues, for humans to receive their just rewards or punishments in an afterlife (Disourse 9.19–33). Conversely, the incarnation of Christ is the ultimate sign to humans in this life of God's providence, and his resurrection was a demonstration to them of the possibility of their own future resurrection.

God and Humans in the Qur'an

Theodoret was not alone in using arguments for providence to encourage the adoption of a new religion. Two centuries after his death, we find many of the same arguments and examples marshaled in the Qur'an.

Throughout the Qur'an, God is extolled for creating the natural world and subjugating it for humans so that they can gain their livelihood (*maʿāyish*) from it. Verses 15:19–22 and 6:99 are typical of this recurrent motif.

> We have set [*jaʿalnā*] in heaven constellations and decked them out fair to the beholders, and guarded them from every accursed Satan excepting such as listens by stealth—and he is pursued by a manifest flame. And the earth—

We stretched it forth, and cast on it firm mountains, and We caused to grow therein of every thing justly weighed, and there appointed [*jaʿalnā*] for you livelihood [*maʿāyish*], and for those you provide not for. Naught is there, but its treasuries are with Us, and We sent it not down [*mā nunazziluhu*] but in a known measure. And We loose the winds fertilizing, and We send down [*fa-anzalnā*] out of heaven water, then We give it to you to drink, and you are not its treasurers. It is We who give life, and make to die, and it is We who are the inheritors. . . .

. . . It is He who sent down out of heaven water, and thereby We have brought forth the shoot of every plant, and then We have brought forth the green leaf of it, bringing forth from it close-compounded grain, and out of the palm-tree, from the spathe of it, dates thick-clustered, ready to the hand, and gardens of vines, olives, pomegranates, like each to each, and each unlike to each. Look upon their fruits when they fructify and ripen! Surely, in all this are signs for a people who do believe.[33]

In addition to fostering an agrarian lifestyle, God provided humans with some of the basic necessities for life in the Arabian Peninsula. Thus, in verses 16:80–81, we read that God gave humans clothing, armor, movable shelter, and transportation.

And it is God who has appointed [*jaʿalā*] a place of rest for you of your houses, and He has appointed [*jaʿalā*] for you, of the skins of cattle, houses you find light on the day that you journey, and on the day you abide, and of their wool, and of their fur, and of their hair furnishing and an enjoyment for a while. And it is God who has appointed [*jaʿalā*] for you coverings of the things He created [*khalaqa*], and He has appointed [*jaʿalā*] for you of the mountains refuges, and He has appointed [*jaʿalā*] for you shirts to protect you from the heat, and shirts to protect you from your own violence.[34]

In a similar vein, we learn that God created (*khalaqnā*, "We created") domesticated cattle (Q 36:71–73) and beasts of burden and riding animals (Q 16:7–8) for the use of humans. Paralleling Theodoret, God also taught bees to build hives and produce honey, which humans can use for medicine (Q 16:68–69). In language reminiscent of the ancient Near Eastern sky gods, God is also said to have "sent down" (*anzala*) iron and cattle. Thus, in verse 39:6 we read that God "sent down for you eight cattle in pairs," and in verse 57:25, "And We sent down [*anzalnā*] iron, wherein is great harm and benefits for people."[35] One could also render this as "caused to descend," suggesting that God directed the angels to

[33] Here and elsewhere, I have used Arberry's translation in *The Koran Interpreted*.

[34] The punctuation has been slightly modified. For the creation of garments that protect the wearer from violence (i.e., armor), see the section on David below.

[35] I have modified Arberry's translation. Ancient Egyptians may have believed that the sky's canopy was made of iron and fell to earth as meteors. See Lesko, "Egyptian Cosmogonies," 117.

do it (see below); either way, a deity in heaven is ultimately responsible for the descent of material culture to earth.

In addition to providing some of the necessities for life on land, God also provided for life on the sea. Thus, He created (*khalaqnā*) ships for humans to ride the waves, and He subdued the sea so that humans may eat its creatures and extract ornaments to wear (Q 16:14).[36]

Several linguistic ambiguities in these passages impede our understanding of God's role in creating culture. First, who is intended by the pronoun *We*? This nebulous word occurs throughout the Qur'an, but its object is not always clear. Moreover, some of the creative acts attributed to "He" are also attributed to "We," as seen above. Is it God acting alone, God and his angels acting in concert, or God's angels acting alone at God's behest?

Sometimes the referent of "We" in the Qur'an seems to be distinct from the angels. For example, in 2:34 "We" addresses the angels: "And when We said to the angels, 'Bow yourselves to Adam.'" But in other instances, it seems that "We" means just the angels or God and the angels. Thus in 4:163, we read that "We" revealed (*awḥaynā*) to Solomon and gave David the Psalms, but that God spoke to Moses directly:

> We have revealed to thee as We revealed to Noah, and the Prophets after him, and We revealed to Abraham, Ishmael, Isaac, Jacob, and the Tribes, Jesus and Job, Jonah and Aaron and Solomon, and We gave to David Psalms, and Messengers We have already told thee of before, and Messengers We have not told thee of; *and unto Moses God spoke directly*. (My italics)

As the passage above indicates, Moses is the only person in the Qur'an to whom God speaks directly (*kallama*), an act that is always described in the third-person singular (Q 2:253, 7:143). Indeed, the people of Muḥammad's time asked, "Why does God not speak to us [*yukallimunā*]?" (Q 2:118), to which the Qur'an replies elsewhere: "It belongs not to any mortal that God should speak to him [*yukallimahu*] except by revelation, or from behind a veil, or that He should send a messenger and reveal whatsoever He will, by His leave" (Q 42:51). One could perhaps claim, on the basis of this passage, that God's revelation constitutes direct speech. But revelation, at least in this passage, seems to be contrasted with direct speech; thus, it is coupled with speaking behind a veil or a message relayed by a messenger.

In his treatment of the troublesome pronoun, Neal Robinson argues that it refers to God alone, and he contrasts his position with that of earlier Western scholars who write that it usually refers to the angels alone.[37] To make his point, Robinson lists a number of parallels between the "We" verses of the Qur'an and the "I," "He," or "God" verses. For example, 5:44 says that "We" sent down the

[36] Presumably, the ornaments are the "pearls and coral" mentioned in 55:22.

[37] Robinson, *Discovering*, 225–29.

Torah, whereas 3:3 says that "He" sent it down. Robinson acknowledges that "We" could be thought of as angels who execute God's commands, but he dismisses this idea because reading some verses in this manner would give the angels too much power vis-à-vis God. Thus, verse 12:76—"Whomsoever We will, We raise in rank"—cannot conceivably refer to angels and must refer to God. This reasoning seems a bit circular, and in light of the passages above and with no clear indication to the contrary, I am more inclined to agree with earlier scholars who argued that the "We" of the Qur'an usually refers to angels, with the caveat that it is probably a select group of angels (such as Michael and Gabriel) speaking for themselves and God. These angels, like the angels in the Enoch literature and *Jubilees*, are the prosecutors of His decrees and the bearers of His gifts of culture (legal, material, or otherwise) to humans. Little wonder that one of these gifts, the Qur'an, is conveyed to Muḥammad by an angel, Gabriel (Q 2:97).

Whatever the referent of "We," it is important to note for our purposes that the angels do not act independently of God's decree (I will return to this point when I discuss the cultural roles of demons and angels); God is the ultimate author of the acts predicated of "We" regardless of how they are carried out.

Another ambiguity in the passages quoted above is the meaning of terms such as *jaʿalnā* ("We made"), *anzalnā* ("We sent down"), and *khalaqnā* ("We created"). This ambiguity is reflected in A. J. Arberry's translation of the Qur'an, the standard translation for modern scholars. Thus, he renders the term *jaʿalā* more literally as "We have set" in relation to God's creation of the stars but more figuratively as "appointed" in relation to the creation of the rudiments of a pastoralist lifestyle. The distinction is perhaps not so important with regard to the creation of the natural world, but it is important in verses where God takes credit for material culture humans could have created.

I do not wish to enter the medieval Muslim debate about the interpretation of the anthropomorphic imagery of God in the Qur'an. But it is important to note that adopting a literal or a figurative reading of these passages affects how we understand the roles of God and humans in the creation of culture. If we accept Arberry's more figurative rendering of *jaʿala* as "appointed," we understand that God wanted humans to have material culture but that humans created it. If we understand it more literally, then God Himself created tents and clothing made of cattle skins for humans and sent down iron from the sky.[38] In the latter reading, the Qur'anic God seems more reminiscent of the Near Eastern sky gods of old, who sent down material culture for humans, than of the God of the Bible. But like the problems surrounding the reading of "We," it is enough to acknowledge that God ultimately condones creating the rudiments of an agrarian and seafaring lifestyle.

God's creation (or sanction) of these rudiments, particularly iron and tents,

[38] Ironically, the ʿAbbāsid Caliph al-Ma'mūn, who was more inclined to the figurative interpretations of Muʿtazilīs, adopted a literal reading of the word *jaʿala* as *khalaqa* ("He created") to bolster his contention that the Qur'an was not eternal but rather created (see "Miḥna," *EI*²).

would have surprised the Yahwist—these are the very cultural phenomena for which Cain's descendants had received such bad press. But as we have seen, the scope of God's cultural gifts had widened considerably by Muḥammad's time in scripture and in learned discussions of providence. The fact that the Qur'an includes several stock examples of God's providence found in antique treatises on providence—such as the hive making of bees—reinforces the notion that Muḥammad was continuing the conversation.

There are some cultural phenomena that God explicitly does not take credit for in the Qur'an. For example, the Qur'an states that "God did not designate [*jaʿala*]" various kinds of camels to be sacrificed (Q 5:103). Although early Muslim tradition attributes this innovation to ʿAmr b. Luḥayy (see chapter 3), the Qur'an does not tell us if humans were responsible for this distasteful innovation; it could just as well have been demons (see below). The institution of monasticism is another human invention of which God disapproves (Q 57:27), although He recognizes that Christians invented it (*ibtadaʿūhā*) in a sincere wish to fulfill God's command to seek His good pleasure.

God is more critical of another human behavior, sodomy. As in the Hebrew Bible, the people of Lot are the primary culprits. But unlike the Bible, the Qur'an makes it clear that Lot's people were the first to engage in the act: "And Lot, when he said to his people, 'What, do you commit such indecency as never any being in all the world committed before you?'" (Q 7:80). The act is condemned by God because it is a subversion of the natural order that He ordained. Thus, Lot warns his people not to leave their wives "that your Lord created for you" to "come to male beings" (Q 26:165–66), which is a "transgression" (Q 26:166). So whereas God condemns monasticism because humans took one of His commandments too far, He condemns sodomy because humans have subverted the natural order that He decreed.

It is significant that sodomy originated in a town (*qarya*), which the Qur'an generally portrays as a breeding ground for human waywardness. It is not that God dislikes civilization and urban living. On the contrary, God facilitates the establishment of urban civilization, as in the case of the people of Thamūd: "And remember when He appointed you successors after Ad, and lodged you in the land, taking to yourselves castles of its plains, and hewing its mountains into houses. Remember God's bounties, and do not mischief in the earth, working corruption" (Q 7:74).

But the problem with towns, some of which are agricultural settlements (see below), is that they can lead to pride in human achievement and to a neglect of the worship of God because humans are sheltered from the vicissitudes of the natural world that make them dependent on divine good favor. It is an argument we have already seen in Philo's discussion of providence. (Nomads are also criticized in the Qur'an, but it is not for being ungrateful to God; rather, it is for being hypocritical and failing to fight for the new religion.)[39] God sends

[39] See Qur'an 9:90, 9:97–99, 9:101, 9:120, 48:11, 48:15–16, 49:14.

messengers and warners to remind the people to worship God, but the examples adduced in the Qur'an make it clear that city dwellers often fail to pass muster because their regular supply of food and shelter makes them ungrateful to their ultimate Provider: "God has struck a similitude: a city that was secure, at rest, its provision coming to it easefully from every place, then it was unthankful for the blessings of God; so God let it taste the garment of hunger and fear, for the things they were working" (Q 16:112).

Thus, the Qur'an counsels Muḥammad's audience to contemplate the end of the people of past civilizations who achieved a great deal materially but failed to listen to His messengers, lest they meet the same end.

> What, have they not journeyed in the land and beheld how was the end of those before them? They were stronger than themselves in might, and they ploughed up the earth and cultivated it more than they themselves have cultivated it; and their Messengers came to them with the clear signs; and God would never wrong them, but themselves they wronged. Then the end of those that did evil was evil, for that they cried lies to the signs of God and mocked at them. (Q 30:9)

The evil end promised by the Qur'an is not further ignorance of God but a divinely ordained disaster that effaces wayward urbanites from the earth and leaves only the ruins of their cities behind as a warning. Thus, the punishment meted out to the people of Lot's time is continually reenacted: "How many a city We have destroyed that flourished in insolent ease!" (Q 28:58).

Again, the Qur'anic story of Thamūd is a good example of this general pattern. God sends Ṣāliḥ, one of the people of Thamūd (Q 7:73), to remind them of their duty to worship God (Q 7:73). Although Ṣāliḥ warns them that they will not be secure in their gardens, springs, sown fields, or houses that they have hewn out of stone (Q 26:146–49), only a few powerless people believe it (Q 7:75). As punishment for failing to heed Ṣāliḥ's call and hamstringing a sacred she-camel, they are destroyed by an earthquake (Q 7:78).

This explication of the moral dangers of settled life is not the same as the Yahwist's disdain for urban living. Muḥammad is no primitivist: God creates numerous elements of civilization, He facilitates the establishment of cities, and He is critical of monasticism, a primitivist lifestyle. But Muḥammad also worries that the benefits of a settled agricultural lifestyle, with reliable sources of food and shelter, cause humans to be ungrateful to their ultimate Provider. Thus, he reminds his settled audience again and again that their ease is the result of God's good pleasure, either through His provision of the cultural phenomena that make it possible or through His indulgence of their waywardness.

Who is this audience of agriculturalists? In the Qur'an, they are described as polytheists (*mushrikūn*) and contrasted with the community of believers, who are traders.[40] This does not fit with the traditional story of Mecca as a barren

[40] See Crone, "Quranic Pagans."

city of pagan traders, but it does explain why Muḥammad spends so much time discussing the subject of God's providence. It is to warn the unbelievers that if they ignore God's new message because of the comfort their livelihood affords them, God can take it away from them and give it to others. Thus, the Qur'an warns, "Those who disbelieve—neither their wealth nor their progeny will profit them against God" (Q 3:10).[41] Rather, their end will be the same as that of Pharaoh and his people (3:11), whose sown lands, great cities, and wealth were destroyed by God and whose enemies, the Israelites, were given vast lands as an "inheritance," raising them from abasement to dominion (Q 7:127–37, 26:52, 44:17–29, 28:3–6). The Qur'an's author warns that the same will happen to the godless cities of his day and that the righteous shall inherit them (7:94–101). Indeed, it affirms that this has already happened to the People of the Book (Jews or Christians) who supported the Muslims' enemies, reminding the audience that God "bequeathed upon you their lands, their habitations, and their possessions, and a land you never trod. God is powerful over everything" (33:27).

This final passage brings us to the point of the Qur'an's musings on divine providence: they are to serve as a warning to those who reject God's newest revelation on account of their material power; they can be brought low and replaced by the righteous. "The earth," writes the Qur'an's author, "shall be the inheritance of my righteous servants" (21:105). This "earth" is not just God's gift of an otherworldly paradise but His sanction of taking land here on earth if its stewards have neglected to worship Him properly.

Qur'anic Culture Heroes

In addition to making God or His angels directly responsible for creating civilization, the Qur'an also depicts Him as acting through mundane intermediaries (which we have already seen with the bees). In this, the Qur'an's author draws on Jewish stories and noncanonical biblical literature that have a more positive view of God's role in creating civilization than that found in Genesis. If he is aware of the latter's negative etiologies of culture, he chooses to ignore them in support of his larger argument for God's providence.

Adam and Cain

In the Hebrew Bible and other Jewish scripture, Adam is responsible for bringing a great deal of culture to humans, either through his own inventiveness or after receiving it as a gift from angels. In contrast, the Qur'an does not clearly credit Adam with the creation of any cultural phenomenon. For example, God, not Adam, is the source of names: "And He taught Adam the names, all of them" (Q 2:31). The Qur'an does not make clear what Adam was naming, in

[41] My translation.

contrast to the Hebrew Bible.[42] But the point is that God is ultimately responsible for teaching Adam these names.

We find a similar pattern with regard to the making of garments. As in the Hebrew Bible (Gen. 3:7), Adam and Eve stitch together leaves of paradise to cover themselves when their shame (*sawʾātihimā*) is revealed after they eat the forbidden fruit (Q 7:22, 20:121). However, whereas the Genesis account depicts Adam and Eve as naked before this point, the Qur'an indicates that they are clothed before committing their transgression. Thus, in verses 20:118–19 God tells Adam that "it is assuredly given to thee neither to hunger therein [i.e., paradise], nor to go naked, neither to thirst therein, nor to suffer the sun."[43] But then Satan tempts them and strips off their garments, revealing their shame (Q 7:27), which prompts them to sew garments from leaves to cover themselves.

Just as he is not credited with inventing clothing, Adam is also not credited with inventing farming or learning of it from the angels. Of course, it is reasonable to assume that Muḥammad was familiar with these legends. But he chooses not to mention the etiology.

This trend of ignoring the negative etiologies in biblical scripture continues with the Qur'an's treatment of the innovations of Cain and his descendants. Although the Qur'an alludes to the story of Cain and Abel (Q 5:27–31), it does not mention Adam's two sons by name or recount the inventions of Cain and his descendants. Again, this is not to say that Muḥammad was unfamiliar with the biblical account of the Cainites. But he chooses to attribute Cainite inventions such as iron and tents to God and not to wayward humans.

Although the typical cultural innovations of the Cainite line are not mentioned in the Qur'an, there is one etiology associated with Cain: the burial of humans underground. According to the Qur'an, Cain is at a loss as to what to do after killing his brother. God sends a raven, who scratches the ground in order to show him how to hide his brother's nakedness (Q 5:31). This story has its roots in rabbinic Jewish lore,[44] but there is a significant difference. In the Jewish story, the body of Abel is left exposed on the ground because Adam and Eve do not know what to do with it. Adam then observes a raven dispose of a dead raven by burying it underground; Adam follows suit. Aside from the question of who sees the raven, the main difference between the stories is that in the Jewish version, Adam intuits the innovation of burial on his own. In the Qur'anic story, Cain also intuits the practice, but with God's help behind the scenes. As with the other antediluvian etiologies in the Qur'an, the main point is, again, that God (this time through a bird) is the ultimate source of culture.

[42] This omission allowed Muslim authors to posit that Adam had invented the writing for some, or all, human languages (e.g., Ibn Nadīm, *Fihrist*, 7; Suyūṭī, *Wasāʾil*, 156).

[43] The Qur'an does say that God sent down a garment to humans: "O Children of Adam! We have sent down [*anzalnā*] on you a garment [*libāsan*] to cover your shameful parts" (7:26). But it is unclear if this happened before Adam sinned or after (as in the Genesis account).

[44] For references, see Ginzberg, *Legends* 5:142n31.

Abraham: Monotheist and Temple Builder

The blurring of the lines between human intuition and divine grace as distinct modes of cultural initiation is also found in the story of Abraham's discovery of monotheism. On the one hand, God says that He showed Abraham the heavens so that he might discern God's existence (Q 6:75). On the other hand, the account that follows this statement has Abraham contemplating the heavens and finally coming to worship God alone as a result of his own reasoning (Q 6:76–79). As in the story of Cain and the raven, God works subtly to guide human intuition.

A useful contrast might be drawn with a similar story in Josephus's *Antiquities*. As in the Qur'anic story, Abraham intuits monotheism after contemplating the heavens. However, God is not involved.[45] In contrast, the Qur'an tells us that God is working behind the scenes of this drama, pulling the levers but letting Abraham believe he has discovered monotheism through his own rational faculties. As with so many other stories about prophets in the Qur'an, God manages His chosen mouthpieces very carefully but often unbeknownst to them.

Although there are echoes of Josephus's etiology in the Qur'an, Abraham is not explicitly credited with discovering monotheism. Rather, he and his son Ishmael are credited (somewhat obliquely) with being the first to build a temple dedicated to the worship of God. In 3:96 we read that the "house," or temple, at Bakka (identified by Muslim exegetes as Mecca) was the "first house established for people" as "a blessing and guidance for all beings." Elsewhere we are informed that God picked out the site of the house for Abraham (Q 22:26), who, along with his son Ishmael, raised its foundations (Q 2:127). Consequently, it is called the "station of Abraham" (Q 3:97). As with the story of Adam, God plays a significant part in this cultural creation, telling Abraham and Ishmael where to build the temple, if not how.

The association of Abraham with the building of a place of worship is not unprecedented in Jewish scripture; in the Hebrew Bible he is twice credited with building altars (Gen. 12:7, 8). But there is no mention that these are the first altars dedicated to God or that Ishmael assisted in building them. Moreover, there is certainly no mention of Abraham or Ishmael building a temple in Arabia.

The story of Abraham building the Kaʿba in Mecca need not have originated with Muḥammad. There is evidence of pre-Islamic Arabs who considered themselves the descendants of Ishmael and the adherents of Abraham's religion,[46] so the story could have easily originated with such a group. But it is surprising, if we assume a pagan audience,[47] that Muḥammad chose to depict a

[45] Josephus *Antiquities* 1.156, in *The Works of Flavius Josephus*.

[46] Sozomen *Ecclesiastical History* 6.38; see Crone, *Meccan Trade*, 190n104.

[47] The traditional dating of sura six—the sura that discusses Abraham's discovery of monotheism—as Meccan would indicate that the author of the Qur'an was addressing a pagan audience.

foreigner as the builder of the first temple, particularly a local one. One suspects that the audience was more biblically oriented than suggested by the standard account, which has them as crude idolaters.[48]

David the Armorer

We see a similar depiction of God guiding a chosen human intermediary to create culture in the Qur'an's depiction of David as an armor smith. The legend is related as follows:

> And We gave David bounty [*fadlan*] from Us: "O you mountains, echo God's praises with him, and you birds!" And We softened for him iron [*wa-alannā lahu al-hadīd*]: "Fashion wide coats of mail [*iʿmal sābighāt*], and measure well the links [*wa qaddir fī al-sard*]."—And do ye righteousness, for surely I see the things you do.[49]

That this is meant to be an etiology of coats of mail is made clear in verse 21:80: "And we taught him [David] the fashioning of garments for you, to fortify you against your violence [*ba'sikum*]; then are you thankful?"

It should not surprise us that the Qur'an depicts David as originating material culture or that it associates him with iron armor. In the Hebrew Bible, David invents material culture (1 Chron. 23:5), handles coats of mail,[50] and endorses the use of iron weapons.[51] This seems to have been reflected in pre-Islamic lore about David—pre-Islamic poetry often mentions the "fabric [*nasj*] of David,"[52] which may be a vague reference to his armor. Indeed, the association between David and the invention of some sort of armor would have fitted well with Arab lore about Arab kings, who are primarily remembered for originating garments and arms, just like the Qur'anic David. Thus Khims, a king of Yemen, is said to have been the first to wear the garment (*burd*) that bears his name.[53] Another king of Yemen, Mālik al-Aṣbaḥ, is remembered as the first person for whom *aṣbaḥī* whips (named after him) were made.[54] In the north, the pre-Lakhmid king Jadhīma al-Abrash[55] (fl. fourth century AD) was the first

[48] See Hawting's *Idea of Idolatry*.

[49] Q 34:10–11 (trans. Arberry).

[50] David was Saul's armor bearer (1 Sam. 16:21); he tried on Saul's coat of mail (1 Sam. 17:38); and he kept Goliath's coat of mail (1 Sam. 17.54).

[51] 2 Sam. 23:7.

[52] Wensinck, *Jews*, 110; Horovitz, *Koranische*, 109–10; Speyer, *Erzahlungen*, 382 (a summary of earlier secondary sources); Paret, "Dāwūd," *EI*²; Déclais, *David*, 174–76.

[53] Jawharī, *al-Siḥāḥ* 3:87.

[54] ʿAskarī, *Awā'il* 1:13. The epithet *aṣbaḥ* means one who has black hair with a reddish tinge (see Lane, *ṣabaḥa*, in *Arabic-English Lexicon* 2:1643.

[55] He was called al-Abrash ("speckled") or al-Waḍḍāḥ ("leper") on account of his leprosy (Ziriklī, *Al-Aʿlām* 2:114).

to wear sandals (*niʿāl*)[56] and to build a mangonel (*manjanīq*).[57] His nephew and founder of the Lakhmid dynasty, ʿAmr b. ʿAdī (fl. early third century AD), was the first to wear a neckband (*ṭawq*).[58] There is even one Arab king, Sayf b. Dhī Yazan (d. ca. 574 AD), associated with iron weapons. He is said to have been the first person to use iron spearpoints.[59]

Perhaps the best parallel with an Arab king is found in the *Kitāb al-tījān*, a book on south Arabian antiquities by Ibn Hishām (d. ca. 213 AH/828 AD). In it, he writes—on the authority of Ibn ʿAbbās by way of Muḥammad b. al-Sā'ib[60]—that a Yemeni king named Shammar Yarʿash was "the first king to command the making of long, wide coats of mail [*al-durūʿ al-sawābigh al-mufāḍa*], of which only the forearms and hands [are uncovered]."[61] Ibn Hishām goes on to remark that Shammar made the Persians, Byzantines, Omanis, and Yemenis each send one thousand of these coats every year. Of these, the Persians made the best coats of mail.[62]

Despite these parallels with Arab kings, the Qur'anic David is different in one significant manner: he fashions iron into armor with his own hands after God softens it and tells him how to shape it. As we have seen, this is not something early Jewish and Christian scripture would attribute to God or to a biblical hero. God has nothing to do with iron, and those who originate smithcraft are sinful; moreover, the application of this technology to the crafting of weapons and armor leads to bloodshed and ruin.

The suspicion of smithcraft and of those who practice it went beyond Judaism and Christianity, as may be inferred from Hesiod's linkage of the deterioration of the five races and the development of ironsmithing. It was, as Fritz Graf points out, a suspicion held by many in the ancient Mediterranean world. Roman poets such as Tibullus (d. 19 BC) lamented the invention of iron weapons, and Ovid (d. 18 AD) regarded the mining of the earth as one of the horrible achievements of the iron race of men.[63] Prefiguring Qur'an 57:25, Pliny remarks, "Iron is an excellent or a detrimental instrument for human life, according to the use we put it to."[64] But elsewhere he focuses on the destructive results of metallurgy: "Nothing [is] more pernicious (than iron) for it is employed in

[56] Ibn Qutayba, *Maʿārif*, 554.

[57] Ibid.

[58] ʿAskarī, *Awā'il* 1:132.

[59] Ibid., 137.

[60] Quite a few south Arabian firsts are related on the authority of Muḥammad b. al-Sā'ib and his son Ibn al-Kalbī (see chapter 3).

[61] Ibn Hishām, *Tījān*, 250. Ibn Hishām quotes a poem by the early Islamic poet Abū Dhuʿayb that links David and the Yemeni king (here referred to by his title, Tubbaʿ): "Upon them both were coats of perforated mail that / David had made or Tubbaʿ fashioned the long coats of mail" (*Tījān*, 251).

[62] Ibid., 251.

[63] Tib. 1.10.1–6; Ov. *Met.* 1.138ff. (cited in Graf, "Production," 322).

[64] Pliny *Natural History* 34.138 (translated in Graf, "Production," 326).

making swords, javelins, spears, pikes, arrows—weapons by which men are wounded and die, and which causes slaughter, robbery and wars."[65] This is not to say that everyone living around the Mediterranean feared metallurgy; on the contrary, I cited positive etiologies of metallurgy in the section on early Greek mythology. Yet the sentiment was common.

Fritz Graf has suggested that this fear of metallurgy in the Mediterranean world arose from a general anxiety about the transformation of substances from one form to another, which was viewed as an alteration of the natural order of the physical world. That is why it is also sometimes coupled with the use of dyes, as in the *Book of the Watchers*. Like divination, dyeing, metallurgy, and alchemy are all transgressions of natural boundaries.[66] But the fact that metallurgy is consistently linked with violence in the texts we have surveyed suggests there was a more rational reason for this fear: humans disliked the technology that transformed iron into lethal weapons.

As necessary as metallurgy may have been for civilized life, its invention was often attributed to groups living on the margins of society. This is not without some semblance of reality, for, as Sawyer puts it, "the peculiar powers of the smiths, which set them apart from the rest of society, tended to lead to the development of a distinctive and exclusive religion" among blacksmithing groups in many parts of the world.[67] Thus the Yahwist attributes the development of metallurgy to transient blacksmiths whom he portrays as outcasts, and Pliny records that antique catalogers of inventions variously attributed its origins to the Dactyls or the Telchines, groups of sorcerers living on the fringes of Greek society.[68]

The suspicion of smiths and the perception of them as outcasts also existed among the pre-Islamic Arabs. As in the Hebrew Bible, they associated ironworking with transient ironworkers, who were not to be trusted.[69] As one proverb has it, "If you hear of the night travel of the blacksmith [*al-qayn*], he will [still] be there in the morning." The meaning, according to the early Arabic philologist al-Aṣmaʿī (d. ca. 213 AH / 828 AD), is that the blacksmith goes to an oasis where a settled population (*ahl al-māʾ*) lives. He is not very successful in plying his trade, so he informs the people that he will leave in the evening. However, his intent is not to leave but to fool the people into hiring him before his supposed departure. He does this so often that he is no longer believed. Ac-

[65] Ibid., 34.39 (translated by Sawyer, "Cain," 165n10).

[66] Graf, "Production," 327–28.

[67] Sawyer, "Cain," 157, citing Forbes's examples in *Studies in Ancient Technology* 8:71–78.

[68] Graf, "Production," 323–25. In Philo of Byblos's *Phoenician History*, Chrysor, one of two brothers who discovered iron and how to work it, is said to have practiced divination and the writing of magical formulas (see chapter 4).

[69] This attitude continued after the appearance of Islam (see J. Chelhod, "Ḳayn," *EI*²). Dyers were also regarded as liars in Arab society, again mirroring the wider Mediterranean suspicion of those who change the outer form of a substance (see Beg, "Ṣabbāgh," *EI*²).

cording to another philologist, Abū ʿUbayd al-Harawī (d. 224 AH / 838 AD), this proverb is told to someone who is known to lie so that his honesty will return.[70] This distrust of blacksmiths also explains a line from the pre-Islamic poet Aws b. Ḥajar: "Umayya set out early in the morning with a pledge. / She betrayed you. Verily, the blacksmith is not trustworthy."[71]

That blacksmiths were viewed with suspicion in pre-Islamic society is further confirmed by the lore surrounding al-Hālik b. ʿAmr b. Asad, who is remembered as the first person to work iron among the Arabs of the desert.[72] On account of his innovation, his descendants are called "the blacksmiths" (*al-quyūn*),[73] and, according to Balādhurī, "they were reviled" (*yuʿayyarūn*) because of it.[74] A similar disgust for blacksmiths among post-Islamic Arabs is reflected in a poem by Ashhab b. Rumayla, a Companion of the Prophet:

> How odd! Is the blacksmith riding the horse
> While the sweat of the blacksmith on horses is filth?
>
> Rather, when he sits, his tools
> Are the tongs, the anvil, and the firebrand.[75]

Like the descendants of al-Hālik, Jewish smiths living in Arabia may have also been the object of opprobrium in Arab and Jewish society because of their trade. There is not much clear literary evidence for this, but it might be inferred from the contrasting descriptions of the three main Jewish tribes of Yathrib (later called Medina after the Prophet settled there): the Qaynuqāʿ, the Qurayẓa, and the Naḍīr. According to Muslim sources, the Qaynuqāʿ, a Jewish tribe of goldsmiths and armorers, had no land and had to live by trade and smithing alone.[76] The Qurayẓa and the Naḍīr, on the other hand, possessed land and were agriculturalists. Moreover, these two tribes are often mentioned separately from the Qaynuqāʿ,[77] and when the Persians appointed tax collectors on behalf of the empire, they gave the job to the Qurayẓa and the Naḍīr, titling them, and not the Qaynuqāʿ, "kings" of Yathrib.[78] Even the name of the Qaynuqāʿ tribe—a combination of *qayn* ("blacksmith") and *qāʿʿ* ("low")—suggests a low social status.

Perhaps the story of David the armorer arose among the Qaynuqāʿ or a similar

[70] Ibn Manẓūr, *Lisān* 13:351, under the root q-y-n.

[71] Aws b. Ḥajar, *Diwān*, 129; Ibn Manẓūr, *Lisān* 13:351 (q-y-n).

[72] Balādhurī, *Futūḥ*, 274; Ibn Manẓūr, *Lisān* 10:507 (h-l-k). The term *hālikī* ("sharp") is said to come from his name.

[73] Ibn Manẓūr, *Lisān* 13:351 (q-y-n), 10:507 (h-l-k).

[74] Balādhurī, *Futūḥ*, 274.

[75] Jāḥiẓ, *Ḥayawān* 1:315.

[76] Ṭabarī, *Taʾrīkh* 7:87.

[77] For the differences between the three Jewish tribes, see Wensinck, *Jews*, 31.

[78] Ahmad, *Muhammad and the Jews*, 33.

tribe of Jewish smiths.[79] It would certainly have benefited a group of Jewish smiths like the Qaynuqāʿ, who were heavily involved in the manufacture of armor and weapons.[80] Indeed, the Qur'anic story has all the elements of a story created by a disadvantaged social group that wants to legitimate the use of a despised cultural phenomenon in the eyes of their coreligionists. Compare, for example, the depiction of David as a smith in the Qur'an and the depiction of Enoch in the *Astronomical Book*. In both cases, those who originated these legends wanted to validate a craft or science that was viewed with suspicion by their contemporaries; for the authors of the *Astronomical Book*, it was astronomy, and for the anonymous promulgators of the David legend, it was smithcraft. To ensure that the association between a biblical hero and questionable technology was acceptable, the responsibility for producing the technology was shifted away from the hero to God and His angels. Like the earlier authors of the *Astronomical Book*, therefore, the promulgators of the David myth found it useful to conceive of positive cultural development as resulting from divine inspiration rather than from human invention, grace rather than reason. If God Himself gave humans an otherwise objectionable craft through His prophet, who could complain?

Instead of being of local Jewish provenance, which is admittedly very speculative, there is evidence that the story of David the armorer originated among Jews or Christians living in the Iranian cultural sphere of influence. As in Arabia and the Mediterranean world, Iranians had mixed feelings about iron. On the one hand, iron had a positive origin in Zoroastrian religious texts: it came, along with other metals, from the body of the first human, Gayōmart, when he died.[81] On the other hand, Iranian prophecies held that the fourth and final age of the world, called the Iron Age, would be a time of wickedness and suffering.[82] As in Hesiod, the implication is that iron weapons were the cause of much of this misery.

Despite this ambivalence toward iron in Iranian religious literature, there is some indication that ironsmithing was revered in more secular mythology—the premier Iranian culture heroes, the first kings, are celebrated as inventors of weapon and armor smithing, at least in post-Islamic records of pre-Islamic Iranian lore. Thus in his *Ta'rīkh*, Ṭabarī notes that "the Persian scholars" say that Jamshīd, one of the first Iranian kings, "originated the manufacture of swords and weaponry."[83] He also records that "someone" said that Jamshīd "ordered the

[79] A large number of blacksmiths also inhabited the Jewish settlement at Khaybar (see Heck, "Arabia," 567n85).

[80] For a description of the type of armor and weapons manufactured by the Qaynuqāʿ, see Ṭabarī, *Ta'rīkh* 7:87, and Ibn Saʿd, *Ṭabaqāt* 2:26. There is even a story in Islamic lore that after Muḥammad defeated the Qaynuqāʿ, he found David's suit of armor among the spoils (Wensinck, *Jews*, 109–10).

[81] Carnoy, *Iranian Mythology*, 294.

[82] Boyce, "Middle Persian," 49.

[83] Ṭabarī, *Ta'rīkh* 1:348–49.

production of swords, coats of mail [*al-durūʿ*], *bīḍ* swords, and other kinds of weapons as well as iron tool(s) for craftsmen."[84] Similarly, Firdawsī records that Jamshīd "wrought arms" and "made iron yield." He also "fashioned it to helmets, hauberks, breastplates, and coats of armour both for man and horse."[85] Although we should be cautious in accepting these depictions of Jamshīd as authentic records of pre-Islamic Iranian lore (see chapter 4), it seems reasonable to suppose that they reflect a positive Iranian attitude toward metallurgy and ironsmithing.[86]

The association between Iranians and armor smithing is also found in pre-Islamic Arabic poetry, which often depicts Iranians as wearing mail. This mail is described as *musarrad,*[87] "made of interlinking rings." The word *musarrad* ultimately derives from the Avestan word for coats of mail, *zrāda*, which becomes *zrih* in Middle Persian and finally *sard* in pre-Islamic Arabic.[88] This is the very word used in the Qur'anic passage about David and his armor: "Fashion wide coats of mail, and measure well the links" (*wa-qaddir fī al-sard*) (34:11).

There is one more reason to suspect that the story of David the armorer has Iranian roots: its parallel with the third-century Armenian translation of the *Book of Adam* cited earlier, which may have been written during Sassanid rule. Here is the passage again:

> Due to envy and malice, Adam, who had lived in that garden, had to go out. And he cried, without enjoying food, five days long, until an angel came. And he [the angel] comforted him and gave him tools. And the angel brought him the tools of the forging art, the fire tongs and the hammer and taught him, on the command of God, how they could be tools. As a result, there came afterward among the grandchildren of Adam Tubal, an artisan of iron and copper equipment. And he [Adam] was not as experienced as Tubal.[89]

In some earlier translations of the *Life of Adam*, Adam is taught the basics of agriculture by the archangel Michael after his penitence;[90] this is also found in our Armenian translation of the *Book of Adam*.[91] But the latter text is unique in

[84] Ibid., 349. Note the parallel with the Yemeni king Shammar, cited above, and the praise of Persian coats of mail.

[85] Firdawsī, translated by Warner and Warner in *Shahnama of Firdausi* 1:132.

[86] The fact that in Iranian mythology Kāvih Ahangar ("Kāvih the Blacksmith") is responsible for ending foreign rule is further evidence, as is the king Hōshang's invention of ironsmithing (see chapter 4).

[87] Goldziher, *Muslim Studies* 1:99.

[88] Jeffery, *Foreign Vocabulary*, 169.

[89] *Book of Adam* 2.1 (my translation from Erwin Preuschen's *Die Apokryphen Gnostischen Adaschriften*, 24; see Ginzberg, *Legends* 5:83n31).

[90] See 20:1b of the Georgian and Armenian translations of the *Vita Adae* (the *Book of Adam* and the *Penitence of Adam* respectively), edited by Anderson and Stone, in *Synopsis*, 21E.

[91] Preuschen, *Die Apokryphen Gnostischen Adamschriften*, 33. The same angel who taught Adam smithcraft also taught him how to plow with an ox and sow a field.

portraying smithcraft and its tools as the gifts of an angel.[92] Indeed, this may be the only instance in Jewish or Christian scripture in which metallurgy is portrayed in a positive light; even Tubal is exonerated by his association with his ancestor's art. This suggests that the motif is of Iranian origin, or in other words that Adam is taking the role of Jamshīd in the Iranian tradition.

Some version of this story was known to early Muslims, as evidenced by the following account of Adam in Ṭabarī's *Ta'rīkh*:

> Then, an anvil, a mallet, and a pair of tongs were sent down to him [*unzila ʿalayhi*]. When Adam was cast upon the mountain, he looked at an iron rod growing on the mountain and said: This comes from that, and he began to break up trees that had grown old and dry with the mallet and heated that (iron) branch until it melted. The first thing (of iron) he hammered was a long knife, which he used for work. Then he hammered the oven, the one which Noah inherited and that boiled with the punishment in India.[93]

As in the story of Adam in the Armenian *Book of Adam*, blacksmithing tools are sent down to Adam; however, we do not know what occasioned these gifts or who brought them to him. Presumably it was the angels, since the tools "descended upon him," and it must have been a good thing if God had sanctioned it. But even if that is so, Adam is left to his own devices, and no angel teaches him to use the tools. Exploring his natural environment, he makes an inductive leap—"This comes from that"—and is able to invent smithcraft on his own, a faint echo of Democritus's concept of technological evolution.[94] Despite this important difference, both accounts tell basically the same story: Adam receives ironworking tools from the heavens.

Although one can posit that Muḥammad heard such stories about Adam and patterned his depiction of David accordingly, this seems implausible. Muḥammad would not refer to a legend that his audience knew nothing about, particularly since he cites it to prove a wider point about the grace (*faḍlan*) of God or

[92] John, a seventh-century AD Coptic bishop of Nikiu in Egypt who wrote a chronology of world history at the time of the Arab invations, does note that Tubal "was a brass and iron smith before the deluge; for he had received wisdom from God" (*Chronicle* 11.2, translated by Charles in *Chronicle of John*). My thanks to Lennart Sundelind for pointing me to this source.

[93] Ṭabarī, *Ta'rīkh* 1:297. (Ginzberg notes that "there are Arabic legends concerning a book of Adam" and refers readers to Grünbaum's *Neue Beiträge* [66]. There, Grünbaum relates a passage from Ṭabarī [67] that parallels the above quotation from the *Life of Adam*.) Several pages later, Ṭabarī cites a report from Ibn ʿAbbās that states that anvils, tongs, mallets, and hammers were sent down with Adam (Ṭabarī, *Ta'rīkh* 1:300). As for the oven, this is one interpretation of the word *al-tannūr* in the Qur'an, which is said to have boiled (*fāra*) and brought on the Flood (Q 11:40, 23:27). Some early authorities held that this oven was located in India. Others say that *al-tannūr* does not mean "oven" at all but rather "springs." See Ṭabarī's compilation of the various interpretations in his *Jāmiʿ* 12:39–40.

[94] Metallurgy and the production of tools are the fifth stage in Thomas Cole's reconstruction of Democritus's theory of technological evolution (Cole, *Democritus*, 26).

God and his angels (34:10). Given the Persian vocabulary in the Qur'anic description of David's armor and the striking parallel with the Armenian story of Adam the smith, a more plausible argument is that both stories emerged in areas under Iranian rule where, perhaps, Jews and Christians fashioned their culture heroes in terms that would have been appreciated by a governing elite that revered metallurgy and the heroes who invented it. That the pagan Meccan audience was familiar with the story should,[95] like the story of Abraham's discovery of monotheism, cause us to either question the traditional dating of some of the suras in the Qur'an or to rethink the traditional account of Meccans as idol worshipers who were unfamiliar with biblical scripture.

Whatever the origin of the legends or the nature of the Qur'an's audience, Muḥammad seems to have drawn on a scriptural tradition in which the working of iron was sanctioned by God: He had sent it down to humans and also taught David how to turn it into armor. As in the *Book of the Watchers*, knowledge of smithcraft descends from the heavens to humans. But it now descended as a token of God's grace rather than on the wings of fallen angels.

Why did Muḥammad draw on this tradition when his Arab and Jewish audience was suspicious of smithcraft? Perhaps it was to prove a wider point: even a technology that was regarded with suspicion and could harm humans (as the Qur'an acknowledges) was originated by an all-powerful Creator. We find the same point made with regard to the origins of magic.

Fallen Angels and Scheming Demons

Although fallen angels are not responsible for teaching humans metallurgy in the Qur'an, there is some echo of the story of the Watchers: demons and angels teach humans magic. Thus we read in verse 2:102 that demons teach people magic in order to mislead them. But even though demons teach humans magic, the Qur'an is unclear as to who originated it.

> They [some of the People of the Book] followed what the demons recited against the power of Solomon. Solomon did not disbelieve; rather, the demons disbelieved, teaching the people magic and what descended upon the two angels in Babylon, Hārūt and Mārūt. [These two angels] did not teach anyone without [first] saying, "We are a temptation, so do not disbelieve." They [the demons] learned from them what separates a man and his wife. They could not harm anyone with it save by the permission of God. They learned what harms them and not what benefits them.[96]

[95] Suras 21 and 34, in which David is depicted as an armorer, are traditionally dated as Meccan.

[96] My translation. In addition to the story of Hārūt and Mārūt, another echo of the Watchers story may be found in Q 9:30, where the Jews are criticized for worshiping ʿUzayr as a god. Although ʿUzayr is typically identified as Ezra, Patricia Crone argues in a forthcoming article, "*The Book of Watchers* in the Qur'an," that he may be Asael from the *Book of the Watchers*.

There are several ambiguities in this passage. First, it is not clear if demons first taught humans magic in the time of Solomon or sometime prior to that. Second, it is unclear if humans first learned of magic through demons. We know from other verses in the Qur'an that sorcerers existed during the time of Moses (Q 7:112, 10:79), so perhaps humans at that time or earlier had developed magic before demons supplemented their knowledge. Third, it is unclear whether demons learned every kind of magic from Hārūt and Mārūt or just a few select dark arts, such as the ability to sow discord between a man and his wife.

What is clear in the passage is that at least some of the dark arts came from two angels in Babylon, Hārūt and Mārūt, who had received them from an anonymous source. This is an interesting combination of the lore surrounding Babylon as the origin of the occult sciences and the story of the Watchers. Moreover, there are several parallels between the Qur'anic depiction of Hārūt and Mārūt and the Watchers in Jewish pseudepigrapha. In *1 Enoch*, angels rebel against God and teach humans forbidden arts, particularly magic. They also create discord by having sex with women. In *Jubilees*, the Watchers have sex with women, but they do not rebel against God and they do not directly teach humans forbidden arts. They do write down their astrological teachings, which cause a problem when Cainan later discovers them.

In the Qur'an, the two angels do not have sex with women or rebel against God. We get the sense that they are fallen, since they are stationed in Babylon, but we are not explicitly told this. In a distant echo of the sexual discord caused by the angels, they teach knowledge of how to create disharmony between a man and his wife. So we have the basic elements of angels (perhaps fallen) teaching occult arts and causing sexual discord.

These parallels are not as interesting as the contrasts, which give us some sense of the Qur'anic perspective on the origins of culture. One difference is that God is involved with magic, although the Qur'an seems to be deliberately obscure about His role. Thus, it says that some knowledge of the occult arts "descended" on Hārūt and Mārūt, but it does not forthrightly claim that God sent the knowledge down. Moreover, it relates that demons are not able to use one of these arts to harm humans except by God's leave; we are not told whether God ever gives them permission to do so. It seems, therefore, that Muḥammad is trying to avoid the stigma attached to magic without admitting that something as powerful as magic is not within God's purview.

One final difference is that God allows angels to give this knowledge to others as a kind of moral temptation. This is not part of the *Book of the Watchers* but does have a parallel in *Jubilees*, in which God allows the chief demon, Mastema, to retain some of his retinue so that they can continue their function of leading humans astray.[97] It also fits well with the Qur'anic notion that God and wayward angels collaborate to separate righteous humans from the ungodly.

[97] *Jubilees* 10.7–10.

This collaboration began with the first fallen angel, Iblīs, or Satan. When God casts Iblīs out of the company of angels, Iblīs asks for a special dispensation, which God grants. Iblīs then vows to lie in wait for humans and lead them astray (Q 7:11–17, 15:28–39, 17:61–65, 38:71–85). "I will command them," he boasts, "and they will alter God's creation" (Q 4:119). Iblīs even manages to lead the people to idol worship in Muḥammad's own time: "Hast thou not regarded those who assert that they believe in what has been sent down to thee, and what was sent down before thee, desiring to take their disputes to idols, yet they have been commanded to disbelieve in them? But Satan desires to lead them astray into error" (Q 4:60).

Despite his boastfulness and seeming rebelliousness, the Qur'an makes it clear that Satan and God are working together. In verses 38:82–83, we learn that his temptation of humans is by God's leave and that he will be able to affect only the corrupt. For God's part, He allows Satan to tempt humans so that the true believers will be separated from the false, who will fall prey to Satan's promises of earthly rewards (Q 17:63–64, 38:82–84). In the passage on Hārūt and Mārūt, God allows demons and fallen angels to perform a similar function by teaching the knowledge of magic to humans.

Conclusion

Although the Qur'an's presentation of cultural history has the same characters found in early Jewish scripture, their roles and their cultural creations are profoundly different: God sends down iron and teaches a biblical hero how to shape it into armor; He makes tents and regulates the use of magic through angels. This would have been inconceivable to the authors of the Hebrew Bible and *1 Enoch*, but not to later Jewish and Christian authors, who had softened the primitivism of these earlier texts by crediting good angels and biblical heroes with the creation of the rudiments of civilization.

Although the authors of these scriptures were responding to immediate intellectual concerns, empire provided the backdrop for their musings and shaped their understanding of cultural origins. The authors of *1 Enoch* grappled with the scientific legacy of their Babylonian conquerors; the authors of *Jubilees* fashioned their heroes to compete with those of the Greeks and others conquered by Alexander; and the authors of the Armenian translation of the *Book of Adam* may have patterned Adam on the culture heroes of their Iranian Sassanid rulers.

The broadening scriptural scope of God's involvement in civilization was complemented by antique Jewish and Christian arguments for God's divine providence, a discourse of which the Qur'an is a part. Indeed, it is the culmination of these two trends. The Qur'an's author deliberately avoids negative etiologies of culture and focuses instead on biblical legends that widen the range of beneficial culture given by God in accordance with antique thinking about divine providence. Thus, he employs a positive etiology of armor smithing—a craft that was viewed with suspicion by his audience—as part of a larger argument that God has provided the rudiments of civilization. Since God is a beneficent, all-powerful Creator, it follows for Muḥammad that He must have created everything that is beneficial to humans—He even has a hand in a dangerous art like magic. Far from censuring civilization, therefore, the goal of Muḥammad was to convince his skeptical audience that God had provided everything for them, including a new religion. If they let life's comforts prevent them from embracing the new religion, their material civilization would be inherited by God's righteous slaves, the Muslims.

THREE

Who Was First? Protography and Discovery Catalogs

> Before we quit the consideration of the nature of man, it appears only proper to point out those persons who have been the authors of different inventions.
>
> —Pliny, *Natural History*

> This is a book in which I have compiled the knowledge that befits a person of noble station who is set apart from the rabble by being cultured and by being preferred in learning and eloquence over the masses. This is so that he might study it and perfect his soul by memorizing it since he cannot do without this knowledge when he attends the salons of kings, hobnobs in the gatherings of nobles, and attends the study circles of scholars.
>
> —Ibn Qutayba, *al-Maʿārif*

THE ARAB CONQUEST of the Near East in the seventh century spurred intensive writing about cultural milestones, formalized in lists of "firsts" (Ar. *awāʾil*) in the ninth century, establishing an Arabic genre of the same name. Although the Muslims may have been indebted to the Greeks and Romans for the form of these lists, they did not preserve any Greco-Roman lore in them, drawing instead from Judeo-Christian, Arab, and Iranian legends. Nevertheless, the social dynamics that led to the rise of the genre in Greece and its maintenance in Rome—intense cultural innovation, borrowing, and competition—were also found in the early centuries of Islam and account for much of the interest in who was first. Since these lists are usually about human inventors rather than divine benefactors, they often encode the ethnic identity of the authors and touch on cultural tensions between foreigners and natives, which were particularly acute during and after the establishment of foreign rule.

Invention, Progress, and Dependency: Classical Greek Cultural History

The origin of the inventor catalog goes back to seventh-century BC Greece when innovators of all stripes began clamoring for recognition of their achievements.[1] Poets and musicians wanted acknowledgment, as did artisans and architects. Philosophers too wished to have their names linked with their discoveries, as indicated by Thales' (ca. 624 BC–ca. 546 BC) desire to have his name linked to a mathematical discovery. A desire for public recognition and fame motivated claims to originality, just as it fueled charges of plagiarism and criticism of previous work as hidebound.[2]

In the early sixth century, this celebration of innovation and desire for individual recognition gave birth to Greek protography, which sought to answer the question "who was the first to discover something."[3] One of the first recorded protographs is found in the sixth-century epic poem *Phoronis*, in which Phrygian sorcerers are said to be the "first" (*prōtoi*) to "discover" (*heuron*) smithcraft. Although the author acknowledges that smithcraft is the art of the god Hephaestus, as we saw in chapter 1, he or she attributes its human invention to foreign neighbors of the Greeks.[4] This penchant for ascribing inventions to gods rather than to humans is mirrored by the sixth-century author Xenophanes of Colophon (ca. 570 BC–ca. 478 BC), who wrote, "The gods have not revealed all things to men from the beginning; but by seeking men find out better in time."[5] This means not that the gods ceased to be regarded as cultural benefactors but rather that some people ceased to regard them as the sole benefactors. As Copenhaver observes, "When human effort was thus recognized as the benefactor of the human condition, divine jealousy ceased to be seen as a great impediment to discovery and divine favour was no longer viewed as its unique source."[6]

Even the gods were refashioned from "bringers" of culture to "inventors" of culture. In the *Hymn to Hermes*, a text of uncertain date,[7] Hermes invents the fire drill, the lyre, and musical pipes. At the beginning of the hymn, Hermes finds a tortoise. He proceeds to scoop out its insides with a chisel and then fashions a lyre out of the shell.[8] Thus, according to the text, he "was the first to make a singer of a tortoise."[9] Later he gives the lyre to Apollo, and then he "invented the skill of a new art, for he made the blaring pipes which can be heard from afar." Hermes displays this inventiveness again when he fashions a fire drill, a stick used to make fire. According to the hymn, after making the lyre, Hermes steals the cattle of Apollo. Then, "intent on the skill of making fire," he gathers wood and undertakes the following operation:

[1] For overviews of Greek and Roman protography, see Kleingunther, *Protos Heuretes*, and Thraede's articles "Erfinder II" and "Das Lob des Erfinders." The first epigraph, Pliny's *Natural History*, is from 7.57, and the second, Ibn Qutayba's *al-Maʿārif*, is on 1.

[2] Zhmud, *Origins*, 27–32.

[3] Ibid., 12, 32.

[4] Ibid., 24.

[5] Xenophanes, frag. 18, translated by Kirk and Raven in their *Presocratic Philosophers*, 179.

[6] Ibid., 193–94.

[7] Athanassakis, *Homeric Hymns*, 77 .

[8] Ibid., lines 4.41–42, 47–56.

[9] Ibid., line 4.24.

A fine branch of laurel he took and peeled with his knife
[lacuna in the text]
tight-fitted in his palm, and up went the heated smoke.
For Hermes was the first to give us fire from fire-sticks.
He gathered many dry sticks and made a thick
and sturdy pile in a sunken pit; and the flame shone afar,
giving off a blast, as the fire burnt high.
While the power of glorious Hephaistos kindled the fire.[10]

Similarly, in *Prometheus Bound* the Greek dramatist Aeschylus (d. ca. 456 BC) has Prometheus boast that he had "invented" numbers, the combining of letters, animal domestication, the harnessing of horses to chariots, the boat, pharmacology, soothsaying, and mining for metals; in short, "every art possessed by man comes from Prometheus."[11] It was a small step for Aeschylus's younger contemporary Sophocles (ca. 496 BC–406 BC) to attribute the development of agriculture and animal domestication not to the god Prometheus but to humanity's own ingenuity.[12]

The positive evaluation of cultural innovation and the increasing emphasis on human ingenuity as the driving force behind technological innovation in the fifth century crystallized in the theories of cultural development expounded by the Sophists and Democritus (ca. 460–370 BC). The Sophists, who appeared in the fifth century, seem to have originated speculation on the origins of *technai* in human prehistory.[13] Protagoras, for example, wrote a lost work titled *On the Original State of Man* and taught that early humans had to cooperate to survive in a harsh physical environment.[14] Prodicus of Ceos (d. ca. 395 BC) speculated that the cultural advances of early humans were shaped by their environment.[15]

It is in this milieu that Democritus articulated his theory of prehistorical cultural formation (*Kulturentstehungslehre*), which speculated on the origins of culture before the advent of writing and thus written history of culture (*Kulturgeschichte*).[16] According to Democritus, basic technology did not come at unconnected intervals, without any apparent relationship between one discovery and the next; rather, it was part of a larger pattern of evolutionary development, with one human invention leading to another.[17] The Sicilian historian Diodorus Siculus (d. after 21 BC) preserved something of this theory when he wrote the following:

[10] Ibid., lines 4.108–15.
[11] Aeschylus *Prometheus Bound* 454–505, in *Works*.
[12] Sophocles *Antigone* 341.
[13] Zhmud, *Origins*, 46.
[14] Dodds, *Ancient Concept*, 10; Henrichs, *Sophists*, 141.
[15] Beagon, *Elder Pliny*, 417; Henrichs, *Sophists*, 141, 144; Barnes, *Presocratic Philosophers*, 154, 156.
[16] Henrichs, *Sophists*, 141; Zhmud, *Origins*, 48, 51.
[17] Cole, *Democritus*, 26. Although Democritus's theory of cultural development survives only in fragments, Cole argues that much of it can be gleaned in the work of later second- and first-century BC authors.

> As for the first-born men, it is said they endured a precarious and subhuman existence. They roamed about individually in search of food, plucking the most digestible plants and natural fruits from the trees. The attacks of wild beasts taught them the advantage of mutual assistance; and, once thrown together by fear, they gradually came to recognize each other's features . . . [And they] refined their power of speech . . . [agreeing] with each other on verbal symbols for everything they encountered . . . . With none of the useful things of life as yet discovered, these first men lived but miserably . . . But in the course of time, taught by experience, they sought the shelter of caves for the winter and put aside for later use those foods capable of being preserved. And, after gaining knowledge of fire and other conveniences, by degrees they discovered the arts and other things of advantage to human existence. For generally speaking, necessity itself served as man's tutor in all things.[18]

In his schema, arts such as music and sciences like astronomy emerged at the same time after the essential technai were invented.[19]

Authors who accepted naturalistic explanations of cultural development, such as Prodicus of Ceos, fitted the Greek gods into this schema, depicting them as human inventors who were later deified by people on account of their discoveries.[20] Some even believed that the idea of gods was invented for the sake of public morality; Plato's uncle Critias (d. 403 BC) attributed the fraud of gods to a priest, whom he described as a "first discoverer."[21]

The euhemerizing trend in Greek philosophical thinking on the origins of culture in the fifth century is mirrored by the historiography of the time, which located innovation in historical time rather than in the distant mythical past.[22] Thus Herodotus (d. ca. 425 BC) recounts a number of inventors in his *History*, but he focuses on human rather than divine or semidivine inventors.[23] He even goes so far as to replace Minos, a legendary king of semidivine parentage, with the human Polycrates as the first to rule the seas.[24] A similar tendency to attribute inventions to humans rather gods with is found in the works of Herodotus's predecessor Hecataeus of Miletus (d. ca. 476), who credited the Aetolian king Oresteus with the invention of wine rather than the god Dionysus.[25]

Throughout his work, Herodotus puts a high premium on direct observation as the basis for human historical inquiry, followed by reports from knowledge-

[18] Diodorus Siculus *Library* 1.8.1–9. See Copenhaver, "Historiography of Discovery," 194.

[19] Cole, *Democritus*, 42–43; Zhmud, *Origins*, 51–52.

[20] Henrichs, "Sophists," 141.

[21] Dodds, *Progress*, 8; Van Groningen, *Grip of the Past*, 34.

[22] On the Greeks' discomfort with speculation on the remote past, see Dillery, "First Egyptian Narrative," 99.

[23] Zhmud, *Origins*, 34.

[24] Herodotus *Histories* 3.122.

[25] Zhmud, *Origins*, 34.

able native informants (although not without due skepticism).[26] Thus, when he wanted to check the reliability of the Greek stories concerning Heracles, he traveled to Phoenicia.[27] And when he wanted to know about the history of the Persian king Cyrus, he consulted some Persians "who desire not to magnify the story of Cyrus but to tell the truth."[28]

Herodotus's emphasis on direct knowledge led him to be very cautious about assigning cultural innovations to a particular person. Instead, he preferred to attribute cultural firsts to entire peoples, thinking, perhaps, that this more readily lent itself to empirical verification.[29] Herodotus's treatments of cultural history, therefore, tend to be ethnographic.

Throughout his *History*, Herodotus attributes a number of cultural firsts to various peoples.[30] Although he does mention a few Greek firsts, he credits the development of most Greek culture to foreigners.[31] Thus, the Lydians were the first to mint and use gold and silver coins, "sell by retail," and invent the games played by Greeks;[32] the Carians were the first to wear "crests on their helmets and devices on their shields" and make grips for their shields;[33] in images of Athena her attire was taken from Libyan women;[34] the sundial and the division of the day into twelve came from Babylonia;[35] and, finally, the Greek alphabet came from the Phoenicians.[36]

Herodotus was particularly impressed with the antiquity and cultural achievements of Egypt, which he visited before 430 BC while it was occupied by the Persians. During his trip, he noticed a number of Egyptian religious practices and beliefs that were similar to those in Greece. He concluded that Greece must have borrowed these from the Egyptians, a conclusion encouraged by the native priests he spoke with.[37] Among the Greek appropriations were the Egyptian helmet and shield,[38] the practice of dating by years and dividing the year into twelve (2.4), the act of worshiping gods in temples and carving images of them in stone (2.4), the names of gods (2.43, 2.51–53), ceremonial religion (2.58), mystery cults (2.171), the doctrines of the immortality of the soul and reincarnation (2.123), fortune-telling based on the day a person is born (2.82), geometry (2.109.3), dividing the land and assessing it for tax revenue (2.109),

[26] Momigliano, "Greek Historiography," 5. Concerning Herodotus's skepticism toward his native informants, see Herodotus *Histories* 2.123, 7.152.

[27] Herodotus *Histories* 2.44–45.

[28] Ibid., 1.95.

[29] Copenhaver, "Historiography of Discovery," 195.

[30] Most of the following firsts from Herodotus are taken from Copenhaver's "Historiography of Discovery," 195–96.

[31] For Greek firsts in Herodotus, see Herodotus *Histories* 1.163, 1.23, 1.25, 3.122.

[32] Ibid., 1.94.

[33] Ibid., 1.171.

[34] Ibid., 4.189.

[35] Ibid., 2.109.

[36] Ibid., 5.58.

[37] Moyer, "Limits," 21, 27, 35–37, 62, 71–72.

[38] Herodotus *Histories* 4.180. Henceforth, these are listed in the text.

and possibly trade (2.167). He even alludes to a Pythagorean practice that originated in Egypt (2.81.2). Not surprisingly, Herodotus's native informants were happy to confirm a number of his conclusions (2.4).

Herodotus's assertion that most Greek culture was a foreign import is based on his assumption that cultural similarity between an old society and a young society indicated that the latter had derived its culture from the former. He believed, like other thinkers in antiquity, that most of the important cultural innovations had been discovered in the distant past. Therefore, as Copenhaver observes, "he refused to entertain the idea that a new development might occur independently in several places, and so he insisted on a diffisionist and monocentric version of the history of culture."[39]

For Herodotus, the older a civilization was perceived to be, the more likely that it was responsible for the invention of human culture; its antiquity ensured its cultural priority. He quite rightly considered Egypt one of the most ancient civilizations on earth,[40] and so he believed that most cultural innovations worth mentioning had originated there. Since the Greeks were the new kids on the Mediterranean block, Herodotus concluded a priori that they must have derived many of their cultural innovations from the Egyptians. Regarding Greek ceremonial religion, for example, he writes: "It would seem, too, that the Egyptians were the first people to establish solemn assemblies, and processions, and services; the Greeks learned all that from them. I consider this proved, because the Egyptian ceremonies are manifestly very ancient, and the Greek are of recent origin."[41] This approach became standard for later Greeks who visited Egypt.

Herodotus's theory of Greece's cultural dependence on Egypt was shared not only by later historians;[42] Greek philosophers also made these assumptions, particularly Plato. In his *Timaeus*, for example, Plato relates a story told by the Greek lawmaker Solon (d. ca. 559 BC), who had traveled to Egypt. According to Plato, Solon recognized Greece's cultural inferiority to Egypt, a recognition that was reinforced by an ancient native priest (*à la* Herodotus).

> "O Solon, Solon, you Greeks are always children: there is not such a thing as an old Greek." And on hearing this he [Solon] asked, "What mean you by this saying?" And the priest replied, "You are young in soul, every one of you. For therein you possess not a single belief that is ancient and derived from old tradition, nor yet one science that is hoary with age."[43]

[39] Copenhaver, "Historiography of Discovery," 196.

[40] Herodotus *Histories* 2.2. Herodotus's native priestly informants reinforced this belief (2.142–46).

[41] Ibid., 2.58.

[42] For the elaboration of Herodotus's methodology by later Hellenistic and Greco-Roman historians, see Murray, "Herodotus"; Nimis, "Egypt in Greco-Roman History."

[43] Plato *Timaeus* 21e–22b, in *Plato in Twelve Volumes*. Just as the mere mention of Solon and Egypt together in the same history (i.e., Herodotus's *Histories*) was enough to lead authors such as

However, Plato then turns the Herodotean scheme on its head when he has the priest relate that the Greeks are actually a thousand years older than the Egyptians but did not retain the arts of civilization because their written records were wiped away by successive floods—floods that the Egyptians had escaped.[44]

According to Plato, Socrates had similar attitudes about Greece's cultural dependence on Egypt. In one conversation, Socrates related that he had heard that the Egyptian god Theuth (Thoth) "invented numbers and arithmetic and geometry and astronomy, also draughts and dice, and, most important of all, letters." Theuth, according to Socrates, then showed his inventions to the Egyptian king Thamus, who reminded him that "one man has the ability to beget arts, but the ability to judge of their usefulness or harmfulness to their users belongs to another."[45] Although Socrates does preface his remarks by expressing his uncertainty as to the truth of the report, the report indicates that, at least in the time of Plato, it was still common to attribute the invention of the sciences prized by the Greeks to an Egyptian god.

Not everyone agreed with the "orientalizing tendency"[46] of Herodotus and other Greek authors. Some Greeks responded that their countrymen had laid the theoretical underpinnings for later cultural achievements by other nations; others held that foreign societies had taken their cultural innovations from Greek wise men who had traveled in the East.[47] The Greek historian Ephorus (d. 330 BC) was particularly antagonistic toward the idea that the Greeks had borrowed from foreign cultures.[48]

Nevertheless, the Peripatetic philosophers who formalized writing on the subject of discoveries (*peri heurēmatōn*) in the fourth and third centuries were willing to concede foreign influence.[49] Although their lists of firsts do not

---

Plato to posit that he had spent his early years studying with Egyptian teachers, so too did Plato's statements about Egypt lead later authors to assert that Plato had traveled there and studied with Egyptian priests; this, despite the absence of any mention of such a trip in his voluminous writings (Lefkowitz, *Not Out of Africa*, 82). Thus the Greek historian Strabo (d. after 21 AD) writes that he actually visited the place in Egypt where Plato studied (Strabo *Geography* 17.1.29). Similar stories were circulated in the fourth century BC about the influence of Zoroaster. See Momigliano, *Alien Wisdom*, 7, 93, 142–43, 146–47.

[44] Plato *Timaeus* 22e–24a, in *Plato in Twelve Volumes*. See Dodds, *Progress*, 14; Vasunia, *Gift*, 218–26.

[45] Plato *Phaedrus* 274c–274e, in *Plato in Twelve Volumes*. The king goes on to express his displeasure with the invention of writing, which he contends, contrary to Theuth's assertion, will not be an aid to memory but will make men lazy and not encourage them to memorize (275a).

[46] This phrase comes from Copenhaver, "Historiography of Discovery," 196.

[47] Ibid.

[48] See Copenhaver's "Historiography of Discovery," 196, and his introduction to Polydore Vergil's *On Discovery*, xxi.

[49] This goes against the opinion of Copenhaver ("Historiography of Discovery," 196), who argues that Peripatetics such as Theophrastus and Strato followed Ephorus in being "strongly opposed to the claim that Greece depended on Egypt and the East for inventions."

survive intact, we can get some sense of the content of this genre, which classicists call heurematography, from the fragments of Theophrastus's (ca. 371 BC–ca. 287 BC) works. One fragment comes from his *On Discovery*, in which he writes that Hyperbius of Corinth discovered the potter's wheel.[50] In the *Robe*, he writes that the Egyptians first discovered letters, followed by the Phoenicians,[51] and Syracuse "invented the art of words."[52] In fragments that probably derive from his *On Discovery,* Theophrastus names the following firsts: Prometheus was "the first to give men a share in philosophy";[53] Phoenicians invented stone quarries;[54] the Tirynthians, a Greek tribe, invented towers;[55] the Phrygian Delas invented coppersmithing (see the section titled "Invention, Progress, and Dependency" above for the Phrygians' invention of smithcraft);[56] and Polygnotus, born in Thasos (fl. ca. 460 BC), was the first in Greece to paint.[57] Theophrastus's predecessor Aristotle also wrote on the subject and named a number of alternative firsts to those of Theophrastus, including foreign firsts.[58]

Given the fragmentary nature of the surviving excerpts from treatises on discoveries, we cannot be sure of their form. They might have been catalogs of discoveries with little commentary, or they could have been detailed in narrative. Whatever the case, it took about two centuries for the genre to take shape after an initial century of social competition and cultural innovation. As we saw in chapter 1, early Greek myth deals with origins, but stories on the subject were not explicitly stated as "firsts." In the seventh century, the social environment fostered competition and a desire for public recognition, which led to a concern with priority as reflected in storytelling and historiography. Growing appreciation for intellectual achievements led to the first protographs in the sixth century and theorizing in the fifth on the secular processes of prehistorical cultural development—theorizing that informed and reflected advances in sciences such as medicine (see chapter 5). As Greek learning became more systematized in the fourth century at the hands of the Peripatetics, so did protography, again by Peripatetics.

From the beginning, Greeks had acknowledged their cultural debt to civilizations in Egypt and the East. Not everyone was happy to admit this debt, as the

[50] Theophrastus, frag. 734, in Fortenbaugh, Huby, Sharples, and Gutas, *Theophrastus of Eresus.*

[51] Ibid., frag. 735.

[52] Ibid., frag. 736A.

[53] Ibid., frag. 729.

[54] Ibid., frag. 732.

[55] Ibid., frag. 732.

[56] Ibid., frag. 731. Clement of Alexandria credits Delas with the invention of bronze smelting (*Stromata* 1.16.75).

[57] Theophrastus, frag. 733, in Fortenbaugh, Huby, Sharples, and Gutas, *Theophrastus of Eresus.*

[58] According to Pliny, he held that the Cyclopes had invented towers, Lydus from Scythia invented coppersmithing, and Euchir was the first in Greece to paint (Pliny *Natural History* 7.56). In *Metaphysics* 1:981b, Aristotle relates that the mathematical sciences originated in Egypt.

case of Ephorus demonstrates. Nevertheless, on the eve of Alexander's conquest of the Near East, many Greeks, including Alexander's teacher Aristotle, believed they were the heirs of its civilizations.

What to Do about the Greeks? Roman Discovery Catalogs

The Romans, like the Greeks, wrote catalogs of firsts and acknowledged their cultural debt to foreigners. They also borrowed heavily from Greek protography and discovery catalogs. But unlike the Greeks, Roman authors rarely mentioned their own people's achievements. This modesty was exploited to good effect by Christian apologists who wished to blunt the Roman charge of being cultural traitors by arguing that Romans themselves were heavily influenced by outsiders. Yet both groups—Roman pagans and their Christian opponents—had difficulty coming to terms with the abiding influence of the Greeks on their thought and used the Greeks' protographical material and forms to come to terms with it.

Although there were far fewer catalogs of discoveries in the Roman era,[59] the catalog of Pliny the Elder (d. 79 AD) is the most extensive of any that survive from antiquity. The work, included almost as an afterthought in book 7 of his *Natural History*, is "overwhelmingly Greek in content and inspiration," as one modern commentator puts it.[60] Indeed, it is due to Pliny that we have many of the fragments of Greek protography cited in the previous section.

Pliny summarizes his Greek material in the form of a list, relating one discovery after another. He attributes inventions to gods, demigods, peoples, and individuals, sometimes giving multiple claimants, foreign and Greek, for each first. On the subject of the alphabet, for example, he writes, "I have always been of [the] opinion that letters were of Assyrian origins, but other writers . . . suppose that they were invented in Egypt by Mercury [Hermes]; others, again, will have it that they were discovered by the Syrians; and that Cadmus brought from Phoenicia sixteen letters into Greece."[61] Significantly, he does not mention any Roman firsts, a point I will return to later.

Pliny does not explain why he includes a catalog of inventors in his survey of nature, but it can be inferred from the introduction of book 7. Humans, he explains, are born with nothing and have to learn to cope with the harshness of life by inventing things. In this, they are helped by nature, which prods them to invent by necessity and provides them the objects they need to survive.[62] Many of these discoveries are derived through divine revelation,[63] nature itself being

[59] Beagon, *The Elder Pliny*, 418–19.
[60] Ibid., 416.
[61] Pliny *Natural History* 7.57.
[62] Ibid., 7.1.
[63] Ibid., 37.59–60.

created by gods for the benefit of humans.[64] These are Stoic doctrines,[65] and as we saw in the last chapter they sometimes framed discussions of the origins of the arts and sciences. Pliny's list of discoverers, therefore, is probably meant to persuade his audience of the truth of these doctrines.[66]

This explains why Pliny includes a list of discoverers but not why he relies on Greek authorities. He does write at the beginning of book 7 that he is quoting the Greeks because they "have proved themselves the most careful observers, as well as of the longest standing,"[67] but he does so defensively, as if his audience might criticize him for using Greek works. Indeed, Pliny himself was concerned about the influence of Greek learning. This concern goes back to the early days of Roman expansion when senators such as Cato the Elder worried that adopting Greek customs and modes of thought would undermine Roman traditions and austerity.[68] And yet many of these senators, like Cato, had also mastered Greek learning,[69] which could hold a certain amount of "social cachet."[70] Still, the cultural dilemma remained;[71] thus Cicero could profess a love of ancient Greek learning and see Rome as its true heir while deploring the influence of contemporary Greeks.[72] By the first century BC, higher education was in Greek, and by the end of that century, Horace could complain with some accuracy, "Captive Greece captured her savage conqueror and brought the arts to rustic Latium."[73] Pliny echoes Horace's complaint when he remarks in the *Natural History*, "Through conquering we have been conquered."[74]

Pliny's exclusion of Roman technological accomplishments in his list of Greek and barbarian innovations is thus meant to portray Romans as the standard-bearers of previous foreign civilizations while shaming them for failing to advance on them. He writes as much in book 2, where he observes that there is no original research being done by Romans and that scientific knowledge is fading due to moral decline.[75] The reason is that Romans are mimicking the luxurious lifestyle of contemporary Greeks, which is sapping the vitality of Romans, who should instead be living according to nature and learning its secrets.[76] Of course, Pliny was aware that Rome had just experienced two centuries of incredible technological innovation, much of which he documents

[64] Ibid., 27.1–2.

[65] Pliny was influenced by Posidonius. See Wallace-Hadrill, "Pliny the Elder," 84.

[66] Wallace-Hadrill, in "Pliny the Elder," makes this point more generally of Pliny's project in the *Natural History* (85).

[67] Pliny *Natural History* 7.1.

[68] Adams, *Caligula*, 33; Mellor, "Graecia Capta," 93.

[69] Momigliano, *Alien Wisdom*, 20.

[70] König and Whitmarsh, "Ordering Knowledge," 23.

[71] Mellor, "Graecia Capta," 112.

[72] Adams, *Caligula*, 32, 35–36.

[73] Mellor, "Graecia Capta," 105.

[74] Pliny *Natural History* 24.5.5 (see Isaac, *Racism*, 225).

[75] Pliny *Natural History* 2.117–18; see Wallace-Hadrill, "Pliny the Elder," 95–96.

[76] Wallace-Hadrill, "Pliny the Elder," 94.

outside his list of inventions. But presumably he viewed these innovations as practical improvements, not theoretical advancements like those made by the ancient Greeks.

Another author who compiled a list of Greek protographical material for a Roman audience was the obscure Hyginus, who wrote a handbook on Greek mythology titled *Genealogies* (later known as *Fabulae*) sometime in the second century AD.[77] In the only surviving manuscript, there are two discovery lists at the end of the work. Either of these may have been a later addition, but the original work included at least one discovery list, as testified by Pseudo-Dositheus in his 201 AD excerpt of the work.[78]

The two discovery lists that survive are drawn almost exclusively from protography in Greek,[79] not all of which was written by Greeks.[80] Like the list of Pliny, Hyginus mentions Greek and barbarian discoveries in equal measure but ignores Roman discoveries. Hyginus's protographical interests overlap with many of Pliny's: carpentry tools, cities, clothing manufacture, farming practices, government, metallurgy, weaponry, musical instruments, religious practices, medicine and astronomy, sports, and transportation. However, Hyginus does not draw on Pliny's list and contradicts him on several firsts. For example, Hyginus gives Tyrrhenus as the inventor of trumpets (274.19), not his son Pysaeus as it is in Pliny.[81] Moreover, Hyginus draws on different sources from those of Pliny. Thus, he credits the Egyptian goddess Isis with discovering sailing, which is absent in Pliny.[82]

Although not stated, the arrangement and content of the *Genealogies* suggests that Hyginus intended it to be a handbook on Greek myth, including its etiologies, for Romans who wished to be conversant on the subject. Some, like Pliny, were no doubt conflicted over the Roman debt to Greek culture, as indicated by Pliny's apology to his readers for using Greek sources. Nevertheless, knowledge of Greek lore was a "touchstone" of cultured society,[83] and so being conversant in Greek protography was a sign of the cultured man.

A similar ambivalence toward Greek learning and lore is found in the discovery catalogs of the early Church Fathers. On the one hand, the Fathers were products of Greek education like their pagan Roman counterparts and thus valued it and recognized its social capital. On the other, they had embraced a

[77] Hyginus used to be identified with the librarian Gaius Julius Hyginus (ca. 64 BC–17 AD), although most scholars reject this now. See Scott and Trzaskoma, *Apollodorus*' Library, xliii–l.

[78] See the translation of his preface and index ibid., 193–94.

[79] Ibid., xlvi, xlviii–xlix.

[80] For example, Hyginus relates that Oannes was the first to figure out astronomy (274.16), which ultimately derives from the *Babyloniaca* of Berossus, a Babylonian priest who lived in the late fourth century and early third century BC (see chapter 4).

[81] Hyginus *Genealogies* 274.19.

[82] Ibid., 277.

[83] Smith and Trzaskoma, *Apollodorus*' Library, liii–liv.

religion that had sprung from Judaism, which the pagan elite considered alien and threatening to Roman values (see chapter 4). Eusebius of Caesarea captured this dilemma in his *Preparation for the Gospel*:

> For in the first place any one might naturally want to know who we are that have come forward to write. Are we Greeks or Barbarians? Or what can there be intermediate to these? And what do we claim to be, not in regard to the name, because this is manifest to all, but in the manner and purpose of our life? For they would see that we agree neither with the opinions of the Greeks, nor with the customs of the Barbarians.[84]

In response, the early Christian elite developed strategies to maintain a connection to Greek and Jewish culture while differentiating Christianity from them.

One of the most stinging pagan criticisms leveled at Christians was that their parent religion, Judaism, was derivative of older civilizations and, based on the assumption that older equals wiser, had not invented anything of note. Thus, the Roman philosopher Celsus (fl. mid-second century AD) asserted that the Jews were neither learned nor ancient like the Egyptians, Assyrians, Indians, Persians, and others; thus, they had contributed nothing to humanity.[85] Even after Christianity had the upper hand politically, pagan intellectuals continued to use this line of argument. Thus, the emperor Julian (d. 363 AD) denied the originality of the Jews in *Against the Galileans*, contending that the Jews never contributed anything to civilization, unlike Oannes of the Chaldeans and Hermes of the Egyptians.[86] The Christians' response was twofold. One was to argue that Greek, and thus Roman, culture was in general derivative of barbarian culture. In making this argument, they made long lists of barbarian discoveries based on Greek sources. The second response was to argue that the Hebrews' primary contribution to humanity was philosophy, an argument that I will return to in chapter 5.

Tatian (ca. 120 to after 170 AD) was one of the first to use a list of firsts in arguing that Greek culture was barbarian derived. Indeed, he opens his *Address to the Greeks* with a list of derivations, prefacing them with "Be not, O Greeks, so very hostilely disposed towards the barbarians, nor look with ill will on their opinions. For which of your institutions has not been derived from the barbarians?" He proceeds to cite foreign firsts from Greek protographical literature: Babylonians invented astronomy, Egyptians geometry, Tyrrhenians the trumpet, and so on.[87]

Clement of Alexandria (ca. 150–ca. 215 AD) adopts the same line of attack in his *Miscellanies*, arguing that "barbarians were inventors not only of philosophy, but almost of every art." He provides a long list of these arts, citing Greek protog-

[84] Eusebius *Preparation for the Gospel* 1.2.1.
[85] Origen *Contra Celsum* 1.14.
[86] Adler, *Time*, 62n74.
[87] Tatian *Address to the Greeks* 1. See Droge, *Homer or Moses?* 86–90.

raphers such as Theophrastus to "confirm the inventive and practically useful genius of the barbarians, by whom the Greeks profited in their studies."[88]

In his *Preparation for the Gospel*, Eusebius of Caesarea (ca. 260–ca. 339) quotes from Clement's list for the same effect,[89] arguing that the "Greeks, by going about among the barbarians, collected the other branches of learning, geometry, arithmetic, music, astronomy, medicine, and the very first elements of grammar, and numberless other artistic and profitable studies."[90] They are "convicted of having stolen everything from barbarians, not only their philosophical science, but also the common inventions which are useful in daily life."[91]

Although this is a disparate collection of pagan and Christian discovery catalogs, they share two characteristics. First, despite the fact that the catalogs' authors are non-Greeks, they rely on Greek-language sources written mainly by Greeks. Second, they all relate barbarian firsts. However, Pliny includes Greek firsts to show that Romans are the heirs of the Greeks and to shame them for not living up to their inheritance because they are enervated by contemporary Greek culture; Hyginus relates the same to help Romans impress each other and Hellenes with their knowledge of Greek lore. Conversely, Christian authors ignore or dismiss Greek firsts to demonstrate that Greek civilization is not novel but barbarian derived. They do so to blunt the pagan charge that elite Christians are betraying their culture, which was heavily Greek, by adopting a "barbarian" religion.

Whether playing up ancient Greek accomplishments or belittling them, pagan Romans and Christians were united in using discovery catalogs to work out the status of Greek culture vis-à-vis their own ethnic identity. In contrast, Jewish authors at this time showed little interest in debating the origins of culture. This was not the case several centuries earlier in the Hellenistic period (see chapter 4), but one would be hard pressed to find any cultural innovations attributed to prophets in rabbinic literature other than legal and ritual practices. Thus in Dov Noy's extensive survey of rabbinic lore pertaining to origins,[92] the few cultural firsts attributed to the prophets are related to farming and ascribed to Noah, who invented several farm implements.[93] But even this is not firm evidence of rabbinic cultural etiologies in our period, since it is first found in the *Tanhuma Bereshit*, which may have been compiled as late as the ninth century AD.[94] Its content and possible late date suggest that it may have been part of a new wave of speculation on the origins of culture whose epicenter was not Athens, Rome, or Jerusalem but Mecca and Baghdad.

[88] Clement *Stromata* 1.16.

[89] Eusebius *Preparation for the Gospel*, 10.6. Eusebius does not make his own list but does address the barbarian origins of Greek letters (10.5).

[90] Ibid., 10.1.

[91] Ibid., 10.4.

[92] Noy, "Motif-Index," 154–61.

[93] See Noy, "Motif-Index," 156, citing Ginzberg, *Legends* 1:147 and 5:168, no. 6.

[94] Waxman, *History of Jewish Literature*, 139.

Ishmael or Yaʿrub? Early Muslim Protography and Discovery Catalogs

For a variety of reasons, there is a lot of protographical material in early Islamic literature. One might point to the Qur'an's concern with the subject or the influence of late-antique historiographical practice. Whatever the proximate cause, the fundamental driver of early Muslim protography was the rapid Arab conquest of the Near East. The conquests engendered competition between Muslims over religious priority, which was tied to income and led to writings on such topics as who was the first Muslim or who was the first to fight in a certain battle.[95] There was also competition between the Arab tribes over which tribe was better and between rival schools of judicial thought over which was more authentic. Moreover, the conquests touched off centuries of cultural innovation, particularly in Arabic literature and the sciences (for the latter, see chapter 5). As in seventh- and sixth-century BC Greece, this innovation fueled interest in inventors. Finally, the conquests brought together two advanced civilizations, Roman and Persian. As the Romans had done before them, the conquering Arabs had to work out the status of the learning associated with the prior civilizations, which really meant determining the identity of the new Islamic civilization. Was it Arab, Greek, Persian, or something altogether new?

Firsts Attributed to Biblical Figures

The earliest Muslim discovery catalogs (the catalogs were called "firsts," *awāʾil*)[96] reflect the identity and scholarly interests of Muslims in ninth-century Iraq who were oriented toward Arabia and the Qur'anic sciences—for example, traditionists (those who collected the words and deeds of Muhammad and his Companions), philologists, exegetes, genealogists, and prosopographers. The protographical material they used was based on biblical and Arab lore, some of it pre-Islamic and some of it created in the first two centuries of Islam.

A lot of early Muslim protography was exegetical. Thus, when the Qur'an says "we taught him [David] the fashioning of garments for you" (Q 21:80), the early Muslim exegete Muqātil b. Sulaymān (d. 150 AH / 767 AD) remarks, "This means coats of mail from iron; David was the first person to make them."[97]

Firsts could also be inferred from the Qur'an even if the plain sense of a verse did not warrant it. Thus in verse 28:38, Pharaoh asks his adviser Hāmān to make bricks out of clay and build a tower so he can ascend to the god of Moses.

[95] Afsaruddin, *Excellence and Precedence*.

[96] The best bibliographical surveys of awāʾil lists are Franz Rosenthal's "*Awāʾil*," in the *Encyclopedia of Islam* (2nd ed.), and ʿAbd al-ʿAzīz al-Mānīʿ's English introduction to his edition of Ibn Bāṭīsh's (d. 655 AH / 1257 AD) *Ghāyat al-wasāʾil* (al-Mānīʿ, "An Edition of *Ghāyat al-wasāʾil*").

[97] Muqātil, *Tafsīr* 3:88–89.

On this basis, Muqātil comments elsewhere (at the end of sura 40) that Pharaoh was the first to bake bricks and build with them.[98] Similarly, in verses 21:82 and 38:37, we are told that demons (*shayāṭīn*) served as pearl divers (*ghawwāṣūn*) for Solomon. Based on this, Muqātil remarks that Solomon was the first to extract pearls from the ocean.[99] It is unclear if Muqātil invented these firsts himself or drew on stories circulated by early Islamic storytellers. Whatever the case, these sorts of biblical firsts seem to have been deduced from the text of the Qur'an—whether formally by an exegete or by storytellers.

In addition to these etiological deductions, a few firsts attributed to biblical figures were derived from etiologies found in Jewish and Christian lore. Some of these had a basis in the Hebrew Bible. Thus, Muqātil states that Nimrod was the first to rule the whole earth (commenting on Q 2:258).[100]

Other etiologies were derived from Jewish and Christian pseudepigrapha that were circulating in the Middle East. We have already seen one example of this in the last chapter where some version of the *Life of Adam* reappears in Ṭabarī's *Ta'rīkh*. Other retellings of the Fall found in the *Ta'rīkh* echo other versions of the *Life of Adam*.[101] In one version of the story found in Ṭabarī, God supplies Adam with the fruits of paradise and teaches him "how to make everything"; it is unclear whether this instruction is confined to the preparation of food or extends to the creation of other culture.[102] In another version, God gives Adam thirty kinds of fruit, presumably so he can grow them on earth.[103] In yet other reports, Adam gathers the branches of various trees in paradise (with God's indulgence) before his expulsion or wears a wreath upon his head made of leaves from these trees; when he falls to earth in India, these leaves drop to the ground and grow. This is the origin of the perfumes (and, according to one report, fruits) that are found in India.[104]

These reports are similar to the depiction of Adam in a Greek translation of the *Life of Adam*, at one time incorrectly labeled the "Apocalypse of Moses." In it, Adam approaches the angels in paradise after the judgment of God (but before his expulsion), beseeching them to let him take fragrant herbs so that he may use them as an offering to God after his expulsion. The angels approach God with Adam's request, and God allows him to take "sweet spices and seeds for his food" (29.1–6).[105]

Another version of the Fall in the *Ta'rīkh* has an angel teach Adam the rudiments of farming after his expulsion. Adam grows hungry after his exile

[98] Ibid., 723.

[99] Ibid., 89, 647.

[100] Ibid., 1:215.

[101] Although Ṭabarī (d. 310 AH/923 AD) is a rather late source to be used in a section on early awā'il, the pseudepigraphical material he records is probably from this earlier period.

[102] Ṭabarī, *Ta'rīkh* 1:297.

[103] Ibid., 298.

[104] Ibid., 296–97.

[105] Gary Anderson and Michael Stone, the two principal authorities on the *Life of Adam*, have

because he does not know how to feed himself. He asks God for food, and God obliges by sending Gabriel with seven grains of wheat.[106] Gabriel then shows him how to sow the seeds. Once Adam has harvested the wheat (at God's command), Gabriel gives Adam stones with which to grind the wheat and then stones and iron with which to make fire by striking them together. Having produced fire, Adam is able to bake bread, making him "the first to bake bread in the ashes."[107]

This account is similar to stories found in the Armenian *Penitence of Adam* and the Georgian *Book of Adam*. In the former, Adam and Eve grow hungry after they are exiled because they do not know how to provide for themselves. After Adam repents, God teaches him "sowing and reaping" (20.1b). In the *Book of Adam*, Michael, not God, teaches Adam farming after he repents: "Then God hearkened to Adam's prayer and sent him the angel Michael who brought him a seeds [*sic*], sealed with the divine seal, destined to be brought to Adam. Then he taught him sowing and the work related to it, so that thus they might be saved, (they) and all their descendants (20.1b)."[108]

Ṭabarī dislikes this version of events because it does not comport with his understanding of verse 20:117–19: "Adam! This (Iblīs) is an enemy to you and your spouse. So let him not drive both of you out of Paradise, so that you will be miserable! You do not have to go hungry or be naked in it, nor to be thirsty there or suffer from heat."[109] The misery that God warns Adam of, Ṭabarī avers, must be

> the difficulty for him to obtain what would remove his hunger and his nakedness. It refers to the means by which his children obtain food, such as ploughing, sowing, cultivating, irrigating and other such difficult and painful tasks. If Gabriel had brought him the food which he obtains by sowing without any more trouble, there would not have been much to the misery here with which his Lord threatened him for obeying Satan and disobeying the Merciful One.[110]

---

compiled and translated the various versions and placed them online (http://www3.iath.virginia.edu/anderson/vita/vita.html). For this section, I have used their translations of the Greek, Armenian, and Georgian translations of the *Life of Adam*.

[106] According to Ibn ʿAbbās, the fruit of the forbidden tree was wheat (Ṭabarī, *Taʾrīkh* 1:299).

[107] Ibid., 298.

[108] The Ikhwān al-Ṣafāʾ have a similar story in their *Rasāʾil* (2:230). In it, Adam and Eve wander distraught in the wilderness, unable to feed themselves. Once they repent, God sends an angel, who teaches them how to farm, make bread, cook, spin thread, sew, and make clothing. Later, the descendants of al-Jānn (the forefather of the jinn—see Ibn al-Kalbī's account of Gayōmart below) mix with the children of Adam and Eve and teach them crafts (*al-ṣanāʾiʿ*), planting and tillage (even though their parents had already learned it from the angel), building, and beneficial and harmful things (*al-manāfiʿ waʾl-maḍārr*—this is a possible allusion to magic, as it mirrors the language used in the Qurʾanic account of Hārūt and Mārūt).

[109] Ṭabarī, *Taʾrīkh* 1:300.

[110] Ibid.

In support of this position, Ṭabarī cites a report by Ibn ʿAbbās in which God punishes Adam by casting him upon the earth, where God charges him to "toil that you will earn your living." Adam is taught (it is not clear by whom) how to work iron so that he can fashion a plow. Over a period he is sequentially taught the various steps involved with growing wheat and making bread.[111]

It is not immediately clear how this report substantively differs from the story of Gabriel teaching Adam the rudiments of farming; perhaps in the latter, Adam does not go hungry long enough to live up to the Qur'anic promise that he will be "miserable." What is clear is that Ṭabarī does not like the pseudepigraphal version of events, which, as we saw in chapter 2, was meant to soften the negative etiology of farming found in the Hebrew Bible. Although he protests that this version does not comport with the Qur'an, there is nothing in the Qur'an that explicitly contradicts the pseudepigraphal account. On the contrary, Muḥammad seems to go out of his way to praise farming and to avoid mentioning etiologies that may have cast a negative light on it. Nevertheless, Ṭabarī's reading of the Qur'anic passage is much closer to the Yahwist understanding of cultural origins than that of late-antique Christian pseudepigraphers.

Another important pseudepigraphal source of biblical firsts for Muslims was *The Book of the Cave of Treasures*. Composed in the sixth century AD but perhaps based on a fourth-century original,[112] the *Cave of Treasures* details events from the creation of Adam to the birth of Christ. Characterized by Brock as "a christianized re-telling of the biblical narrative,"[113] the reworked story of Adam and his progeny exercised an important influence on Eastern Christianity.[114] Since it was also translated into Arabic and informed the histories of some later Muslim chronographers (see below), we will survey its contents here.[115]

At the beginning of the *Cave of Treasures*, we read the standard account of early human culture: Adam gives names to animals,[116] Adam and Eve fashion clothing to cover their shame, and God makes Adam and Eve garments of skins.[117] God also expels Adam and Eve from Paradise and curses the earth because of their sin. Once expelled, Adam and Eve take refuge in a cave, which Adam names the "Cave of Treasures."[118] In an interesting twist, Adam is not made to work the cursed earth for his livelihood; rather, God exempts him from "the operation of the curse," and Adam becomes the "first priest"[119] after

[111] Ibid., 299.

[112] James Charlesworth, *The Pseudepigrapha and Modern Research*, 91.

[113] Brock, "Jewish Traditions," 227.

[114] For a survey of the authors who used *The Cave of Treasures*, see Götze, "Schatzhöhle," 51–94.

[115] This summary is based on Budge's English translation of the Syriac *Book of the Cave of Treasures*.

[116] Ibid., 53.

[117] Ibid., 65.

[118] Ibid., 69.

[119] Ibid., 70. In paradise, God had made Adam "king, and priest, and prophet" (53).

consecrating the cave as a "house of prayer for himself and his sons."[120] Adam then establishes a covenant with his son Seth to take over the office when he dies, and Seth passes it on to his son, and so forth.[121] Once Adam dies, his body is the first to be buried in the earth.[122]

Before his death, Adam's primary directive to Seth is to keep his descendants separate from those of Cain.[123] Following his father's instructions, Seth sequesters his descendants on the top of the mountain around the Cave of Treasures, whereas the descendants of Cain stay below.[124] Seth's descendants prosper, for they do not have to toil on the earth for their livelihood. Instead, "they fed themselves with the delectable fruits of glorious trees of all kinds, and they enjoyed the sweet scent and perfume of the breezes which were wafted forth to them from Paradise."[125]

While Seth's progeny is living a life of ease, Cain's descendants Jubal and Tubal-Cain are busy inventing all kinds of musical instruments.[126] Thus Jubal "made reed instruments, and harps, and flutes, and whistles, and the devils went and dwelt inside them. When men blew into the pipes, the devils sang inside them, and sent out sounds from inside them."[127] Similarly, Tubal-Cain fashioned cymbals and drums.[128] Satan is pleased with these inventions, since he sees them as a means of corrupting humans;[129] he does not, however, inspire their creation.

Since the Cainites had no government and no work to occupy them, they busied themselves with eating, drinking, engaging in sex, and "dancing and singing to instruments of music." This debauchery created laughter, which seduced the progeny of Seth.[130] And thus in the days of Jared, Seth's progeny began to descend the mountain to be with the children of Cain, where they were corrupted,[131] the sons of Seth being irresistibly drawn to the sexual charms of the daughters of Cain.[132] In the end, Satan ruled the camp.[133]

In the Muslim world, the book was translated into Arabic from Syriac,[134] and some version of it was used by a number of historians, including early chronog-

[120] Ibid., 69.

[121] Ibid., 72.

[122] Ibid., 73. Contrast this with the account in the Qur'an that intimates Abel was the first to be buried in the earth (see chapter 2).

[123] Ibid., 72.

[124] Ibid., 73–74.

[125] Ibid., 75.

[126] Ibid., 87.

[127] Ibid.

[128] Ibid.

[129] Ibid., 88.

[130] Ibid.

[131] Ibid., 84.

[132] Ibid., 90.

[133] Ibid., 89.

[134] The Arabic version has been edited by Bezold, *Die Schatzhöhle*.

raphers such as Ṭabarī (d. 310 AH / 923 AD) and Yaʿqūbī (d. 292 AH / 905 AD).[135] It also worked its way into several statements attributed to Ibn ʿAbbās, one of the Companions of the Prophet. One is found in Ṭabarī's *Taʾrīkh*.[136] Another is found in Ibn al-Kalbī's (d. ca. 204 AH / 819 AD) history of idol worship, *al-Aṣnām*.

> The sons of Seth were bringing the body of Adam to the cave. They were glorifying him and blessing him. A man among the sons of Cain, son of Adam, said: "O sons of Cain! The sons of Seth have an enclosure they circle around and glorify and you have nothing." Whereupon he chiseled an idol for them. He was the first person to make them.[137]

Ibn al-Kalbī further relates that the people kept making idols to capture the spirits of departed kin until God destroyed them with the Flood.[138] But it was all for naught, since ʿAmr b. Luḥayy, a forefather of the Khuzāʿa tribe, reintroduced idolatry to the Arabs.[139]

In addition to the *Cave of Treasures* and the *Life of Adam*, the pseudepigraphal story of Enoch seems to have been the source of at least one first: in Ibn Hishām's (d. 213 or 218 AH / 828 or 833 AD) *Sīra*, we learn that Idrīs was the first to write with a pen.[140] Although Ibn Hishām does not explicitly equate Idrīs with the biblical Enoch, the nature of the first indicates that this is whom he has in mind. Indeed, by the time of Ibn Hishām, the equation of Idrīs with Enoch seems to have gained some currency.[141]

Other biblical firsts were based on Jewish and Christian stories in which no first is mentioned. For example, Ibn Saʿd (d. 230 AH / 845 AD) relates in his *Ṭabaqāt*, on the authority of the Prophet, that Adam was the first person to relinquish part of his lifespan for another human, David.[142] This is based

[135] For the influence on Ṭabarī and Yaʿqūbī, see Götze, "Schatzhöhle," 60–71, 153–55.

[136] Rosenthal notes in his translation of Ṭabarī's *Taʾrīkh* that a report from Ibn ʿAbbās has a parallel in *The Cave of Treasures* (362n1113).

[137] Ibn al-Kalbī, *al-Aṣnām*, 51.

[138] Ibid., 51–53.

[139] Ibid., 8, 54. ʿAmr b. Luḥayy is frequently cited in early Islamic literature as the first person to introduce idolatry to the Arabs (see, for example, Muqātil, *Tafsīr*, commenting on Q 5:103, 5:509; Ibn Isḥāq in Ibn Hishām, *Sīra* 1:81; Zubayrī, *Nasab*, 8).

[140] Ibn Hishām, *Sīra* 1:23.

[141] One of the earliest instances of the identification of Idrīs and Enoch is found in Muqātil's commentary on verse 19:57 (the verse commented upon is embedded in Muqātil's interpretation):

> "Mention" to the people of Mecca "in the book," meaning the Qur'an, "Idrīs" who is the grandfather of the father of Noah and whose name is Enoch [*Akhnūkh*] (upon him be peace), that "he was truly a friend" meaning that he believed in the unity of God (exalted and glorified be He), "a prophet and that he was raised up to an exalted place," meaning in the Fourth Heaven, in which he died and at that time he called out to the King [*lil-malik*—or perhaps *malak*, "angel"] who sends the Sun in its course." (Muqātil, *Tafsīr* 2:631)

[142] Ibn Saʿd, *Ṭabaqāt*, 12. Also see Ṭabarī's discussion of this story in his *Taʾrīkh* 1:327–32.

on a rabbinical legend in which the same story is recounted but not presented as a first.[143]

Other biblical firsts were the product of Arab tribal rivalries. Thus, according to Abū Ḥayyān al-Tawḥīdī (d. 414 AH / 1023 AD), those who aligned themselves with the northern tribal confederation of Muḍar held that Ishmael, their purported forefather, was the first to speak Arabic, whereas those who aligned themselves with the southern tribal confederation of Qaḥṭān believed that Yaʿrub, the son of the first Arab, Qaḥṭān, was the first to do so.[144]

Something of this protographical division between northern and southern Arabs is preserved in the *Ṭabaqāt* of Ibn Saʿd (d. 230 AH / 845 AD). In his biography of Ishmael, Ibn Saʿd relates that Muḥammad b. ʿAlī, the fifth Shīʿī imam and a Hāshimite (a Muḍarī clan and thus descended from Ishmael), maintained that his forefather was the first to speak Arabic; before him, the people of Arabia and the prophets spoke Hebrew.[145] In support of this position, Ibn Saʿd writes that his former employer, al-Wāqidī (d. 207 AH / 822 AD), related that several scholars believed that Ishmael had been inspired to speak Arabic from the day of his birth.[146] However, Ibn Saʿd also relates that Muḥammad al-Kalbī (d. 146 AH / 763 AD), the father of Ibn al-Kalbī and of Yemeni descent, denied this, saying that it was impossible for Ishmael to speak a language that differed from that of his father, Abraham.[147] Rather, Ibn al-Kalbī relates elsewhere that it was Yaʿrub who was the first to speak Arabic (citing the people of Yemen as his authority).[148] Perhaps as a compromise between the competing claims, Ibn al-Kalbī records in his *Nasab al-khayl*, through his father on the authority of Ibn ʿAbbas, that Ishmael was the first to speak *ḥanīfī* Arabic, the Arabic used in the Qur'an.[149]

Other biblical firsts were, like the story of Abraham and the Kaʿba in the Qur'an, the result of Muslim attempts to legitimate the use of pre-Islamic pagan customs and architecture by connecting them with biblical figures. Thus, al-Wāqidī tells us in his *Maghāzī* that Abraham was the first to erect the stone boundary markers (*anṣāb*) of the *ḥaram* of Mecca.[150] Similarly, Ibn Abī Shayba (d. 235 AH / 849 AD) relates in his *Muṣannaf* that Hagar was the first to walk between al-Ṣafā and al-Marwa,[151] a pagan practice that became a part of Muslim pilgrimage.[152]

Finally, some biblical firsts were purely the product of polemics between

[143] See Ginzberg, *Legends* 5:82n28 for the sources.

[144] Tawḥīdī, *Baṣā'ir* 4:81.

[145] Ibn Saʿd, *Ṭabaqāt*, 33–34.

[146] Ibid., 34.

[147] Ibid.

[148] Balādhūrī, *Ansāb* 1:7.

[149] Ibn al-Kalbī, *Nasab al-khayl*, 28. For more sources on the origins of Arabic, see Suyūṭī's *Muzhir* 1:8–34.

[150] Wāqidī, *Maghāzī* 2:842. According to a report in Kulaynī's *al-Kāfī*, Maʿadd b. ʿAdnān was the first to set up the boundary markers (4:211).

[151] Ibn Abī Shayba, *Muṣannaf* 8:328, no. 30.

[152] "Saʿy," in *EI*^{2}.

Muslim scholars. For example, the traditionalist Ibn Sīrīn (d. 110 AH / 728 AD) held that Iblīs was the first to use analogical reasoning.[153] This etiology was directed against Abū Ḥanīfa and his followers, who used analogical reasoning to derive judicial rulings not expressly stated in the Qur'an and hadith; indeed, Ibn Abī Shayba, who cites the tradition in his chapter on awā'il, follows this chapter with one titled "Book of the Refutation of Abū Ḥanīfa."[154]

As with the Qur'an, many of the firsts attributed to biblical figures in early ʿAbbāsid literature have to do with the rudiments of civilization. As mentioned above, Ibn Hishām, drawing on some version of the Enoch story, relates that Idrīs was the first to write with a pen. Drawing on other pseudepigraphal sources, Ṭabarī transmits reports that have an angel teaching Adam how to create fire and engage in agriculture or have either God or an angel teaching him how to work iron so as to fashion a plow. Although such reports were compatible with the Qur'an's positive evaluation of civilization, they did not sit well with Ṭabarī, who believed that Adam should have had to work harder to obtain his food as punishment for his sin. Thus, we see a reemergence of the Yahwist's negative view of the origins of agriculture, even though the Qur'an and the biblical pseudepigrapha available to Muslims militated against it.

Not all Christian pseudepigrapha could be used to widen the scope of beneficial culture; they could also narrow it. For example, the negative etiology of musical instruments in Genesis resurfaces in the *Cave of Treasures*. If Muḥammad knew of the etiology, he pointedly avoided it just as he avoided the other sins of Cain's children. Nevertheless, it made its way into Arabic tradition and contributed to the condemnation of musical instruments in some Muslim literature.[155]

Despite the negative etiology of musical instruments, most of the firsts attributed to biblical figures in early ʿAbbāsid literature follow the Qur'anic model in three respects. First, the creation of fundamental aspects of civilization is ascribed to biblical heroes. Second, the cultural phenomena are disconnected and authors do not attempt to link one to another. Third, the creation of elements of Arab culture is credited to biblical heroes, either to legitimate the use of some vestige of pagan religion or to affirm the Abrahamic identity of the Arab people. But as we saw with the debate over the origin of Arabic, not all Arabs were happy to subsume their past into biblical history. We can see the same sort of tribal pride behind several cultural firsts attributed to pre-Islamic Arabs.

Firsts Attributed to Pre-Islamic Arabs

In addition to biblical firsts, a number of pre-Islamic Arab firsts are mentioned in early Islamic literature. But unlike biblical firsts, it is often impossible to

[153] Ibn Abī Shayba, *Muṣannaf* 8:334, no. 74.

[154] Ibid., 363.

[155] See, for example, Bayhaqī's inclusion of musical instruments in his list of negative cultural firsts (*Maḥāsin*, 395–96).

know if any of these etiologies are authentic representations of pre-Islamic lore, since we rarely have pre-Islamic written sources to compare them with. In the few cases that we do, it seems that some of these firsts were products of Muslim etymological speculation. Take, for example, the case of ʿAlas Dhū Jadan, who, as Abū al-Faraj relates in his *Aghānī*, was the first person to sing in Yemen.[156] Abū al-Faraj maintains that he was one of the Tabābiʿa, Himyarī kings descended from Qaḥtān through Sabaʾ al-Asghar.[157] According to Ibn Qutayba, ʿAlas ruled briefly after the invading Ethiopian army drove Dhū Nuwās into the ocean, although it is said he soon suffered an identical defeat.[158] This gave him the dubious distinction of being the last Arab king to rule Yemen before the rise of Islam.[159] In contrast, others sources say ʿAlas was one of the kinglets (*aqyāl*) of Yemen, meaning he did not rule the entire country.[160]

The confusion over the history of ʿAlas Dhū Jadan arises from the fact that there were several people with this name. One reason for this is that in pre-Islamic times, *Dhū Jadan* indicated affiliation with the Sabaean Jadan clan.[161] Thus, the dam inscription of Abraha at Marib metions two "commanders, Wāṭih and ʿAwdah, both Dhū Jadan."[162] If ʿAlas came from this clan, he would have been known by its cognomen. The title could have also been based on a geographic location, as some Muslim authors note that *jadan* is the name of either a desert (*mafāza*) or a basin (*baṭn*) in Yemen.[163]

Despite the residual memory of the tribal or geographic referent of the title Dhū Jadan in Islamic sources, the dominant interpretation of the meaning of the name is based on the dubious etymology of *jadan* as the Ḥimyarī word for "voice."[164] In this reading, *Dhū Jadan* would mean "Possessor of the Voice." Thus Ibn al-Kalbī and others contend that ʿAlas was called Dhū Jadan "on account of

[156] Abū al-Faraj, *Aghānī* 4:221. Al-Bayhaqī attributes the same first to a certain "ʿAnbas" in his *Kitāb al-maḥāsin wa'l-masāwī*, where he lists it as a negative innovation (395). The different name given for ʿAlas was probably the result of graphical confusion. To the latter point, al-Zabīdī notes a similar confusion in genealogical sources over the names ʿAlas and ʿAbs in reference to this Ḥimyarī king (*Tāj al-ʿarūs* 12:447).

[157] Abū al-Faraj, *Aghānī* 4:221.

[158] Ibn Qutayba, *Maʿārif*, 637.

[159] Somewhat incongruously, Sijistānī writes that ʿAlas was one of the "long lived," claiming that he lived for three hundred years (*Muʿammarūn*, 430).

[160] See Ibn Durayd, *Jamharat al-lugha* 1:451; al-Bakrī, *Muʿjam* 2:18; Zamakhsharī, *Rabīʿ al-abrār* 2:582.

[161] See Bosworth's translation of Ṭabarī's *Ta'rīkh* 5:236n585.

[162] For a translation, see Sidney Smith, "Events," 438.

[163] Al-Bakrī, *Muʿjam* 2:582; Zamakhsharī, *al-Jibāl*, 143; Yāqūt, *Muʿjam* 2:114. Ibn Durayd asserts that Janad is the name of a geographic location in Yemen, whereas Dhū Jadan is the name of the Ḥimyarī kinglet (Ibn Durayd, *Jamharat al-lugha* 1:451).

[164] Abū al-Faraj, *Aghānī* 4:221. I have been unable to find *jadan* used as "voice" in Ethiopic or South Arabian dialects. However, the Ethiopic word *gadām* ("desert" or "plain") is phonetically similar to *jadan* and close to the meaning given by al-Bakrī and others (see the entry for *gaddama* in Leslau's *Comparative Dictionary of Geʿez*, 183).

the beauty of his voice."[165] This etymology is probably also the inspiration for the following anecdote about the discovery of his tomb,[166] recorded in the *Aghānī*:

> One of the men of the people of Sanʿāʾ reported to me that they were digging a grave in the time of Marwān and they happened upon a vault that had a door. They saw a man upon a throne (sitting) as if he were the greatest man who had ever existed. He was wearing a signet ring of gold and a turban of gold and by his head was a tablet of gold on which was written: "I am ʿAlas Dhū Jadan, the kinglet [*qayl*]. My friend will receive success from me and my enemy woe. You have searched and attained. I am a man of one hundred years of age. Wild beasts heeded my voice."[167]

Perhaps this etymology of *jadan* arose from the reputation of a certain Dhū Jadan al-Ḥimyarī, a poet to whom several verses are attributed.[168] Although most authors do not specify who this person was, Ibn al-Kalbī and Abū al-Faraj identify him as ʿAlas the Ḥimyarī king.[169]

Whatever the truth of this identification, we can be fairly certain that Abū al-Faraj's assertion that ʿAlas was the first person to sing in Yemen is not a record of pre-Islamic lore. It is neither found in works written prior to the tenth century nor recorded in any earlier awāʾil works, histories of pre-Islamic Arabs, or the *Tījān* of Ibn Hishām (see below), who recorded a large number of cultural firsts by Yemeni kings and would not have missed an opportunity to attribute another one to them. Thus, it is reasonable to assume that this etiology was the result of etymological speculation in the tenth century, which transformed ʿAlas from an obscure Ḥimyarī king with a short reign into a long-lived poet and musical innovator.

One can find similar etymological etiologies in Khalīl b. Aḥmad's (d. between 160 and 175 AH/776 and 791 AD) *Kitāb al-ʿayn*, one of the first Arabic lexicons. For example, we read that Nabateans are called that (*nabaṭ*) because they were the first to draw water from (*isṭanbata*) the earth (*istanbaṭa* is derived from the same three-letter root as *nabaṭ*).[170] Moreover, the first person to make

[165] Abū al-Faraj, *Aghānī* 4:221. See also Yāqūt, *Muʿjam* 2:114; Zamakhsharī, *Rabīʿ al-abrār* 2:582.

[166] Tomb discovery is a common trope in Islamic lore about Yemeni kings. See, for example, the many instances of this trope in Ibn Hishām's *Tījān* (e.g., pp. 75–78) and al-Hamdānī's *Iklīl*, 74–103.

[167] Abū al-Faraj, *Aghānī* 4:221. Zamakhsharī asserts that his power to compel animals with his voice was also the subject of Ḥimyarī proverbs (*Rabīʿ al-abrār* 2:582).

[168] One of his most frequently cited poems concerns the destruction of citadels in Yemen after the Ethiopian invasion. See Ibn Hishām, *Sīra* 1:50–51; Ṭabarī, *Taʾrīkh* 5:208–10; al-Azraqī, *Akhbār Makka* 1:103–4. Yāqūt attributes these poems to ʿAlqama Dhū Jadan, a grandson of ʿAlas (*Muʿjam* 1:535).

[169] Ibn al-Kalbī, *Nasab Maʿadd* 2:545; Abū al-Faraj, *Aghānī* 4:221. In the *Aghānī*, Abū al-Faraj attributes a poem to him that was later versified by Ṭuways, a famous singer of the Umayyad era (4:223).

[170] Khalīl b. Aḥmad, *al-ʿAyn* 4:184.

ḥanafiyya swords was al-Aḥnaf b. Qays, a chief of the Banū Saʿd during the time of ʿAlī.[171] Finally, Hāshim, the great-grandfather of Muḥammad, was the first to grind up and mix (*hashama*) *tharīd,* a dish of crushed bread mixed with soup; hence his name Hāshim, "the one who grinds."[172]

Other pre-Islamic Arab firsts reflect different tribal loyalties and may have been the product of Islamic-era rivalries. For example, some Muslim authors of Yemeni descent glorified their southern ancestors by attributing a number of firsts to Yemeni Arab kings. Ibn Hishām (d. ca. 213 AH / 828 AD), whose family was of Yemeni Ḥimyarite origin, records a number of these in his *Kitab al-tījān*, a work on Yemeni antiquities. Several of them are reported on the authority of Wahb b. Munabbih,[173] a Yemeni of Persian descent. Ibn al-Kalbī, also of Yemeni descent, mentions a number of pre-Islamic firsts by Yemeni kings in his genealogy of Yemeni tribes, *Nasab Maʿadd wa'l-Yaman al-kabīr*: Dhū Aṣbaḥ was the first to have *aṣbaḥī* whips made for him;[174] Dhū Yazan was the first to have iron tips made for his spears;[175] Dhū al-Manār was first to place a fire along his path to light his way;[176] and Imru' al-Qays was the first to weep over abodes (an allusion to a trope in pre-Islamic poetry).[177] In contrast, Ibn al-Kalbī attributes very few firsts to Qurashīs and other northern Arabs in his other major genealogical work, *Jamharat al-ansāb al-ʿarab.*

Awā'il Lists

Protography having been a subject of scholarly interest for two centuries, Muslims in Iraq began to compose lists of firsts (awā'il). Some did so as a way of organizing hadith, the words and deeds of Muhammad and his Companions. Ibn Abī Shayba (d. 235 AH / 849 AD), who was born in Kufa and lived in Baghdad, compiled more than three hundred firsts of biblical figures and early Muslims mentioned by the Prophet or his Companions in a chapter titled "Firsts," perhaps one of the first Arabic lists of its kind.[178] The only two pre-Islamic Arabs he mentions are both negative: ʿAbbās b. ʿAbd al-Muttalib instituted usury,[179] and ʿAmr b. Luhayy (see above) started idol worship.[180] Slightly later authors

[171] Ibid., 1:365.

[172] Ibid., 4:311.

[173] For example, Wahb maintains that Luqmān b. ʿĀd, a king of Yemen, was the first to cut a hand for theft (Ibn Hishām, *Tijān*, 84). This first was also claimed by Ibn Qutayba for a Meccan patriarch (see below).

[174] Ibn al-Kalbī, *Nasab Maʿadd* 2:542.

[175] Ibid., 545.

[176] Ibid., 547. Ibn Hishām records the same first in his *Tijān* (136).

[177] Ibid., 599.

[178] There were earlier books called *Kitāb al-awā'il,* but they do not survive, and it is unclear if these works were about cultural firsts or something else.

[179] Ibn Abī Shayba, *Muṣannaf* 8:352, 356.

[180] Ibid., 326, 336–37.

such as Ibn Abī ʿĀsim (d. 287 AH / 900 AD) and al-Ṭabarānī (d. 360 AH / 971 AD) maintained the same form and similar content but wrote their awāʾil lists as stand-alone monographs by that title.

Other authors compiled lists of firsts that would be of interest in court and learned salons. For example, Ibn Qutayba, a contemporary of Ibn Abī Shayba, wrote a list of firsts in his *Maʿārif*, an encyclopedic handbook for secretaries.[181] In it, he remarks that his book contains the knowledge a secretary needs to be successful at court. He further remarks that small bits of information concerning precedent and the deeds of ancestors matter a great deal at court.[182] That etiological discussions often took place at court and learned salons is attested by several other Muslim authors. Al-Azraqī (d. ca. 250 AH / 864 AD), for example, reports that the Umayyad caliph Sulaymān b. ʿAbd al-Malik (d. 99 AH / 717 AD) asked his entourage who was the first to light the fire on the mountain of Qazaḥ, near the plain of Muzdalifa (one of the stopping points during a pilgrimage).[183] Similarly, Masʿūdī relates that the caliph Muʿtamid (d. 295 AH / 908 AD), who loved musical instruments, entered a salon one day and asked who the first person to make an *ʿūd* was. One of his boon companions answered that it was Lamech, a son of Methuselah.[184] Etiological speculation also seems to have been a feature of learned salons in Baghdad. For example, the bookseller Ibn Nadīm relates that he once asked the logician Ibn al-Khammār (d. after 407 AH / 1017 AD) who the first philosopher was in a salon held by ʿIsā b. ʿAlī (d. 334 AH / 946 AD), an influential secretary of Iranian descent. Drawing on Porphyry, Ibn al-Khammār replied that the first philosopher was Thales.[185]

Unlike the hadith lists above, Ibn Qutayba includes positive pre-Islamic Arab innovations in his list of firsts. Most of these are achievements by northern Arabs, perhaps to offset the pro-Yemeni etiologies found in early Islamic literature. One of the most important culture heroes in Ibn Qutayba's list is al-Walīd b. al-Mughīra, a prominent member of the Makhzūm clan of the Quraysh tribe who served as a judge in Mecca during the jāhiliyya period. He died three months after Muḥammad fled from Mecca.[186] Al-Walīd is supposedly the first person to judge according to a *qasāma* oath,[187] to forbid wine during the jāhiliyya, to remove his sandals in order to enter the Kaʿba, and to cut someone

[181] For a detailed treatment of Ibn Qutayba's list, see Lang's dissertation "Awāʾil in Arabic Historiography." Despite the title, it is primarily focused on Ibn Qutayba's list.

[182] Ibn Qutayba, *Maʿārif*, 1–4.

[183] Al-Azraqī, *Akhbār Makka* 2:183–84.

[184] Masʿūdī, *Murūj* 4:131–32 (Dāghir edition); see Bayhaqī, *Maḥāsin*, 395.

[185] See Ibn Nadīm, *Fihrist* 2:590; Joel Kraemer, *Humanism*, 126. For a general overview of the debate culture at courts, see Joel Kraemer, *Humanism*, 58, 73, 179.

[186] Ziriklī, *Aʿlām* 8:122.

[187] The *qasāma* oath is used when a dead person is found and his killer is unknown. The executor of the blood feud (*walī al-dam*) extracts an oath to God from the people of that place stating that they did not kill him and do not know who his killer is. See Crone, "Qasāma."

for theft.[188] Despite being an enemy of the Prophet, Ibn Qutayba explicitly writes that the Prophet followed al-Walīd's precedent and ratified the use of the qasāma oath and cutting the hand for theft in Islam. Moreover, the people continued his practice of taking off their sandals before entering the Kaʿba.[189]

Another important pre-Islamic Arab hero in Ibn Qutayba's list is Jadhīma al-Abrash (d. ca. 366 AD), who was the third king of Tanūkh, a kingdom centered on al-Ḥīra in the north. He died battling against Zenobia of Palmyra, and control of al-Ḥīra passed to the Lakhmids. Ibn Qutayba relates that al-Abrash was the first to wear sandals, the first to build a *manjanīq* (a type of catapult), and the first king to travel at night using candles.[190]

Like the firsts found in earlier Arabic literature, those attributed to pre-Islamic Arab heroes in Ibn Qutayba's list are striking in how parochial, modest, and mundane they are. There is no attempt to attribute the invention of fundamental aspects of human society to a pre-Islamic Arab hero unless it was something of importance in Muslim Arab culture; thus, Arabs invent the Arabic language, poetry, and song, but not farming, animal domestication, or the building of houses.

In addition to the firsts of northern Arabs, Ibn Qutayba also recorded a number of biblical etiologies (i.e., firsts about biblical figures) that are not found in earlier Arabic literature. Several of these come from Wahb b. Munabbih, who reports that Moses was the first to use the qasāma oath (God revealed it to him),[191] and Idrīs was the first to write with a pen and sew garments and wear them.[192] Among those who do not have an informant, we learn that Solomon was the first to make soap,[193] Joseph was the first to make papyrus,[194] Nimrod was the first to make flat loaves of bread,[195] John, the son of Zachariah, was the first to be named John (Yaḥyā),[196] and, finally, Noah was the first to build a city, after the Flood.[197]

Strangely, most of the biblical firsts in Ibn Qutayba's *Maʿārif* that can be found in early Muslim protography are not included in his awā'il list. For example, Ibn Qutayba writes at the beginning of the *Maʿārif*, on the authority of Wahb b. Munnabih, that Abraham was the first to give hospitality to guests, the

[188] Ibn Qutayba, *Maʿārif*, 551–52.

[189] Ibid.

[190] Ibid., 554.

[191] Ibid., 552. See note 188 above.

[192] Ibid., 552. Goshe's explanation of the origin of the sewing first (*khāṭa*, "to sew") as a corruption of *khaṭṭa*, "to write," is probably right (Goshe, "Das kitāb al-awā'il," 4). Nevertheless, there is an antique account of Hermes' being the first to sew (Cole, *Democritus*, 20).

[193] Ibn Qutayba, *Maʿārif*, 554.

[194] Ibid.

[195] Ibid.

[196] Ibid., 556. This first is derived from the Qur'an 19:7: "O Zachariah, We give thee good tidings of a boy, whose name is John. No namesake have We given him aforetime."

[197] Ibn Qutayba, *Maʿārif*, 558.

first to make *tharīd* (bread crumbled in broth), the first to have his hair turn white, and the first to originate various hygienic practices.[198] All of these can be found in Ibn Saʿd's *Ṭabaqāt*. Why Ibn Qutayba chose not include them in his section on awāʾil is not clear. Nevertheless, like biblical firsts found in earlier literature, a number of the cultural firsts claimed for biblical heroes in Ibn Qutayba's awāʾil list are the rudiments of civilization.

Noticeably absent from Ibn Qutayba's list are Iranian firsts, even though he was Iranian[199] and must have been familiar with them, since he wrote a significant section on the history of Iranian kings in his *Maʿārif*[200] who elsewhere are credited with all manner of firsts (see the next chapter). This omission is striking given that Iranian culture dominated the court in Ibn Qutayba's time[201] and his *Maʿārif* was written to prepare secretaries for serving in that court. This omission was not lost on authors who did not share Ibn Qutayba's exclusive orientation toward Arabia. The Iranian encyclopedist Ibn Rusta (fl. ca. 290 AH / 903 AD), for example, appended a list of Iranian firsts to the end of Ibn Qutayba's.[202] Later awāʾil authors were similarly inclusive. Al-ʿAskarī (d. after 400 AH / 1010 AD) wrote a whole chapter on Iranian firsts in his long monograph devoted to awāʾil.[203] Still, they fitted Iranian mythology into the Abrahamic and Arab framework worked out by Ibn Qutayba and others. As we have seen above, this framework reflects the cultural orientation of Muslims living in Basra, Kufa, and Baghdad who were helping to create the Arabocentric philological and historiographical tradition that became the bedrock of Islamic scholarship.

We have to bear in mind that if this framework later became dominant, in Ibn Qutayba's time it was not. Indeed, the purpose of Ibn Qutayba's list of biblical and Arab firsts was to challenge the dominance of Iranian culture among elites at court in Baghdad, a subject that will be treated in the next chapter.

Conclusion

It is easy to dismiss protographical material as trivia, which it usually is. But that does not mean it is useless as a source for social history. Indeed, the creation of large volumes of protography in a short span of time indicates intense periods of innovation and borrowing and a heightened appreciation of individual achievement.

Because it deals with the status of foreign knowledge and innovation, proto-

[198] Ibid., 30.
[199] Savant, "Place," 41.
[200] Ibn Qutayba, *Maʿārif*, 652–67.
[201] Gutas, *Greek Thought*, 29, 34; Bosworth, *Heritage*, 8–9.
[202] Ibn Rusta, *Aʿlāq*, 196–200. Many of these firsts center on the city of Isfahan.
[203] ʿAskarī, *Awāʾil*, 165–74.

graphical literature can also illuminate ethnic tensions and the ways elites defined themselves against perceived outsiders. This is particularly useful for understanding social dynamics during and after conquests of foreign countries, when ethnic tensions run high. Moreover, documenting the use of protographs as social currency can help historians identify the "markets," or elite groups, who valued them and who determined which institutions they "bought" access to.

In this chapter, I have focused primarily on protographical literature written by those who articulated the culture of the conquerors. The Greeks of Alexander's era saw themselves as the peers and heirs of the Near Eastern civilizations they were about to conquer. They accepted foreign contributions to their culture but were also confident in their own achievements, presaging the skill with which Greek rulers in the Near East would adopt the native traditions of those they conquered while expanding the influence Greek learning (see chapter 4).

Ibn Qutayba and Pliny, in contrast, wrote after the conquests and thus had to differentiate the conquerors' culture from that of the conquered following decades or centuries of foreign influence. Unlike the Greek authors, the two men are modest about the cultural achievements of the conquerors (Roman and Arab), reflecting the conquerors' genuine lack of a native learned high culture comparable to those they conquered. (The Romans had a high culture, but it was heavily indebted to the Greeks.) This lack of sophistication also caused both men to worry about the cultural influence of their imperial predecessors (Greek for Pliny, Iranian for Ibn Qutayba) on the new empires. However, they handled it in very different ways: Pliny acknowledged the influence and employed it to challenge his countrymen to surpass the Greeks, whereas Ibn Qutayba ignored it and encouraged his coreligionists to create a parallel cultural system to supplant it.

I am unaware of a pre-Islamic analog to Ibn Qutayba, an ethnic chauvinist glorifying the cultural achievements of those who conquered his more civilizationally advanced forefathers. If there is, it is hard to imagine one so dedicated to collecting the conquerors' culture myths. Usually, a strategy like Ibn Qutayba's, which prioritized cultural rather than lineal criteria for joining the empire's ruling and scholarly elites, was used to opposite effect—persuading the conquerors to behave more like the conquered. I will consider this opposite effect in the next chapter and return to Ibn Qutayba's motivations in the book's conclusion.

FOUR

Inventing Nations: Postconquest Native Histories of Civilization's Origins

> Mighty deeds of Semiramis are celebrated among the Assyrians, and mighty deeds of Sesostris in Egypt, and the Phrygians, even to this day, call brilliant and marvelous exploits "manic" because Manes, one of their very early kings, proved himself a good man and exercised a vast influence among them.
>
> —Plutarch, *Isis and Osiris*

> Every people is more familiar than others with their own forefathers, pedigrees, and accomplishments. With respect to every complex matter, one must have reference to those people who were (directly) involved.
>
> —Ṭabarī, *Ta'rīkh*

A CENTURY AFTER the Arabs conquered the land of Iran, Iranians began writing histories of their pre-Islamic Iranian kings in Arabic. In most of these histories, the first kings are depicted as inventors of the arts and sciences of civilization.

Something similar happened after the Greek and Roman conquests of the Near East, when native elites wrote histories of their forefathers' contributions to civilization in the language of the conqueror to instill a sense of national pride in past accomplishments after being conquered by a foreign power and to remind the conquerors of their cultural dependence on the conquered people.[1] Such accounts did not necessarily imply a political program; indeed, these histories were usually intended to encourage foreign rulers to behave like native kings, not to drive them out.[2] But their ambiguity meant that they could be appropriated to support revivalist kingdoms, at least in the case of tenth-century Iran.

[1] Edwards, "Philo or Sanchuniathon?" 214. The first epigraph is from Plutarch's *Isis and Osiris* in *Moralia* 5.360b, and the second is from Ṭabarī's *Ta'rīkh* 1:326.

[2] Although these histories sometimes treat the native origins of inventions commonly ascribed to the Greeks, such as rhetoric, law, philosophy, and the sciences, their primary concern is the origin of civilization as a whole. So, despite the norm of considering them together with native histories of Greek inventions, I will treat them separately (see the next chapter). In doing so, I hope to show that the function of the general histories of civilization is different from that of the histories of Greek scholarship and sciences. Whereas the latter is meant to ratify Greek learning, the former celebrates native civilization, placing it on par with or above the preconquest civilizations of the conquerors.

Some readers will no doubt object to the use of "national pride" as anachronistic. That is a fair objection if nationalism is defined solely with reference to modern examples. But as David Goodblatt has recently argued, limiting the concept to the modern period is unwarranted given the strong parallels between ancient and modern identity formation; the definition should be expanded to include the common features of both.[3] One important common feature is that imagined membership in a nation is asserted through appeal to shared blood or shared culture (religion, language, education, etc.).[4] Ancient authors emphasized one or both at different times,[5] and often they were deemed inextricable, with culture construed as an intrinsic part of one's biological descent.[6] The histories I consider in this chapter are nationalistic in the sense that they place the origins of civilization locally and in the distant past and assert or imply that the cultures of other nations are inferior and derivative. Moreover, they make shared ancient culture, rather than kinship, the primary marker of ethnic belonging.

In all three postconquest periods, claims to have originated civilization were bolstered by citing ancient texts attesting to the same. Although this sometimes led to forgeries and frequently to exaggerated claims for the antiquity of a translated text, it also fueled the translation of preconquest histories. Where preconquest texts are available for comparison, the preconquest provenance of the translated material is usually borne out (see below). Thus, the question is usually not whether the postconquest culture myths are authentic but rather why postconquest authors chose particular myths to translate and how they presented them to their multiple audiences to elevate the status of preconquest native civilization.

Postconquest Greek Ethnography

I begin with the aftermath of Alexander's conquests, which united much of the Mediterranean and the Near East politically. Although this political unity did not survive Alexander's death, Greek culture continued to be the elite culture of the ruling class after his Greek generals divided the empire among themselves: the Antigonids in Greece and Thrace; the Seleucids in much of Asia Minor, Syria, and Mesopotamia; and the Ptolemies in Egypt and southern Syria.

The extent to which these elites adopted local culture or native elites adopted Greek culture, a process called "Hellenization" or "Hellenism,"[7] has been the

[3] Goodblatt, *Elements*, 1–15.

[4] Ibid., 17.

[5] Herodotus held that Greekness was the result of common blood and common culture (8.144.2), whereas Isocrates elevated common culture over kinship (*Panegyricus* 50). See Goodblatt, *Elements*, 17–19.

[6] Goodblatt, *Elements*, 25; Isaac, *Racism*, 55–168.

[7] Mellor, "Graecia Capta," 85–86.

subject of intense debate. Johann Droysen's earlier notion of a fusion or hybrid culture, with Greek culture as the driving force, has been rejected in favor of multiculturalism.[8] Still, the question remains as to how autonomous these islands of culture were.

The problem is exemplified by Greek ethnographies of the newly conquered lands written by court officials. Like Herodotus, the authors of these ethnographies could not help but interpret local culture through Greek eyes. But also like Herodotus, they were influenced by their native interlocutors, who shaped the conquerors' interpretations for their own ends.

Foremost among these postconquest ethnographers is Hecataeus of Abdera (fl. late fourth century BC), a Greek trained in philosophy who served Ptolemy I in Egypt. Hecataeus wrote a Greek ethnography of the Egyptians during the first years of Ptolemy I's reign (306/5–300 BC).[9] The work, parts of which survive in paraphrastic form in Diodorus's *Historical Library*,[10] stresses the cultural achievements of Egypt.[11] Although Hecataeus claims to derive the records of these achievements from local priestly informants, it is unclear if the myths are Greek or Egyptian in origin. Some priests, for example, inform him that Hephaestus (the Greek equivalent of the craft god Ptah) was Egypt's first king because he discovered fire,[12] but the myth he relates of Ptah/Hephaestus's discovery of fire when lightning struck a tree does not appear in Egyptian texts. It does, however, parallel a Greek account of Hephaestus by Hellanicus of Lesbos (d. ca. 395 BC).[13]

Hecataeus also relates that Egyptian priests record that Osiris was the first to wean humans from cannibalism—once the goddess Isis discovered wheat and barley, Osiris taught humans how to cultivate and harvest grains.[14] There is not a great deal on cannibalism in Egyptian texts, but the subject was of great interest to Greek authors.[15] Osiris was known as a vegetation god in Egyptian mythology, so his creation of agriculture may have derived from local myth.[16] But

[8] See Momigliano's classic critique of Droysen ("J. G. Droysen between Greeks and Jews") and Cartledge's 1997 survey of the field of Hellenistic Studies (introduction to *Hellenistic Constructs*).

[9] Sterling, *Historiography*, 59–75.

[10] On the derivation of Diodorus's account from Hecataeus, there has been considerable debate. Bar-Kochva (*Pseudo-Hecataeus*, 14) holds that most of book 1 of Diodorus's (first century AD) *Library of History*—from 1.10 through the rest of the book—is a paraphrase of Hecataeus's *On the Egyptians*. Burstein ("Hecataeus," 45) agrees and is unconvinced by Burton's argument that Diodorus probably quoted from multiple sources (Burton, *Commentary*, 16, 34), given his tendency to quote from a single source for all of his major topics (Burstein, "Hecataeus," passim). I am more persuaded of Burstein's argument, since much of Burton's evidence for multiple sources is from early Greek authors, whom Hecataeus is as likely to quote as Diodorus.

[11] Sterling, *Historiography*, 71.

[12] Diodorus Siculus *Library* 1.13.3.

[13] Ibid.; Burton, *Commentary*, 9.

[14] Diodorus Siculus *Library* 1.14.

[15] Burton, *Commentary*, 73; Mendels, "Polemical Character," 107.

[16] Burton, *Commentary*, 74.

Isis's discovery of wheat and barley is not attested in Egyptian myth, indicating that her connection with Osiris led either Hecataeus or his Egyptian informants to equate her with the Greek goddess Demeter, who was associated with wheat and barley.[17]

The priests also tell Hecataeus that Osiris discovered the grapevine and was the first to "deduce" the method for turning it into wine, similar to Hellanicus's contention that the vine was discovered in Egypt. Osiris, they say, taught the rest of humanity how to cultivate crops and make wine, similar to Greek myths about Dionysus, with whom Osiris is equated.[18] All of this is much closer to Democritus's vision of cultural development through human innovation than to native Egyptian and Near Eastern etiological myths in which the gods create culture ex nihilo, a vision consistent with Hecataeus's euhemerism.[19]

Finally, the priests tell Hecataeus of the inventions of Hermes (the Greek equivalent of Thoth), whom he describes as a mortal king of Egypt, in like manner.

> For this god was the first to bring language to perfection; he named many nameless things, and invented the alphabet, and ordained ceremonies governing divine worship and sacrifices to the gods. He was the first to perceive order in the stars and to discern the nature and harmony of musical sounds. He was also the first to establish a school of wrestling and to cultivate the graceful movement and proper development of the body. He invented the lyre, with three strings of sinew to represent the seasons of the year; that is he prescribed three basic tones, treble, bass, and middle: treble is evocative of summer, bass of winter, and the middle tone of spring. And he taught the Greeks eloquence [*hermeneia*], which is why he is called Hermes. In short, they hold him to have been the sacred scribe to whom Osiris confided all things, and on whose counsel he especially relied. And incidentally, it was he who discovered the olive, not Athena as the Greeks pretend.[20]

We have already seen many of these inventions attributed to Hermes in the writings of Plato and the *Homeric Hymns*, although some are unattested and may have been of Egyptian origin, since Thoth was known as a patron of the arts.[21] If we can accept that Diodorus has faithfully summarized the work of Hecataeus, this passage represents one of the earliest syntheses of Greek lore on the Egyptian god Thoth and the Greek god Hermes.

Clearly, Greek myth has made its way into Hecataeus's account of Egypt's cultural achievements. But who was responsible for its inclusion? At the very least, the functional similarity between some Greek and Egyptian gods led Hec-

[17] Ibid.

[18] Diodorus Siculus *Library* 1.15.6–8; Burton, *Commentary*, 10, 17, 76.

[19] Oden, "Philo," 118; Edwards, "Philo or Sanchuniathon?" 214.

[20] Diodorus Siculus *Library* 1.16.

[21] Burton, *Commentary*, 79.

ataeus to flesh out the native god's achievements with Greek myths. More speculatively, Egyptian priests familiar with Greek myth may have suggested the parallels to Hecataeus. This seems unlikely so soon after Alexander's conquest of Egypt but not completely far-fetched given that Herodotus's interlocutors seem familiar with Greek mythology and were trying to convince him of Greece's cultural dependence on Egypt, just as Hecataeus's interlocutors were doing. Moreover, a few years after Hecataeus wrote his book, an Egyptian priest named Manetho would make similar equations between Greek and Egyptian gods (see his section below).

But why would Hecataeus or his interlocutors wish to glorify the civilization of Egypt when it was now ruled by Greeks? For the priests, reminding the Ptolemies of their cultural dependence on Egypt was a way to encourage them to cultivate Egyptian learning and religion, of which they were the guardians. For Hecataeus and the Ptolemaic state, it was a way to "win the approbation of the indigenous power base (i.e., the priests) by celebrating accomplishments of the native civilization and affirming continuity with it."[22]

Glorifying the cultural achievements of Egypt was also a way to advance the Ptolemies' claims to regional power against the other Greek kingdoms that had arisen after Alexander's death.[23] Thus, Hecataeus writes that Egyptian colonists settled other parts of the world after the death of Isis and Osiris. The Egyptian Belus (the Babylonian god Bel) and his followers founded Babylon, where they became known for their skill in astronomy (a skill they took from the Egyptians).[24] Likewise, Egyptian colonists settled Greece and "the nation of the Jews."[25] Not surprisingly, the settlements just happen to be in regions not only renowned for their scientific achievement, making them derivative of Egypt, but at the time (with the exception of Greece) ruled by the Ptolemies' primary rival, the Seleucids.

Hecataeus does not say much about these other settlements, with the exception of the colonists who settled Judea.[26] According to Hecataeus, there were several minorities in Egypt who sacrificed differently from the way the majority did. When a plague came, the Egyptians exiled these minorities. Some of these people went to Greece and others to Judea, which was uninhabited. The leader of the latter group was Moses, who founded Jerusalem and its temple. He also forbade the representation of God in human form, since he believed that God controlled the entire universe. (This feature of Jewish religion would be highlighted by many subsequent pagan authors writing in Greek and Latin.)

[22] Sterling, *Historiography*, 74–75.

[23] Ibid., 75.

[24] Diodorus Siculus *Library* 1.28. Hecataeus notes that the Babylonians called these men Chaldeans.

[25] Ibid., 1.28.

[26] Diodorus Siculus *Library* 40.3.1; see Bar-Kochva, *Pseudo-Hecataeus*, 19, 22; Schäfer, *Judeophobia*, 15–17.

Although Hecataeus is largely favorable toward Judaism, praising Moses for forbidding infant exposure and distributing land equally, he does note that Jews are hostile to outsiders on account of their expulsion from Egypt: "The sacrifices that he (Moses) established differ from those of other nations, as does their way of living, for as a result of their own expulsion from Egypt he introduced an unsocial and intolerant mode of life."[27] However, other peoples expelled from Egypt did not develop misanthropic attitudes, leading scholars to question the earlier consensus that Hecataeus was unreservedly favorable toward the Jews.[28]

Whatever the case, Hecataeus did not reach these conclusions in a vacuum. As Davies has demonstrated, he probably had Jewish priests as informants,[29] mirroring his use of Egyptian priests. Thus, in the immediate aftermath of the Greek conquests of the Near East, native elites were shaping their conquerors' understanding of local culture. Their reasons for doing so would become clearer as they began to write their local histories in the language of their conquerors.

The Empires Write Back: Babylonian, Egyptian, Jewish, and Phoenician Histories of Civilization

Around the same time that native priests shaped Hecataeus's understanding of Egyptian and Jewish history, some of them began to write down their culture myths in Greek. Since these native authors expressed themselves in the language of their conquerors, they provide important evidence in the modern debate about the validity of Droysen's nineteenth-century notion of Hellenism, a syncretism of Greek and Oriental ideas with influence usually running from west to east (except in religion).[30]

The most influential and detailed treatment of these texts is by Gregory Sterling, who argues that they form a distinct genre of "apologetic historiography" that borrows Greek modes of writing and Hellenizes local traditions "in an effort to establish the identity of the group within the setting of the larger world."[31] By blending Greek forms with native content, the texts' authors both "*challenged* and *identified* with Hellenism at the same time."[32]

One Greek mode of writing that Sterling and others adduce as proof of Hellenic influence is the motif of the *Kulturbringer*, the local hero who brings some

[27] Diodorus Siculus *Library* 9.3.4 (in Stern, *Greek and Latin Authors* 1:28).

[28] Schäfer, *Judeophobia*, 16–17; Gruen, *Heritage*, 51.

[29] Davies, "Judaeans in Egypt," 118–20.

[30] For critical assessments of Droysen's legacy, see Momigliano, "Droysen between Greeks and Jews"; Samuel, *Shifting Sands*; Cartledge, introduction to *Hellenistic Constructs*; Moyer, "Limits of Hellenism," 88–89. Recent scholarly assessments of the extent of Hellenization among the native historians are treated below.

[31] Sterling, *Historiography*, 17.

[32] Ibid., 103.

or all of the arts and sciences of civilization to humanity.[33] The motif is found in nearly all of the native histories I will survey below. Sterling argues that native historians used it to show that their forebears had invented the culture that the rulers now enjoyed. Thus, they could adopt the new culture by claiming it as their own.[34]

Sterling's argument needs modification. First, although the Kulturbringer motif abounds in preconquest Greek historiography and is found in nearly all of the native histories mentioned earlier, it is also a commonplace in preconquest Near Eastern myth,[35] so we have to rule out Greek influence in terms of form. Indeed, native authors were frequently translating these myths into Greek. Second, Hellenism is a fluid concept, which makes debates about the extent of identifying with or challenging Hellenism hard to answer.[36] Finally, focusing on Hellenism fails to capture the purposes of these histories. Although many of them sought to correct Greek misunderstandings of the local culture and its origins, they also sought to persuade foreign rulers to identify more closely with the local culture and to denigrate local rivals for the title of cultural superiority. This is not to say that these authors were not mindful of their Greek audience; they were. However, justifying the adoption of Greek culture was not the objective of these histories.

Berossus

One of the first native authors to try his hand at writing a history of local civilization in the Hellenistic age was a Chaldean priest named Berossus (d. after 278 BC), an acolyte of the Babylonian high god Marduk. Berossus, who wrote a history of Babylonia in Greek, was born during the rule of Alexander over Babylon and served his Seleucid successors, probably in the Great Temple of Esagila in Babylon.[37] There are also reports of a Berossus who left Babylon and settled in Kos, an island in the Mediterranean off the coast of modern Turkey, where he established a school for astronomy or astrology. Modern scholars are split over whether or not this is the same Berossus.[38]

As a priest, Berossus had the ability to read cuneiform documents, a skill that was quickly fading as Greek and Aramaic, written in two noncuneiform scripts,

[33] Ibid., 223.

[34] Ibid., 136.

[35] See chapter 1. Dalley ("Semiramis," 27) notes a parallel phenomenon of Near Eastern euhemerism before Euhemerus.

[36] For the problems with the concept of Hellenism and Hellenization, see Samuel, *Shifting Sands*, 9–10; Cartledge, introduction to *Hellenistic Constructs*, 4–5.

[37] Burstein, "Babyloniaca," 5; Kuhrt, "Babyloniaka," 33, 48; Komoróczy, "Berosos," 125; Sterling, *Historiography*, 104.

[38] Verbrugghe and Wickersham, *Berossos and Manetho*, 13–14; Burstein, "Babyloniaca," 5; Sterling, *Historiography*, 104–16. Concerning the Berossus who moved to Kos, Kuhrt, in "Babyloniaka"

came to dominate as literary languages after Alexander's conquest.[39] This would have given him access to the ancient temple records in Esagila.[40] Berossus was also fluent in Greek, which would have made him a very valuable cultural interpreter in the polyglot court of the Seleucid Empire[41] and well positioned to explain the Babylonian past to the region's new rulers;[42] hence the dedication of the book to Antiochus I around 280 BC.[43]

Berossus begins his narrative of Babylonian history not with a cosmogony and anthropogony, but with a framing story about a sea creature, Oannes, who gives humans all the culture they would ever need (see below). Oannes then tells humans about the origins of the world and its creatures. The universe, Oannes tells the Babylonians, "was only darkness and water." In the darkness and water were "wondrous beings with peculiar forms who were able to engender other living beings." These "other living beings" were either hybrids of humans and animals or of two animals. All of these creatures lived in the darkness and water, which was actually a goddess named Thalatth (Tiamat).[44]

After this point in Berossus's narrative, things become a bit confused. There are two stories of the rebellion of the god Bel (Marduk),[45] but it is unclear if Berossus authored both or if one is a later addition. The essence of the story is

(43–44), has observed that this story fits with other Greek legends about sages who bring sciences from the East. The Roman author Vitruvius (fl. late first century BC) is the primary source of this legend. He writes that the Chaldeans are the most skilled in the practice of astrology, and foremost among the Chaldeans in this science was Berossus, who "emigrated from the city in the land of the Chaldeans" to settle in Kos (also the home of the legendary physician Asclepius). See T1a and b in Verbrugghe and Wickersham, *Berossos and Manetho*, 35–36 (T5a and b in Jacoby's *Fragmente*). In keeping with his status as a culture hero for astrology, Vitruvius credits Berossus with inventing the "half-circle sundial cut out of a square block" (T1c, Verbrugghe and Wickersham, *Berossos and Manetho*, 36; T5c in Jacoby's *Fragmente*). Other Roman authors write that he was the father of an Egyptian or Babylonian Sibyl (the Sibyls were women who—the Greeks and Romans believed—could predict future events). See T5 and T8, Verbrugghe and Wickersham, *Berossos and Manetho*, 37, 39 (T7a and T7c in Jacoby's *Fragmente*). Pliny the Elder even writes that there was a statue of him in Athens (T3b, Verbrugghe and Wickersham, *Berossos and Manetho*, 36; T6 in Jacoby's *Fragmente*). Given his iconic status, it is not surprising that some Roman authors attributed several astronomical statements to Berossus (F16, F17a, F17b, F17c, F18, Verbrugghe and Wickersham, *Berossos and Manetho*, 64–66; T5b, F19a, F19b, F19c, F18 in Jacoby's *Fragmente*). Verbrugghe and Wickersham, who produced a complete translation of the Berossus fragments, believe that these statements are by the Babylonian Berossus and a part of his history (*Berossos and Manetho*, 17). But in light of his culture-hero status, they are more likely pseudepigrapha (Drews, "Babylonian Chronicles," 51; Burstein, "Babyloniaca"; Kuhrt, "Babyloniaka," 44).

[39] Verbrugghe and Wickersham, *Berossos and Manetho*, 4.

[40] Drews, "Babylonian Chronicles," 54; Adler, *Time*, 24; Gmirkin, *Hellenistic Histories*, 96n62, 136; Sterling, *Historiography*, 111–12.

[41] Kuhrt and Sherwin-White, *Hellenism*, 7; Rotroff, "Greeks and the Other," 224–25.

[42] Kuhrt, "Babyloniaka," 33.

[43] Ibid., 33. On the date of the book, see Koromòczy, "Berosos," 125; Burstein, "Babyloniaca," 4; Gmirkin, *Hellenistic Histories*, 91.

[44] F1 (Verbrugghe and Wickersham, *Berossos and Manetho*, 45; F1b in Jacoby's *Fragmente*).

[45] Ibid.

basically the same: Bel rebels against Thalatth and cuts her in half. As a result, all of the creatures inside her are destroyed. Out of her first half, Bel fashions the earth, and from her second half he makes the heavens. One of the gods then cuts off his own head.[46] In the first version, the other gods mix the headless god's blood with the earth and create humans. In the second version, the headless god mixes his own blood with the earth, creating humans and animals.

Even more important than the slight differences in the story is the commentary that is present in the first version but is absent in the second. In the first version, the author writes that the story of the headless god "is an allegorical explanation" meant to explain why humans have reason and "share in the gods' wisdom" (they have reason and wisdom because they were made from the blood of a god).[47] In the second version, there is no commentary at all. The absence is significant, for it indicates that the author of the second version unapologetically believed in the historicity of the cosmogony he was relating, whereas the author of the first version wanted to make sure that his audience knew he was using only allegory, a clear appeal to Greek sensibilities.[48]

The first book ends after the rebellion of Bel. The second book begins with a list of the ten antediluvian kings. Here we can insert the story of Oannes, who was half human and half fish and emerged from the Persian Gulf during the "first year" of creation. Seeing that the Babylonians were living "without discipline and order, just like animals," he proceeded to teach them "all those things conducive to a settled and civilized life."

> This monster spent its days with men, never eating anything, but teaching men the skills necessary for writing and for doing mathematics and for all sorts of knowledge: how to build cities, found temples, and make laws. It taught men how to determine borders and divide land, also how to plant seeds and then to harvest their fruits and vegetables. In short, it taught men all those things conducive to a settled and civilized life. Since that time nothing further has been discovered. At the end of the day, this monster Oannes went back to the sea and spent the night. It was amphibious, able to live both on land and in the sea.[49]

Although not stated explicitly, we can infer that Oannes appeared during the reign of the first king, Aloros, of the first city, Babylon. A second Oannes (Oannes the Annedotos) appeared during the reign of the fourth antediluvian king, Ammenon. During the reign of the sixth king, Daonos, four more sea creatures appeared. And during the reign of the seventh king, Euedorankhos,

[46] Verbrugghe and Wickersham believe that the god who cuts off his own head in the first version is Bel (*Berossos and Manetho*, 46n7), but this is not clearly stated in the text. One could just as easily read the passage as referring to an anonymous god.

[47] F1 (Verbrugghe and Wickersham, *Berossos and Manetho*, 45; F1b in Jacoby's *Fragmente*).

[48] Adler, *Time*, 25; Dillery, "Narrative History," 16–17; Gmirkin, *Hellenistic Histories*, 99–100.

[49] F1 (Verbrugghe and Wickersham, *Berossos and Manetho*, 44; F1b in Jacoby's *Fragmente*).

the last sea creature, Odakon, appeared. Odakon, Berossus tells us, "explained in detail what Oannes had originally said in a summary fashion."[50] In other words, he elaborated on the cosmogony related by Oannes; but like the other sea creatures who came after Oannes, he did not give humans any more culture.

Although Oannes had given humans culture, this gift was jeopardized by the first great flood. According to Berossus, the tenth antediluvian king, Xisuthros, was visited in a dream by Kronos (the Greek equivalent of the Mesopotamian god Enki). Kronos warned Xisuthros of the impending flood and ordered him to "bury together all the tablets, the first, the middle, and the last, and hide them in Sippar, the city of the sun."[51] Presumably, these tablets contained all of the knowledge bequeathed by Oannes. Kronos then instructed Xisuthros to build a boat for his family and closest friends and provision it with food, drink, and animals. After the flood ended, Xisuthros and his companions landed in Armenia. He and some of his companions were taken to live eternally with the gods, and the rest were charged by a "voice from the air" to return to Babylonia, dig up the tablets that were buried in the city of Sippar, near Babylon, and give them to humanity. They obediently did so and again renewed Babylonia.[52] After this, history continues unbroken through a succession of rulers, which Berossus details in the remainder of book 2 and all of book 3.

Berossus combined several local Mesopotamian myths and genres to form his narrative. The cosmogony is from the *Enuma Elish*,[53] a Babylonian account that exalts Marduk over the other gods. The text was very important to the city of Babylon, as it was recited during the New Year's festival in the city.[54] Oannes is Uanna of Eridu, the first of the half-fish sages, or apkallē, who is sometimes assimilated to Adapa, a human sage.[55] By Berossus's time, Oannes was believed to be the author of the *Enuma Elish*.[56] Moreover, Oannes and the rest of the sages were firmly joined with their kingly counterparts, as they are in his history.[57] As for the flood account, it is probably a Sipparian recension of the Sumerian story that has the hero as Ziusudra, hence Berossus's Xisuthros, rather than the Akkadian Utnapishtim.[58] The rest of Berossus's account is largely a king list.[59]

[50] F3 (Verbrugghe and Wickersham, *Berossos and Manetho*, 48; F3b in Jacoby's *Fragmente*).

[51] F4a (Verbrugghe and Wickersham, *Berossos and Manetho*, 49; F4b in Jacoby's *Fragmente*).

[52] Ibid.

[53] Burstein, "Babyloniaca," 8–9; Kuhrt, "Babyloniaka," 46; Sterling, *Historiography*, 111–12; Gmirkin, *Hellenistic Histories*, 92.

[54] Dalley, "Near Eastern Myths," 50–51; Gmirkin, *Hellenistic Histories*, 96.

[55] Greenfield, "Apkallu," 73; Dalley, "Semiramis," 18.

[56] Lambert, "Poultices," 59–77.

[57] Kvanvig, *Roots*, 192–93; Sanders, "Writing," 125.

[58] Burstein, "Babyloniaca," 8–9; Kuhrt, "Babyloniaka," 46; Sterling, *Historiography*, 111–12; Gmirkin, *Hellenistic Histories*, 102, 105, 113.

[59] Sterling, *Historiography*, 111–12.

There is one element of Berossus's culture myth that does not seem to fit well with the pre-Alexandrian tradition. In Berossus, the first *apkall* reveals the arts of civilization all at once, whereas in preconquest mythology, a succession of apkallē revealed it over time. This has led some authors to speculate that Berossus shifted the role of Enki to Oannes.[60] That may be the case, but it was probably not due to creativity on Berossus's part, since the apkallē in several pre-Alexandrian texts deliver culture on behalf of Enki.[61]

If Berossus wrote his history for Antiochus I, what would have been the ruler's impression upon reading it? That Babylon is the origin of all the arts of civilization and that it survived only because a succession of kings and sages worked to preserve it.[62] The purpose of this message was twofold. First, it was intended to educate the new foreign rulers of Babylon of their duty to preserve Babylonian custom and wisdom. Second, it was meant to elevate their status as the bearers of this patrimony, the religious scholars, who in Berossus's time portrayed themselves as the heirs of the ancient apkallē.[63]

In addition to writing the history of Babylonia to impress a Greek audience and remind them of their cultural dependence on Babylonia, Berossus may have wanted to correct the perception that all culture originated in Egypt; indeed, Hecataeus had asserted that Babylon and its sciences were founded by Egyptians. Although Berossus does not mention Egypt by name, claiming that all culture originated in Babylon was as much a shot at Egyptians as it was at Greeks.

Manetho

Another priest who tried his hand at "native history" (*patrion historian*, as Josephus calls it)[64] soon after the conquests was Manetho, an Egyptian who may have been the chief priest of Re at Heliopolis during the reigns of the first two Ptolemies (323–246 BC)[65] and perhaps the third (246–222 BC). Manetho was a high-ranking priest,[66] which meant that, like Berossus, he knew the native scripts[67] and was a member of the highest remaining elite institution in his native land (the native pharaohs having been displaced by Persian conquest in 343 BC).[68] Moreover, like Berossus, Manetho's knowledge of Greek literature was

[60] Komoròczy, "Berosos," 150–51; Van Seters, *Prologue*, 68.

[61] See chapter 1.

[62] Burstein, "Babyloniaca," 7–8.

[63] For additional evidence of this by the Babylonian scholars of the time, see Lenzi, "Uruk List," 161–62.

[64] Josephus *Apion* 1.73, in *The Works of Flavius Josephus*.

[65] Sterling, *Historiography*, 118.

[66] Ibid.; Dillery, "First Egyptian," 100.

[67] On the education of Egyptian priests, see Dillery, "First Egyptian," 110.

[68] Moyer, "Limits of Hellenism," 44.

quite good,[69] which meant that he was well positioned to mediate between the native religious institutions and the new foreign court.[70] Little wonder, then, that he helped found or develop the cult of Sarapis patronized by Ptolemy Soter, which was based on a pre-Alexandrian Egyptian cult.[71]

Like Berossus, Manetho may have dedicated his history of his native land to its Greek ruler, in this case Ptolemy Philadelphus.[72] Unlike Berossus, Manetho did not relate how the world or the gods came into being.[73] Moreover, he did not relate the physical geography of Egypt or say much about its customs, making it unlikely that he was slavishly following the Herodotean genre of ethnography.[74] Indeed, even in content, recent scholars have questioned whether Manetho relied on Herodotus or Hecataeus at all (although he was certainly aware of them).[75]

Despite these differences (some of which may be attributed to the transmission of the text), Manetho did parallel Berossus by relating several culture myths beginning in the time of the gods. Giving the Greek equivalent for the Egyptian god Ptah,[76] Manetho stated that the god Hephaestus was the "first person among the Egyptians" and the one "who also discovered fire for them."[77] The second human king of Egypt, Athothis (Iti), "built the palace in Memphis. He was a skilled physician and wrote books on anatomy."[78] Imhotep, the high priest of Re and chancellor of the second pharaoh of the Third Dynasty, Tosorthros (Djoser), is similarly remembered for his medical skills and architectural innovations: "For his medical skill he was esteemed as Asclepius by the Egyptians, and he invented the art of building with cut stones, and he studied writing."[79] Finally, Bocchoris (Bakenranef), the first king of the Twenty-fourth

[69] Mendels, "Polemical Character," 106; Dillery, "First Egyptian," 97. Murray, in "Herodotus," 209, argues that Manetho was far more conversant with Greek culture than his Babylonian counterpart.

[70] Moyer, "Limits of Hellenism," 78.

[71] Stambaugh, *Sarapis*; Moyer, "Limits of Hellenism," 138–49. See Borgeaud and Volokhine, "Sarapis," on the questionable historicity of the legend.

[72] Sterling, *Historiography*, 133.

[73] Ibid.

[74] Ibid., 125–26, 132.

[75] Mendels, "Polemical Character," 93–94, 108; Moyer, "Limits of Hellenism," 131. For the contrary view, see Armayor, "Influence," 8; Dillery, "First Egyptian," 102, 105; Burstein, "Hecataeus," 46; Sterling, *Historiography*, 128.

[76] Greeks equated Hephaestus with Ptah as far back as Herodotus (*Histories* 37.2) on account of the homyphony of the names and the similarity in function. See Asheri et al., *Commentary*, 435.

[77] F2a (Verbrugghe and Wickersham, *Berossos and Manetho*, 130–31; F2 in Jacoby's *Fragmente*). The medieval monk George Synkellos preserved a fragment of Manetho that clearly stated that Hephaestus is a god (Synkellos, *Chronography*, 18, 24).

[78] F2a (Verbrugghe and Wickersham, *Berossos and Manetho*, 131; F2 in Jacoby's *Fragmente*).

[79] Ibid. (Verbrugghe and Wickersham, *Berossos and Manetho*, 134; F2 in Jacoby's *Fragmente*). The text is garbled here and makes Tosorthros the culture hero. See Sethe, who in *Imhotep* suggests that Imhotep's name was dropped through corruption of the text or epitomization.

Dynasty, "made laws for the Egyptians" (Manetho did not credit anyone else with making laws before this time).[80]

For the sequence of culture heroes, Manetho drew on local tradition. All of them, except Bocchoris, are mentioned in the *Turin Canon*, a thirteenth-century BC king list similar to texts on which Manetho based his chronology of gods and pharaohs.[81] As for the culture myths, most of them are pre-Alexandrian. Certainly the architectural and medicinal firsts of the pharaohs are based on pre-Alexandrian tradition,[82] as is Bocchoris's introduction of some Egyptian laws.[83] The equation of Imhotep with Asclepius, associated also with Sarapis as a healing god, makes sense given the Ptolemaic emphasis on both.[84] However, crediting Ptah with creating fire is not clearly found in pre-Alexandrian Egyptian myth, in which the god created civilization all at once. Moreover, the culture myth is strikingly similar to the Greek myths of Prometheus taking fire from Zeus or Hephaestus and Athena (Plato).[85] One suspects, therefore, that this is an addition by the epitomists of Manetho's work because of his equation of the craft god Ptah with the craft god Hephaestus.[86] Indeed, Hecataeus made the same equation, and his accompanying explanation of the culture myth similarly has no basis in Egyptian mythology.[87]

Regardless of whether Ptah created fire in Manetho's original text, his position at the top of the list (instead of Re) indicates a "Memphite point of view."[88] This claim is strengthened by the fact that he presents the non-Memphite dynasties in his history as aberrations and focuses largely on events around Memphis.[89]

Another observation on positioning: the second kings in several dynasties are the primary originators in Manetho's narrative. Athothis builds and writes on anatomy, worship of sacred bulls begins under Kaiechos, and Imhotep founds medicine and invents a new form of rock cutting under Tosorthros.[90]

All of this was probably meant to reinforce the cultural patronage of natives by Manetho's sponsor, Ptolemy Philadelphus. Memphis, the focus of Manetho's narrative, was important to the Ptolemies as a cult center[91] and as a center of

[80] F2a (Verbrugghe and Wickersham, *Berossos and Manetho*, 146; F2 in Jacoby's *Fragmente*). For a discussion of the origin of the tradition of Bocchoris as a lawgiver, see Markiewicz, "Bocchoris."

[81] For Manetho's use of material similar to the *Turin Canon*, see Redford, *Pharaonic King-Lists*, 232; Mendels, "Polemical Character," 91–92, 104; and Moyer, "Limits of Hellenism," passim.

[82] See chapter 1 and Redford, *Pharaonic King-Lists*, 210.

[83] Burton, *Commentary*, 232n5.

[84] Mendels, "Polemical Character," 104.

[85] Diodorus Siculus *Library* 1.13.3; Burton, *Commentary*, 72.

[86] Grimal, *Ancient Egypt*, 47.

[87] Diodorus Siculus *Library* 1.13.3; Burton, *Commentary*, 72.

[88] Dillery, "Egyptian Narrative History," 10. Hecataeus, in contrast, begins with Helius (Re). See Mendels, "Polemical Character," 104.

[89] Dillery, "Quintus Fabius," 10. See also Mendels, "Polemical Character," 103.

[90] Moyer, "Limits of Hellenism," 122.

[91] Mendels, "Polemical Character," 103–4.

government. Ptolemy I had it as an early capital, and the Ptolemies were crowned there.[92] Moreover, Philadelphus was the second king in the dynasty, so Manetho's attention to the cultural achievements of the second pharaohs was meant to encourage his continued patronage of native rites and scholarship.[93] Thus, like Berossus, Manetho wished to help the new foreign pharaohs assimilate to and support local customs,[94] the guardians of which were the priests. As with the relationship between Tosorthros and Imhotep, it could be mutually beneficial.[95]

In addition to encouraging the Ptolemies to cultivate native Egyptian customs, Manetho took the time to detail the negative foreign customs that had crept into Egypt at the hands of the Jews, almost as a caution to the Ptolemies against tolerating inauthentic Egyptian traditions. It is hard to know what portions of this account were written by Manetho, since his history became involved in polemical exchanges between later Alexandrian pagans and Jews over who had contributed more to Hellenistic civilization.[96] Indeed, the only reason it survives is that Josephus quoted it when answering the charges of one of these pagans. I do not propose to solve the problem here; rather, I will present the account and then offer two ways of thinking about it based on whether or not it represents Manetho's thought.

Although Manetho does not mention the Jews by name, his accounts of the Hyksos suggest that he is equating these foreign conquerors of Egypt with the Jews. In one account, Manetho contends that the Hyksos burned towns in Egypt, destroyed the Egyptian temples dedicated to local gods, and oppressed the natives. He writes that these same people were expelled from Egypt and built Jerusalem in a land called Judea.[97] In another account, Manetho writes that one of the Egyptian kings enslaved all of the lepers and polluted the people of Egypt so that he could be given a vision of the gods. Later, he granted the slaves' request to be sent to Avaris, the old capital of the Hyksos. There they appointed Osarsiph, a former priest of Heliopolis, as their leader; Manetho equates this priest with Moses. Osarsiph taught his followers not to worship the gods of the Egyptians or obey their taboos on food. Further, he enjoined them to associate only with each other. He sent his representatives to the people who inhabited Jerusalem (i.e., the Hyksos), who had been exiled from Egypt. The people of Osarsiph defeated the Egyptians, and the inhabitants of Egypt were

[92] Redford, *Pharaonic King-Lists*, 204–5.

[93] Moyer, "Limits of Hellenism," 122.

[94] Redford, *Pharaonic King-Lists*, 205–6; Mendels, "Polemical Character," 110; Moyer, "Limits of Hellenism," 132–33.

[95] Dillery, "First Egyptian," 111.

[96] Schäfer (*Judeophobia*, 17–21) attributes the anti-Jewish material to Manetho, whereas Gruen argues that it is a later addition ("Abuse," 102–4). See Pucci ben Zeev ("Reliability of Josephus Flavius") for a summary of the research on the problem.

[97] Josephus *Apion* 1.73ff., in *The Works of Flavius Josephus*.

more scared of them than they were of the Hyksos until the pharaoh Amenophis finally expelled Osarsiph and his followers.[98]

If we believe that these accounts were not written by Manetho but were added to his work by later Alexandrian pagans who were hostile to the Jews, then the accounts belong in the coming section, which describes the cultural polemics between first-century BC and first-century AD Alexandrian Jews and pagans. If, however, we accept that these accounts of Jewish history were written by Manetho or represent his thought in some form, we can ask why his account was so negative. Of course, it may just have been the product of tension between Egyptians and Jews, as others have argued,[99] and Manetho may have wanted to put the Jews in their place. But even if we accept this claim, why would Manetho include an account of Jewish history in a general presentation of Egyptian history for a Greek audience?

One primary reason may have been Manetho's desire to discredit a local rival who also claimed to be the cultural benefactor of Greece, at least in the realm of philosophy. Before the conquest, Greek authors had little interest in the Jews, if the absence of literary references is any indication. There is one passing reference to the "Syrians of Palestine" who practice circumcision in the *Histories* of Herodotus, but it is unclear whether these are Jews, since he does not designate them as such.[100] After the conquest, the initial Greek impression of the Jews was largely positive, and they were generally depicted as a race of philosophers (see chapter 4). Thus, Manetho would have had a good reason to write a negative history of the Jews in a book meant to impress the Greeks with the antiquity and cultural achievement of the Egyptians. The book was meant to discredit the cultural claims of a local rival. Even if he did not write the account, the later Alexandrian pagans who did would have done so for the same reason.

Artapanus

The only instance of a Hellenistic Jewish author writing a general account of civilization's origins is Artapanus, a second-century Jewish historian who probably lived in Alexandria, Egypt.[101] This is not to say that there were not other Jewish authors writing about the origins of particular aspects of civilization; indeed, there were many, as we will see in chapter 5. But these accounts were focused on the origins of rhetoric, the sciences, and law—in other words, subjects frequently credited to Greek invention and also of particular interest to learned Jews because of their analogs in the Bible.

[98] Ibid., 1:228ff.
[99] Schäfer, *Judeophobia*, 21.
[100] Herodotus *History* 2.104.
[101] Gruen, *Heritage*, 150.

To be sure, Artapanus treated some of these subjects as well. He wrote that Abraham taught the Egyptians astrology[102] and that Moses invented philosophy and writing, leading Artapanus to identify him with Thoth/Hermes, the cultural benefactor of Egypt.[103] Artapanus also equates Moses with the Greek poet Musaeus and makes him the teacher of Orpheus, the father of Greek poetry (the Greeks had Musaeus as either the son or student of Orpheus).[104] Surprisingly, he does not depict Moses as a lawgiver.[105]

In addition to the sciences and rhetoric, Artapanus attributes a number of material inventions to Moses, including the cults, the crafting of ships, machines to lay stones, Egyptian armaments, war engines, machines for drawing water, and the division of the land of Egypt into thirty-six nomes.

> And when grown up he taught mankind many useful things. For he was the inventor of ships, and machines for laying stones, and Egyptian arms, and engines for drawing water and for war, and invented philosophy. Further he divided the State into thirty-six Nomes, and appointed the god to be worshipped by each Nome, and the sacred writing for the priests, and their gods were cats, and dogs, and ibises: he also apportioned an especial district for the priests.[106]

Thus, Moses was not only the progenitor of Egyptian wisdom and Greek poetry but was also stylized as a pharaoh who founded Egyptian civilization.[107] Artapanus depicts Joseph in a similar manner, crediting him with dividing the land and inventing measures.[108]

Artapanus's depiction of Moses as a culture bringer is based not on the culture myths of the Jews but on those of the Egyptians. For example, the Egyptian pharaoh Sesostris is also said to have divided the land of Egypt into thirty-six nomes.[109] Although this contrasts with Berossus and Manetho, both of whom drew primarily on their peoples' culture myths, it still fits the model of native authors privileging local mythology (in this case Egyptian) rather than that of the conquerors.

The fact that Artapanus styles Moses not only as Thoth-Hermes but also as a pharaoh suggests that he, like Berossus and Manetho, was mindful of competing claims to cultural priority among the Greeks and Egyptians. Indeed, much

[102] Eusebius *Preparation for the Gospel* 9.18.1. See Wacholder, "Pseudo-Eupolemus," 103; Gruen, *Heritage*, 151; Reed, "Was There Science in Ancient Judaism?" 8.

[103] Eusebius *Preparation for the Gospel* 9.27. See Droge's discussion in *Homer*, 27; Gruen, *Heritage*, 158.

[104] Eusebius *Preparation for the Gospel* 9.27. Droge, *Homer*, 26; Gruen, *Heritage*, 159.

[105] Sterling, *Historiography*, 181.

[106] Eusebius *Preparation for the Gospel* 9.27.4.

[107] Gruen, *Heritage*, 157–58. Droge, *Homer*, 25–27; Sterling, *Historiography*, 175–76.

[108] Eusebius *Preparation for the Gospel* 9.23.

[109] Diodorus Siculus *Library* 1.54.3 (see Burton, *Diodorus Siculus*, 167–68). Artapanus's Moses shares a number of other parallels with Sesostris (Sterling, *Historiography*, 177).

of his account of Moses's life, which is too long to detail here, rebuts many of the accusations of Manetho against the Jews. The fact that Moses was the source of Egyptian civilization, reinforced by the borrowing of Egyptian culture myths, is evidence that the text was meant to bolster Jewish confidence at a time when the Jews' identity was increasingly under attack (see chapter 5). It may also have been intended to persuade Egyptians of the Jewish origin of their civilization, although there is no evidence that this was effective.[110]

Philo of Byblos

My final instance of postconquest native histories of civilization comes from a Phoenician, Philo of Byblos, who wrote under Roman rule at the end of the first century AD and beginning of the second.[111] His Greek-language history of his native land, called *The Phoenician History*, was meant to correct Greek misunderstandings of the origins of their myths and to rectify their misconceptions about the beginnings of civilization (the former objective is stated explicitly,[112] and the latter may be inferred).

Philo claims that his history is a translation of a book written in Phoenician by Sanchuniathon, an ancient Phoenician sage who lived before the Trojan War (according to Porphyry) or before Hesiod (as inferred from Philo).[113] Although the clear Hellenistic influences in this work and several anachronisms refute this claim,[114] the original work that Philo claims to have translated could have been written sometime after Alexander's conquests and before the first century AD when Philo lived. On the other hand, it could just as easily be thought of as a literary invention by Philo.

According to Philo, Sanchuniathon wanted to know the history of the entire world, so he searched for a history written by Taautos, since he knew that Taautos had invented letters and was the first to keep records. Philo assures us that this Taautos, who, we learn elsewhere, is Phoenician, is the same person the Egyptians call Thoyth, the Alexandrians Thoth, and the Greeks Hermes.[115] Having rediscovered Taautos's account, Sanchuniathon sets about writing a history of the origins of the world.

Sanchuniathon's retelling of Taautos's account is a consecutive history divided into a cosmogony, a zoogony, an anthropogony, and then a list of discoverers; it ends with an account of a civil war between Kronos and his

[110] Sterling, *Historiography*, 184.

[111] Baumgarten, *Phoenician History*, 261; Barr, "Philo of Byblos," 17; Oden, "Philo of Byblos and Hellenistic Historiography," 116.

[112] Eusebius *Preparation for the Gospel* 1.10.40. See Johnson, "Ethnic Argumentation," 43–44; Oden, "Philo of Byblos and Hellenistic Historiography," 122.

[113] Baumgarten, *Phoenician History*, 262, 267.

[114] Ibid., 264, 267.

[115] Eusebius *Preparation for the Gospel* 1.9.23–26.

family.[116] From Sanchuniathon's cosmogony and zoogony (explicitly based on that of Taautos),[117] we learn that in the beginning there was a dark, windy mist and a watery chaos. The wind loved its own elements, leading to a mixture called Desire. Slime was produced from this mixture, from which the rest of the universe was generated.[118] Initially, there were animals that had no sense perception. From these were born living beings with intelligence who were shaped like an egg (we are not told how they acquired intelligence). Then the slime burst into the sun, moon, stars, and the constellations. Because the land and sea were burning, the air burst into light, which gave rise to winds and clouds, which led to rain and floods. When the waters were parted due to the action of the sun, everything came together in the air, generating thunder and lightning. This awoke the slumbering intelligent animals. On account of their fright, male and female animals started moving about the earth and sea.[119]

Next begins the anthropogony and a detailed genealogy of discoverers. The wind, Colpia, and his wife, Baau ("Night"), gave birth to two mortal men, Aion and Protogonos. Aion "discovered the food obtained from trees." Aion and Protogonus gave birth to Genos and his sister Genea, who settled in Phoenicia. When there was a drought, they would raise their hands to heaven toward the sun, whom they considered the sole god. Genos sired three children, Phos, Pyr, and Phlox (Light, Fire, and Flame). The children discovered fire by rubbing sticks together and taught others how to do so. They also sired four giant sons. The offspring of a union between these giants and licentious women were Hypsouranios (also given as Samemroumos) and Ousoos. Hypsouranious "contrived huts out of reeds and rushes and papyrus." He was revered as a god after his death. His brother, Ousoos, "first invented a covering for the body from skins of wild beasts." He was also the first to build a sea vessel. Like his brother, he was revered as a god after his death.[120]

Here, the discovery genealogy skips a few generations because the next inventors come from the family of Hypsouranios and not his direct offspring. Agreus and Halieus, born into the family of Hypsouranios, were "the inventors of hunting and fishing, from whom were named huntsmen and fishermen." Agreus and Halieus sired two males: Chrysor, who is equated with Hephaestus, and an anonymous brother. These brothers were "the discoverers of iron" and how to work it. Other brothers of Chrysor are credited with inventing walls of bricks. As for Chrysor, he "invented the hook, and bait, and line, and raft, and was the first of all men to make a voyage." He also practiced divination and wrote magical formulas, but is not credited with their invention.[121]

[116] Baumgarten, *Phoenician History*, 263. Barr divides it into a cosmogony, a technogony, and a theogony (Barr, "Philo of Byblos," 22).

[117] Eusebius *Preparation for the Gospel* 1.10.5.

[118] Ibid., 1.10.1.

[119] Ibid., 1.10.2.

[120] Ibid., 1.10.7–10.

[121] Ibid., 1.10.11–12.

Again breaking the direct genealogy of inventors, the next discoverers, Technites ("Artificer") and Geinos Autochthon ("Earth-born Aboriginal"), are the descendants of the brothers of Chrysor who invented walls of bricks. They "devised the mixing of straw with the clay of bricks, and drying them in the sun, and moreover invented roofs." Technites and Geinos sired Agros and the Hero of Agros or Agrotes, who were also called "Wanderers" or "Titans." These siblings added courtyards, enclosures and cellars to houses. They were also the ancestors of husbandmen and hunters. Agros and the Hero of Agros gave birth to Amunos and Magos, who "established villages and sheepfolds." Amunos and Magos sired Misor and Suduc, who "discovered the use of salt." Misor sired Taautos, who, as we have already learned, invented alphabetic writing.[122] His sibling Suduc sired eight sons variously known as the Dioscuri, Cabeiri, Corybantes, or Samothracians.[123] One of them was Asclepius.[124] They were the first to invent a ship, and their descendants "discovered herbs, and the healing of venomous bites, and charms."[125]

Here the first genealogy of discoverers ends and a new one begins. Around the time that the descendants of the Dioscuri discovered herbs, Elioun, called "the Most High," and Berouth were born. They sired Uranus and Ge (Earth). Elioun was killed by wild animals, and his children deified him. After his death, his son, Uranus, ruled and married his sister, Ge. They had four sons, El or Cronos, Baitylos, Dagon or Siton, and Atlas.[126]

Sanchuniathon goes on to detail the feuding between Uranus and his son Cronos. Uranus had a lot of children with wives other than Ge, which made her jealous. As a consequence, they separated from each other. Uranus raped her often and tried to destroy the children he had with her. In the end, his son Cronos, with the advice of Hermes Trismegistus (his secretary), overthrew Uranus.[127]

Cronos is credited with several inventions. In the lead-up to his battle against Uranus, Athena, his daughter, and Hermes Trismegistus advise him to make a iron sickle and spear. Later, suspecting his son Sadidos of treachery, Cronos slays him with his iron weapon. After he overthrows Uranus, Cronos "builds a wall around his dwelling, and founds the first city, Byblos in Phoenicia." Cronos's brother, Dagon, is also credited with an invention: he "discovered corn and the plough." In an unrelated genealogy, a man named Pontos is born in Peraia, located in Syria. He gives birth to Poseidon and Sidon. Because of the sweetness of the latter's voice, she is the first to create musical song.[128]

Sanchuniathon ends his account with a more detailed description of the

[122] Ibid., 1.10.12–14.
[123] Ibid., 1.10.14, 38.
[124] Ibid., 1.10.38.
[125] Ibid., 1.10.14.
[126] Ibid., 1.10.15–16.
[127] Ibid., 1.10.16–18.
[128] Ibid., 1.10.18–27.

invention of writing. During the time of Cronos, Taautos "imitated the features of the gods who were his companions . . . and gave form to the sacred characters of the letters." Cronos then appointed Taautos ruler of Egypt.[129] Presumably, this Taautos is the same as Hermes Trismegistus, the adviser of Cronos mentioned earlier.[130]

The Hellenistic elements in Philo's *Phoenician History* are too numerous to catalog here, but I will highlight a few.[131] We have a rationalistic explanation of the universe's origins, a euhemeristic explanation for the origins of the gods, a detailed catalog of human inventions that loosely develop according to Democritus's schema, and finally the archetypal sage Taautos/Hermes, who invents writing (Asclepius also makes an appearance and is associated with the invention of medicine).

Since we know so little about pre-Hellenistic Phoenician mythology, it is difficult to know which of its elements survive this Hellenistic treatment. But comparing it with other earlier myths from nearby regions, one can notice two trends that are peculiar to the eastern Mediterranean: first, the creation of culture is intimately bound to a genealogy. As in the Hebrew Bible, the invention of culture is a family affair in *The Phoenician History*, with pairs of inventors begetting pairs of inventors (with some variation in the pattern).[132] However, the prejudice against material culture is not present.

Second, the discovery of ironworking is consistently mentioned in etiological texts from the eastern Mediterranean and is usually associated with magic. In *The Phoenician History*, Chrysor, who is equated with Hephaestus, and his brother discover iron and how to work it. Chrysor also practices divination and writes magical formulas. In Canaanite mythology, Kothar-wa-Khasis (clearly the inspiration for Philo's Chrysor)[133] fashions two different double-headed maces for Baal so that he can defeat El's son Yamm (see chapter 1). He is also able to endow the weapons with magical powers by speaking certain phrases.[134] In the Hebrew Bible, ironworking is one of the key inventions of the sons of Cain and leads to violence. In the *Book of the Watchers*, ironworking is one of the skills that the wayward angels teach humans, in addition to magic. Again, the biblical stigma attached to ironworking is absent from *The Phoenician History* (and also from Canaanite mythology).

Why was *The Phoenician History* written? Primarily to remind those educated in Greek learning of Greece's, and thus Rome's, cultural dependence on

[129] Ibid., 1.10.35–38.

[130] Baumgarten, *Phoenician History*, 192.

[131] See Baumgarten's commentary on the text for a detailed discussion (in *Phoenician History*). Also Oden, "Philo of Byblos and Hellenistic Historiography," 118–23; Edwards, "Philo or Sanchuniathon?" 219.

[132] Van Seters, *Prologue*, 86.

[133] Baumgarten, *Phoenician History*, 166.

[134] Ibid.

Phoenicia.[135] To this end, Philo downplays the role of one of Phoenicia's rivals, Egypt, by making Taautos/Hermes its ruler. He may have also been trying to minimize the claims of the Jews.[136] This is stated nowhere in his work, but claiming all cultural innovations for Phoenicia is just as much a shot at the Jews as it is at the Egyptians. Philo of Byblos was certainly aware of the good press the Jews were getting and did not like it. In Origen's *Contra Celsum*, we learn that Philo wrote a treatise called *On the Jews,* in which he doubted the authenticity of Hecataeus's account of the Jews; even if it is authentic, he argued, it just meant that Hecataeus was duped by the Jews into writing a favorable account.[137] Thus, it would not be at all surprising if he had written or translated a book on Phoenician history in order to discredit the cultural contributions of the Jews. Once again, local rivalry may have been a principal reason for the generation of cultural history. We see a similar dynamic following the Arab conquests of the Near East.

Iranian Histories of Civilization

After the Arab conquests, the Near East was again united politically, much as it had been during Alexander's lifetime. But in this instance, it took several centuries rather than several years for the empire to disintegrate into competing kingdoms. If the Arab conquerors were impressed with the cultural achievements and antiquity of the civilizations they conquered, we have no record of it during the first century of their rule. There was no Arab Hecataeus. Indeed, we know little about what Arab tribesmen at that time thought about their own cultural history due to a paucity of sources. The most that can be said is that there is no record of Arabs making grandiose claims to have created the rudiments of civilization (see chapter 3). And why should they have done so when the great civilizations of their day had not been able to withstand their onslaught? Thus al-Nābiga al-Jaʿdī (d. ca. 79 AH/698f AD), a Companion of the Prophet who participated in the conquest of Khorasan,[138] gloated in verse: "O men, do you not see how Persia has been ruined and its inhabitants humiliated? They have become slaves who pasture your sheep, as if their kingdom was a dream."[139]

Native elites who wanted to participate in their conquerors' culture had to learn the language of their imperial masters, just as native elites had done after Alexander's conquests. They also adopted their beliefs, which in this case meant

[135] Oden, "Philo of Byblos and Hellenistic Historiography," 120; Edwards, "Philo or Sanchuniathon?" 214; Johnson, "Ethnic Argumentation," 36.

[136] Edwards, "Philo or Sanchuniathon?" 214.

[137] Origen *Contra Celsum* 1.15. This seems to be a reference to a work by Pseudo-Hecataeus (see Bar-Kochva, *Pseudo-Hecataeus*, 184).

[138] "al-Nābigha al-Djaʿdī," in *EI*[2].

[139] Trans. Crone, "Mawlā," in *EI*[2].

adopting their religion, Islam, the consequence of the spread of monotheism in the Near Eastern and Mediterranean worlds. Because Arab society was organized by kinship, these new converts were made clients (*mawlā*, *mawālī* pl.) of Arab tribes.[140]

Despite their assimilation, new converts were not accepted as equals by the conquerors, either legally or socially.[141] As one later source has it: "They used to say that only three things interrupt prayer: a donkey, a dog, and a *mawlā*. . . . If they were present at a meal, they stood while the others sat, and if a *mawlā*, because of his age, his merit, his learning, was given food, he was seated at the end of the table, lest anyone should fail to see that he was not an Arab."[142]

As a consequence, they began to demand equality on the conquerors' terms by appealing to statements of universalism found in the Qur'an (e.g., Q 49:13), much like modern nationalists who turned the belief systems of their European conquerors against them.[143]

The rising tide of converts eventually overwhelmed the political and cultural hegemony of the Arabs in the eighth century, culminating in the ʿAbbāsid revolution in 750 AD and the move of the capital to Baghdad, in the former center of the Sasanian Empire. As Islamic society became more cosmopolitan, the educated elite grew increasingly diverse. Some of these educated Muslim Arabs and non-Arab converts were culturally oriented toward Arabia, as we saw in the last chapter, and others were oriented toward the learned cultures of the previous Near Eastern civilizations, those of Greece and Iran.[144] Thus, rather than there being one dominant elite culture, there were several of them competing for dominance in Iraq.

One group of elites consisted of Iranian functionaries in the Umayyad and then ʿAbbāsid courts, whose numbers swelled with the influx of the revolutionaries from Iran, including *dahāqīn* (sing. *dihqān*), the lower ranks of the landed gentry who administered the rural subdistricts of Iraq and Iran.[145] One of them was Ibn al-Muqaffaʿ (d. 139 AH/757 AD), an Umayyad chancery secretary from a noble Persian family hailing from Fārs Province, the cultural center of the previous empire. His father had sent him to Basra to study Arabic literature, and by 743 AD he had become a secretary for the governor of Fārs. After the ʿAbbāsid revolution, he converted to Islam from Manichaeism and worked for the governor of Basra, where he met his demise for offending the caliph and for his allegedly false conversion.[146]

[140] Crone, *Slaves on Horses*, 49.

[141] See Goldziher, *Muslim Studies* 1:101–4, and Crone, "Mawlā," in *EI*^{2}.

[142] Ibn ʿAbd Rabbih, *al-ʿIqd*, in Lewis, *Islam* 2:204.

[143] Crone, "Imperial Trauma," 114.

[144] See Gibb's comments on the literary struggle between partisans of the Arab and Iranian traditions over the cultural orientation of the empire (Gibb, "Shuubiya," 66).

[145] Crone, "Post-Colonialism," 11–12; Arjomand, "Ibn al-Muqaffaʿ," 11–12; Morony, *Iraq*, 118.

[146] J. Derek Latham, "Ebn al-Moqaffaʿ," *EIr*. Arjomand, "Ibn al-Muqaffaʿ," 13, 24; Khanbaghi, "De-Zoroastrianization," 13, 204n20.

Ibn al-Muqaffaʿ translated several books from Pahlavi into Arabic,[147] most of which were meant to expose the late Umayyad and early ʿAbbāsid court to the traditions of Iranian kingship and advice on how to navigate its intricacies.[148] One of these works was the Sasanian *Xwadāy-nāmag, The Book of Lords*, a history of ancient Iranian kings that began with the first man, Gayōmart, and continued down to the Sasanian present. The final version of the book dates to the reign of the last Sasanian king and was compiled by the dihqān Dānishvar.[149] Although only fragments of Ibn al-Muqaffaʿ's translation survive,[150] one of them (translated into Persian in the tenth century) relates some of the cultural achievements of the first king, Gayōmart, and his son Hōshang. The fragment is dozens of pages long and details Gayōmart's fight against demons working to overthrow him.[151] One part of the fragment relates the origins of kingship and religious sermons.

> Gayūmarth [*sic*] went among all the sons and daughters of Adam and in each city he delivered a sermon [*khutbih*]. He said, "God, honored and glorified, made me your king. Do not sin for God has overlooked one's [Adam's] sins." His was the first sermon among the children of Adam. In that larger group was Cainan. He said, "This group [should] be a patriarchal caliphate and make whomever you want the caliph. Recognize me as king since God, exalted is He, has made me your king. I will not approve of anyone who sins."[152]

The other fragment relates the invention of ironsmithing by Hōshang.

> Gayūmarth raised an army and Hūshang became aware of what had befallen his father. He extracted iron [*āhan*] from the mountain and broke it into pieces. From that he made weapons for war [*salīh*]: he fashioned a terrible club, he made a shield [*separ*], and he made a type of knife. He made those things by divine inspiration [*bih-ilhām īzidī*], not by seeing and hearing. Since that day, whenever his army saw him they called him Hūshang the Weapon-Bearer, meaning all of the horse-armor for battle [*zīn arvāz*] and this nickname remains today. Some say this is the [nickname] of Tahmūrath. Afterwards, Hūshang was sitting at the foot of the mountain with that army and heard the sound of Gayūmarth's deception and his calling to God, and his children saw that the enemy was in sight. They went over the mountain and fought hard. From there they surrounded all of them [the demons] and

[147] Pahlavi was an Aramaic-based script used for Middle Persian; New Persian, which uses the Arabic script, developed in the ninth century AD.

[148] Latham, "Ebn al-Moqaffaʿ." Arjomand, "Ibn al-Muqaffaʿ," 15.

[149] Nöldeke, *Iranian National Epic*, 23–24.

[150] See Mutlaq Khāliq, "Az Shāhnāmih," passim.

[151] Balʿamī, *Taʾrīkh*, 112–28.

[152] Ibid., 123. I have based my translation on Dabiri's "Persian Epics" (92); Dabiri translates most of the passage in his dissertation on Balʿamī's *Taʾrīkh* (see pages 89–93).

> there was great destruction and many were captured. Hūshang made chains from the iron and iron collars and put them in the collars with chains and bound their heads. Since that day, prisons have existed. On account of those arts and the intellect of Hūshang, Gayūmarth was very pleased. Thus, he said to him that after my works are done and my life ended, [you] will be [my] successor and the crown prince after [my] death.[153]

As the passages suggest, Ibn al-Muqaffaʿ held that the ancient Iranian kings were exemplars of both religious and secular rule and offered better guidance on both than contemporary models did. Thus, he writes the following in one of his epistles: "The master of religion among them reached further in the matter of religion, in theory and in practice, than the master of religion among us; and the master of the world (among them) was likewise in his reach and superiority."[154]

It is no accident, therefore, that the first king, Gayōmart, also delivers the first religious sermon in Ibn al-Muqaffaʿ's history of the Iranian kings. Ibn al-Muqaffaʿ is careful, however, to integrate Gayōmart into Islamic salvation history by equating him with the biblical Cainan and not create controversy by equating him with Adam, as other Iranians would later do.[155]

Ibn al-Muqaffaʿ likewise connects Hōshang with biblical history, making him Mahalalel, the son of Cainan. Hōshang is an inventor as well, although Ibn al-Muqaffaʿ is clear to point out that his discovery of ironworking and weapon smithing is the result of divine inspiration and not experimentation. It is these inventions that endear him to Gayōmart and that prompt the latter to designate him his successor. Thus, kingship and beneficial material inventions are closely associated in Ibn al-Muqaffaʿ's rendition of *The Book of Lords*.

Ibn al-Muqaffaʿ's translation demonstrates that at the same time that authors living in Baghdad, Basra, and Kufa were creating genealogies and firsts that connected the Islamic empire to the Bible and Arabia, Iranians in the same cities were translating histories that connected it to Iran.[156] One interesting inter-

[153] Balʿami, *Taʾrīkh*, 126.

[154] See Arjomand, "Ibn al-Muqaffaʿ," 16. In the same vein, Ibn al-Muqaffaʿ wrote, "We have found men before us to have been larger in body and, moreover, more rational; stronger and, moreover, more skillful; longer-lived and, moreover, more experienced . . . ; the most that a scholar of our generation can aspire to is to receive his knowledge from them. . . . After them, nothing more can be said, be it weighty or trivial." See Khalidi, "Progress," 280.

[155] On the controversy surrounding the identity of Adam and Gayōmart, see Dabiri, "Persian Epics," 79–80; Savant, "Finding Our Place," 22. Ṭabarī writes that most Persian scholars consider Gayōmart identical to Adam (Ṭabarī, *Taʾrīkh* 1:319, 325). Similarly, the Iranian astrologer Abū Maʿshar al-Balkhī (d. 272/886) notes in his *Kitāb al-ulūf* that Persians equate the two (Ibn Juljul, *Ṭabaqāt*, 5—see chapter 5). For his part, Ṭabarī accepts that Gayōmart is the father of the Persians and writes that no one disputes this (Ṭabarī, *Taʾrīkh* 1:319). What he and some other Muslims object to is equating him with Adam because Persians do not believe there was a flood or hold that it occurred only in the west of Iran, which would contradict the Qurʾan (ibid., 369).

[156] For efforts to orient the empire toward Iran, see Gutas, *Greek Thought*, 29, 34; Bosworth, *Heritage*, 8–9.

section between the two is found in the writings of Ibn al-Kalbī (d. 204 or 206 AH / 819 or 821 AD), the Arab genealogist we met above, who expended most of his energies recording the kinship ties of the Arab tribes. Nevertheless, he was also interested in Iranian history and recorded some of the legends circulating among the Iranian elite during the early ʿAbbāsids.

In the *Muḥabbar*, a book on Arab antiquities written by his student Muḥammad b. Ḥabīb (d. 245 AH / 860 AD), we find the following report from Ibn al-Kalbī under the heading "Names of Jinn and Humans Who Ruled the Entire Earth, According to Ibn al-Kalbī":

> The first to rule all of it from among the progeny of al-Jānn [the forefather of the jinn][157] was Jayūmart, then his son Tahmūrath, then after him Ūshīng, who is Ūshang [i.e., Hōshang]. Then God (glorified and praised) created Adam (may the blessings of God be upon him) in the time of Ūshīng. Some of the Persians [*al-majūs*][158] say he is Adam, the son of Ūshīng, but not all of them say that.
>
> The first to rule (all) of it among the progeny of Adam was Jam Shādh b. Yiwanjihān (Jamshīd), from the progeny of Cain. He used to cross the world every day just as the sun crosses it: in the morning he was in the East and in the evening he was in the West. He ruled it and the one hundred souls who had appeared between Noah and Adam (upon them be peace).[159]

The sequence of the legendary Iranian rulers differs from Ibn al-Muqaffaʿ's, indicating either a different tradition of Iranian lore or a garbled source. Moreover, the biblical first man, Adam, either displaced the Iranian first man and king, Gayōmart, or was displaced by him. Notably, it is Ibn al-Kalbī's Iranian informants who are doing the equating and displacing. That Gayōmart is made a jinn may have been an attempt by Ibn al-Kalbī or his informants to reconcile Iranian lore about the first man with the Qur'anic depiction of Adam as the first human.

In addition to the *Muḥabbar* account, there are two reports by Ibn al-Kalbī on Persian culture myths found in Ṭabarī's *Ta'rīkh*.

> "We have heard—God knows best!—that the first king to rule the earth was Ōshahanj b. Eber b. Shelah b. Arpachshad b. Shem b. Noah." He continued. "The Persians claim him and assume that he lived two hundred years after Adam's death." He continued. "As we have heard, this king lived two hundred years after Noah, but the people of Fars had him living two hundred years after Adam, with no indication of what was before Noah. . . ."[160]

[157] Kister, "Ādam," 117.

[158] For a translation of *majūs* as "Persians," see "Madjūs", *EI*²; Tavakoli-Targhi, "Contested Memories," 149n1.

[159] Ibn Ḥabīb, *Muḥabbar*, 392.

[160] Ṭabarī, *Ta'rīkh* 1:326.

> . . . I, in turn, was told on the authority of Hishām b. Muḥammad b. al-Sāʾib that (Ōshahang) was the first to cut trees and build buildings and the first to produce minerals and make people understand their use. He commanded the people of his time to use mosques. He built two cities, the first to be built on earth. They were the city of Bābil in the southern region of al-Kūfah and the city of al-Sūs (Susa). He ruled forty years.[161]

In these fragments, Hōshang, not Gayōmart, is the first king and is credited with several inventions that are fundamental to civilization, including the use of minerals, which parallels Ibn al-Muqaffaʿ's account of Hōshang's invention of ironsmithing.

Ibn al-Kalbī's association with these two reports might seem a bit strange, since he is remembered as a genealogist of Arabs, not Iranians. However, according to Ibn al-Nadīm, Ibn al-Kalbī had direct access to Pahlavi texts, which were translated for him by his secretary, Jabala.[162] Perhaps Ibn al-Kalbī's interest in genealogy attracted him to this literature. Indeed, his interest in recording the firsts of Yemeni kings (see chapter 3) may have been meant as a retort to Iranian etiologies he found in these texts. On the other hand, he may not have been reading texts at all, but rather recording popular legends circulating at the time. The account recorded by Ibn Ḥabīb seems to be of this sort, and the culture myths in Ṭabarī's *Taʾrīkh* may have been more of the same.

One thing is certain: The audience for histories of the early Iranian kings had grown in the ʿAbbāsid court between the death of Ibn al-Muqaffaʿ under the second ʿAbbāsid caliph, al-Manṣūr, and the death of Ibn al-Kalbī under the seventh caliph, al-Maʾmūn (d. 218 AH / 833 AD). This is not to say that the early ʿAbbāsid rulers severed their ties with Arabian culture; on the contrary, Arabic court poetry was very oriented toward pre-Islamic Arabia. But they also tolerated a certain amount of boasting by Iranian Muslims at the expense of Arabs, as the Iranian ʿAbbāsid court poet Bashshār b. Burd (d. ca. 168 AH / 784f AD) demonstrated repeatedly in poems such as the following:

> Never did my father sing a camel song, trailing along behind a scabby camel
> Nor approach the colocynth, to pierce it for very hunger
> Nor the mimosa, to knock down its fruits with a stave;
> Nor did we roast a skink, with its quivering tail,
> Nor did I dig and eat the lizard out of the stone ground.[163]

The audience for such sentiments increased dramatically once al-Maʾmūn had deposed his brother Amīn in 813 AD and returned from his governorship in Khorasan to rule as caliph. The new elite at court had little connection with

[161] Ibid., 341.
[162] "Al-Kalbī," *EI*².
[163] *Dīwān* 1:377–80, in Beeston, *Selections*, 50.

the Arabian past—most of them were neither ethnically Arab nor culturally oriented toward the Arabian Peninsula; rather, they were Iraqi gentry or bureaucrats and military men from Iran who were culturally oriented toward the Sasanian Empire.[164] Thus, they set about creating a court culture that reflected and validated their identity.[165] As al-Maʾmūn's contemporary Jāḥiẓ (d. 255 AH / 868f AD) wryly remarked, the ʿAbbāsid Empire at this time was "a Persian [*ʿajamiyya*], Khorasanian empire."[166]

It was during this period of Iranian cultural ascendency that Iranian litterateurs started denigrating the cultural legacy of the Arabs and glorifying the civilizations they had conquered, a trend called Shuʿūbiyya (loosely, "ethnic chauvinism") by its detractors. Some were members of the imperial bureaucracy, and others were poets and courtiers (Bashshār b. Burd, whose anti-Arab poem we have already read, is an early example). None of their treatises survives intact, so we cannot know if they specifically mentioned the firsts of Iranian kings to bolster their claims. But their arguments, summarized by their enemies, certainly ridiculed the Arabs for not having universal kings, cities, or laws and for achieving nothing in philosophy or in the invention of tools and crafts.[167]

Iranians' celebration of their ancient kings, particularly their material achievements, reached its pinnacle in the tenth century, when the caliphate had broken up and Iran and Iraq were ruled again by Iranian dynasties. In this postcolonial moment, which Patricia Crone calls the "tenth-century crisis,"[168] Muslim Iranian historians set about reconciling their Islamic beliefs with their Iranian past. Although they privileged the biblical framework of history,[169] their inclusion of Iranian kings and their inventions implied that Iranians had both a part to play in Islamic salvation history and that they had created the material civilization now reborn under Islam.

The most prominent of these historians was al-Ṭabarī (d. 310 AH / 923 AD), whose family hailed from Ṭabaristān in Iran and who may have been of Iranian origin.[170] Aside from recording the culture myths found in the writings of Ibn al-Kalbī (see above), he mentions a number of firsts associated with the first Iranian kings. Several have to do with Hōshang and include references to his invention of ironsmithing.

> Someone else said: "It was during Ōshahanj's rule that iron was first produced. He made it into tools for the crafts. He assessed the available water in

[164] Kennedy, *Baghdad*, 243.

[165] Ibid., 244.

[166] Jāḥiẓ, *Bayān* 3:366; see Goldziher, *Muslim Studies* 1:137.

[167] These rebuttals were summarized by Ibn ʿAbd Rabbih in his *Iqd*, in Lewis, *Islam* 2:201–4. For the Shuʿūbiyya, see Goldziher, *Muslim Studies* 1:145–48; Norris, "Shuʿūbiyyah," 38.

[168] Crone, "Post-Colonialism," 12, 18–19.

[169] Tavakoli-Targhi, "Contested Memories," 149–75.

[170] Ṭabarī discouraged speculation on his ancestry (Savant, "Finding Our Place," 203).

localities with a stagnant water supply. He urged people to till the soil, sow, harvest, and engage in all (kinds of agricultural) activity. He commanded people to kill beasts of prey and use clothing made from their skins as well as mats and to slaughter cows, small cattle, and wild animals and eat their meat. He ruled forty years. He built the city of al-Rayy. Reportedly, it was the first city built after the city that was Jayūmart's residence, in Dunbāwand of Tabaristān. . . ."[171]

. . . The Persians say that this Ōshahanj was born a king. His way of life and the way he administered his subjects were outstandingly praiseworthy. That gave rise to his surname Fēshdādh, which in Persian means "the first to judge in justice," for *fāsh* (*pēsh*) means "first"; and *dādh* (*dād*) means "justice and legal decision."[172]

There are also firsts associated with Hōshang's descendant Ṭahmūrath.

The Persians, in turn, assume that Tahmūrath ruled over all the climes. He placed a crown [*tāj*] upon his head and, on the day he became ruler, he said: "With God's help, we shall remove the corrupt rebels from God's creation. His rule was praiseworthy, and he was kind to his subjects. He built Sābūr in Fārs and resided there. . . . He was the first to use wool and hair for clothing and carpeting, and the first to use the horses, mules, and donkeys that are part of royal pomp. He ordered people to use dogs to guard and protect cattle from wild beasts and (to use) birds of prey for hunting. He wrote in Persian.[173]

More firsts are attributed to Ṭahmūrath's brother, Jamshīd.

The Persian scholars say. . . . When he was (securely) settled in his realm, he said: "God has given us perfect splendor and great support. We shall do much good to our subjects." He originated the manufacture of swords and weaponry. He also showed (people) how to make brocade, silk, and other textile threads. He ordered garments woven and dyed and saddles with pommels carved to make the mounts more manageable. As mentioned by some(one), he went into hiding after 616 years and six months of his rule had passed, and the country was without him for a year. After the first year to year five of his rule, he ordered the production of swords, coats of mail, *bīḍ* swords, and other kinds of weapons as well as iron tool(s) for craftsmen. From the year 50 to the year 100 of his rule, he ordered the spinning and weaving of brocade, silk, cotton, linen and every other textile thread, the dyeing of material in various colors, cutting it into various patterns, and wearing it. . . . . From the year 150 to the year 250, he fought the Satans and

[171] Ṭabarī, *Ta'rīkh* 1:341–32.

[172] Ibid., 342. The word *Pīshdād* actually comes from the Avestan *Para'a@ta*, meaning "first created" (see "Ho@æang," *EIr*).

[173] Ibid., 345.

> jinn, causing great slaughter among them and humiliating them. They were subjected (to doing forced labor) for him and had to follow his orders. From the year 250 to the year 316, he charged the Satans with cutting stones and rocks from the mountains and making marble, gypsum, and chalk. They also were directed to build buildings and baths with (these materials) and with clay. He also charged them with producing depilatories and with transporting, from the oceans, mountains, mines, and deserts, everything useful for mankind, such as gold, silver, and all other meltable precious metals, as well as different kinds of perfumes and medicines.[174]

These are most of the approximately thirty-one cultural firsts attributed to Iranian kings in Ṭabarī's *Ta'rīkh*.[175] As in Ibn al-Muqaffaʿ's translation of *The Book of Lords*, their inventions are associated with their assumption of kingship. Indeed, in the case of Jamshīd, the inventions are explicitly tied to the legitimacy of his rule: "God has given us perfect splendor and great support. We shall do much good to our subjects." What is also striking about these etiologies is how rationalized they are: most of these inventions seem to build on each other (e.g., iron before craft tools, craft tools before weaponry, etc.).

In Zoroastrian texts recorded after the Islamic conquests, the focus of cultural history is also on Gayōmart and his descendants.[176] For example, in the *Dēnkard*, a Zoroastrian encyclopedia written in the ninth century AD, Gayōmart is said to have been the first to bring religion from the Creator.[177] In the seventh book, we learn that Ahura Mazdā taught Gayōmart's children, Mashye and Mashyāne, how to sow corn and use an ox and "other appliances."[178] Mashye and Mashyāne were also taught other civilizing arts by sacred beings.

> And, owing to the explanation of the sacred beings, Mashye and Mashyāne attained also to the manufacture of clothing, the tending of sheep, house-building, and primitive carpentry, the agriculture and husbandry of the ancients, and the memory of their original state; and these proceeded from

[174] Ibid., 349–50.

[175] A large number are also found in Masʿūdī's (d. 345 AH / 956 AD) *Murūj*, Ibn Nadīm's (d. 380 AH / 990 AD) *Fihrist*, and al-Iṣfahānī's (d. before 360 AH / 970 AD) *Sinī mulūk al-arḍ*.

[176] In the earliest Avestan texts, the *Gāthās*, Gayōmart is not mentioned. As Sven Hartman argues, his name was probably a neologism formed from the synthesis of the words *gaya*, "life," and *marətan*, "mortal," found in the *Gāthās*. The fusion probably arose from a later exegesis of *Yasna* 30, which speaks of the coming together of life and not-life. In later *yasnas* (Avestan liturgical texts), "Gayamarətan" appears as a distinct figure (Hartman, *Gayōmart*, 37). In several places in the Avesta, he is also depicted as a type of prophet. In the *Frawardīn Yasht*, for example, he is described as he "who first listened unto the thought and teaching of Ahura Mazdā" (*Yasht* 13.87, in anon., *Zend-Avesta*, pt. 2). Furthermore, in several yasnas he is praised in the same breath as Zoroaster (13.7, 23.2, 26.5, 67.2). In *Frawardīn Yasht* 13.87, he is also depicted as the progenitor of the Aryan nations. But despite his status as a divine interlocutor, Gayōmart is not depicted as a culture hero.

[177] Anon., *Dēnkard*, bk. 3, chaps. 35 and 143. See the edition of Sanjana, anon., *Dinkard*, in the bibliography. For books 7–8, see West's translation, *Pahlavi Texts*.

[178] Ibid., bk. 7, chap. 1, 11.

them through their lineage, presenting an example and spreading in the world, to artificers among the plenitude of artificers.[179]

Among Mashye's posterity are also important culture heroes. Humanity learned how to attain union with the Beneficent (Sōshyant) from his son, Siyāmak, and his grandson, Fravāk.[180] Fravāk's son, Hōshang, is depicted as the first ruler in the *Dēnkard*.[181] The *Dēnkard* also says that he was the first to rule the seven climes.[182] In addition, he is credited with instituting laws, including the law of cultivation (hence his epithet Pīshdād, "lawgiver").[183]

There are, obviously, some parallels with the etiologies found in Muslim literature; Hōshang, for example, gives laws to humans. But they are far more similar to etiologies found in the Qur'an and biblical pseudepigrapha (see chapter 2) than they are to the rationalized, fully developed story of cultural origins associated with the early Iranian kings we see in Ibn al-Muqaffaʿ, Ibn al-Kalbī, and Ṭabarī. This is not to say that one or the other is an Islamic-era invention, although we must allow for some literary license, given the chauvinistic climate surrounding the production of both groups of literature.[184] Rather, they represent two different streams of thought on cultural origins, one centered in the Sasanian court and the other in the Zoroastrian temples.

The Iranian culture myths related by Ibn al-Muqaffaʿ and others not only owe their creation to the patronage of Sasanian rulers and the pre-Islamic efforts of the landed gentry, the *dahāqīn*; they also owe their survival in versified form to new Muslim Iranian kings and Muslim dahāqīn. These new dynasties frequently claimed genealogical ties to one of the early Iranian kings or promulgated the cultural exploits of their forebears in order to convince their subjects that they were worthy to rule and to demonstrate that they were the inheritors and renovators of a glorious Iranian past. For example, in a poem written for Yaʿqūb al-Ṣaffār (d. 265 AH / 879 AD), the founder of an independent Iranian state, Abū Isḥāq Ibrāhīm b. Mamshādh (fl. mid-fourth century AH / tenth century AD)—a native of Isfahan who had been the boon companion of the caliph al-Mutawakkil (d. 247 AH / 861 AD)—wrote: "I am the son of the noble descendants of Jam [i.e., Jamshīd], and the inheritance of the kings of Persia has fallen to my lot. / I am reviving their glory which has been lost and effaced by the

[179] Ibid.

[180] Ibid., bk. 3, chap. 209.

[181] Ibid., chap. 29.

[182] Ibid., bk. 8, *Nask* 12.

[183] Ibid., bk. 7, chap. 1. For the etymology of *Pīshdād*, see above. As with Gayōmart, Hōshang is not mentioned in the *Gāthās* but is mentioned several times in the Yasht hymns (e.g., Farvardin Yasht, v. 137); however, no details are provided about his life and exploits. Also similar to Gayōmart, the mythology surrounding him as the first king may have arisen from a later etymology of his name: the authors of the *Dēnkard* assert that Hōshang means "one who aims at kingship" (*Dēnkard*, bk. 3, chap. 209, in anon., *Dinkard*, vol. 1).

[184] There are other instances where Zoroastrian lore was influenced by the Arab conquests. See Choksy, *Conflict*, 60–66.

length of time."[185] And a few lines later, we find an echo of Bashshār b. Burd's sentiments: "Our fathers gave you your kingdom, but you showed no gratitude for our benefactions. / Return to your country in the Ḥijāz, to eat lizards and to graze your sheep; / For I shall mount on the throne of the kings, by the help of the edge of my sword and the point of my pen!"[186] Abū Manṣūr Ṭūsī (d. 350 AH / 962 AD), a governor of Nishapur under the Iranian Sāmānid dynasty with aspirations to rule Khorasan, made a similar claim in the tenth century to be a descendant of Jamshīd (through his son). He also had his vizier Abū Manṣūr Maʿmarī oversee the compilation of a *Book of Kings* (*Shāhnāmih*),[187] which mentioned the numerous cultural exploits of ancient Iranian kings (see the following paragraphs). That contemporary rulers claimed to be related to these kings to add luster to their rule is remarked on critically by al-Bīrūnī, who censured both Abū Manṣūr Ṭūsī and the Būyids in his *Āthār* for forging genealogical ties to these rulers.[188] Finally, the two largest Persian-language collections of Iranian etiologies—Balʿamī's (d. 363 or 382 AH / 974 or 992 AD) translation of Ṭabarī's *Ta'rīkh*, which includes the etiologies found in Ṭabarī as well as the fragment of Ibn al-Muqaffaʿ about Gayōmart and Hōshang, and Firdawsī's (d. 411 AH / 1019f AD) *Shāhnāmih*—were both sponsored by the Sāmānids (although Firdawsī completed his work under the patronage of Maḥmūd of Ghazna). Firdawsī's would become the Iranian national history par excellence.

Whereas the Iranian courts sponsored the promulgation of the cultural exploits of ancient Iranian kings, the dahāqīn supplied the material. According to an account that was later attached to Firdawsī's *Shāhnāmih* (called the "Older Preface" by modern scholars of the *Shāhnāmih*), when Abū Manṣūr Ṭūsī wanted to create a compilation of the stories of Iran's ancient kings (see above), his vizier reportedly gathered four dahāqīn from various regions of Iran and had them write the stories (or "books," *nāma-hā*) of the kings.[189] This compilation of stories, which was completed in April 957 AD, began with "the first king [*kay*], who was he who established the practices of civilization in the world and brought men out of [the condition of beasts]" (i.e., Gayōmart).[190] It included a number of other culture myths preserved in Thaʿālibī's (d. 429 AH / 1038 AD) Arabic *Ghurar* and Firdawsī's *Shāhnāmih*, both of whom consulted the text.[191]

The following reasons given in the "Older Preface" for compiling the stories

[185] Stern, "Persian National Sentiment," 541.

[186] Ibid., 542.

[187] Meisami, *Persian Historiography*, 20–21.

[188] Bīrūnī, *Chronology*, 44–51 (see Meisami, *Persian Historiography*, 21).

[189] Minorsky, "Older Preface," 266. This and the following translations from the "Older Preface" are by Minorsky. Bīrūnī's quotation from it is in his *al-Āthār al-bāqiya*. Bīrūnī, *Chronology*, 119. Zeev Rubin accepts, with Nöldeke (*Iranian National Epic*), that such a compilation existed and that it was a source for Firdawsī's *Shāhnāmih*, although he notes that many other scholars disagree (see Rubin, "Ibn al-Muqaffaʿ," 64n58).

[190] Minorsky, "Older Preface," 266.

[191] Nöldeke, *Iranian National Epic*, 62–67; Khāliqī Mutlaq, "Az Shāhnāmih," 16, 47–48; Omidsalar, "Source," 340; Meisami, "Two Views," 262.

of ancient Iranian kings are pertinent to our discussion of why these etiologies were promulgated:

> As long as the world has existed, people have sought knowledge, held Speech great, and considered it the best memorial, because in this world men become greater and richer through knowledge. As men have understood that nothing permanent remains of them, they strive that their names remain and their vestiges stay unbroken, such as (spreading) prosperity, or making places strong, or courage, daring and giving one's life, or promoting wisdom for the benefit of men, or inaugurating new practices. . . .[192]
>
> . . . [T]hey called the book *Shāhnāmih* (*Book of Kings*) so that men of knowledge may look into it and find in it all about the wisdom of the kings, noblemen and sages, the royal arrangements, nature and behaviour, good institutions, justice and judicial norms, decisions and administration, military organization in battles, storming of cities, punitive expeditions and night attacks, as well as about match-making and respecting honour. They compiled this Book of Kings (*Shāh-nāmih*) and brought it out and in it there are matters which while being said (strike) the reader as important and everybody has some utility to derive from the book. . . .[193]
>
> . . . And the reading of this book (brings) the knowledge of the affairs of the kings and the rewards given to a lot of people for accomplishing the affairs of this world, comfort to the afflicted and medicine to the weary. And people read this book of the affairs of the kings for two purposes: the one is because when they learn the actions, the conduct and the ceremonial of the kings, they will be able to get on with anyone in administration; the other is that the book contains stories both pleasant to (their) ears and suitable to (their) strivings, for it contains good and clever matters, such as (the opposition between) the rewards of Good and the retribution of Evil, animadversion and mildness, rudeness and gentleness, daring and restraint, engagements and issues, advice and admonition, wrath and contentment, and the wonder of the affairs of the world.[194]

In short, the compilation was to teach Iranian Muslims about their pre-Islamic heritage and the glory of their kings, which was tied to their inventions.

Firdawsī, a dihqān, offers similar reasons for his tenth-century AD versification of the book's stories about Iranian kings.

> Thirty long years I labored,
> I revived ancient Persia [*ʿAjam*] in this Persian tongue.[195]

[192] Minorsky, "Older Preface," 265.

[193] Ibid., 266–67, slightly edited.

[194] Ibid., 268.

[195] *Shāhnāmih* 9.381, in Shahbazi, *Ferdowsī*, 124. References to verses follow the Moscow edition of Bertel et al.

To him [Firdawsī's patron] will I raise a memorial
That stands high as long as man exists.
In this history of earlier rulers
And nobles and mounted warriors of old,
Are found accounts of wars and feasts, of judgments and sayings,
Of the events of remote periods of ancient time;
Narration of rules of wisdom, religion, restraint and judgment
Likewise guidelines for obtaining happiness in the other world.
Of these, whatever he deems pleasant and acceptable,
Will benefit him in this very living world.[196]

At the beginning of his epic poem, Firdawsī gives a detailed list of the early Iranian kings' inventions—a list that rivals those found in Ṭabarī. For instance, the verses on Hōshang's achievements cover much the same ground as Ṭabarī's, with the addition of his discovery of fire:

Hōshang, a just and prudent sovereign,
Assumed his grandsire's crown. For forty years
Heaven turned above him. He was just and wise.
He said: "I lord it o'er the seven climes,
Victorious everywhere. My word is law,
I practise bounteousness and equity;
So hath God willed."
He civilised the world,
And filled the surface of the earth with justice.
He was the first to deal with minerals
And win the iron from the rock by craft.
He gained more knowledge and, inventing smithing,
Made axes, saws, and mattocks. Next he turned
To irrigation by canals and ducts;
Grace made the labour short. As knowledge grew
Men sowed and reaped and planted. Each produced
The loaf whereof he ate, and kept his station.
Till then men lived on fruit in poor estate
And clad themselves in leaves. Religious rites
Existed, Gayōmart had worshipped God.
Hōshang first showed the fire within the stone,
And thence through all the world its radiance shone.[197]

As we can see in Firdawsī's introduction to Gayōmart's inventions, they are an integral part of his effort to revive Iranian culture and connect Iranian Muslims with their past.

[196] *Shāhnāmih* 6.323, ibid., 127.

[197] *Shāhnāmih*, in Firdawsī's *Shahnama of Firdausi*, 122–23. I have altered the transliteration of the names.

What saith the rustic bard [*dihqān*]? Who first designed
To gain the crown of power among mankind?
Who placed the diadem upon his brow?
The record of those days hath perished now
Unless one, having borne in memory
Tales told by sire to son, declare to thee
Who was the first to use the royal style
And stood the head of all the mighty file.[198]

Regardless of whether these etiologies were in circulation before the coming of Islam or were the product of eighth- and ninth-century cultural polemics (or perhaps a bit of both), it is no accident that many of them were written down for the first time during a period of Iranian resurgence. For the reasons outlined above, they served the purposes of various Iranian elites who wished to culturally orient Islamic society toward pre-Islamic Iran. It is also no accident that the focus of these etiologies is Gayōmart and his progeny, since their exploits served as a useful foil to the cultural history associated with Adam and his progeny. Perhaps for this reason the "pride of *dihqāns*" is denounced in one tradition attributed to Muḥammad,[199] and the Iranian legends spread by one of the Prophet's enemies are condemned in another.[200] A similar feeling lies behind the reaction of the ʿAbbāsid governor of Khurāsān, ʿAbd Allāh b. Ṭāhir (d. 230 AH / 844 AD), to an Iranian legend presented to him in a book.

The prince stated, "We are the people who read the Qur'an. We desire nothing besides the Qur'an and the accounts of the Prophet. To us such books as this are useless, and this book is the work of Zoroastrian scholars (*moghān*), and in our view unacceptable." He then gave orders that the book be thrown into water and issued a decree commanding that wherever books written by the older Persians (*ʿAjam*) and Zoroastrian scholars (*moghān*) were kept, they must all be burnt.[201]

Strikingly, ʿAbd Allāh b. Ṭāhir was of Iranian descent. So too was Ibn Qutayba,[202] one of the most famous Muslim Arabophiles (see chapter 3). Although Ibn Qutayba wrote a significant section on the history of Iranian kings in his *Maʿārif*,[203] he does not mention a single Iranian cultural first in his awā'il list or elsewhere. He would adopt a similar attitude toward the Hellenistic sciences (see chapter 5).

[198] Ibid., 118.
[199] See Goldziher, *Muslim Studies* 1:104.
[200] Bosworth, "Heritage," 16.
[201] Dawlatshāh, *Tadhkirat al-shuʿarā'*, 30 (in Shahbazi, *Ferdowsī*, 120).
[202] Savant, "Finding Our Place," 41.
[203] Ibn Qutayba, *Maʿārif*, 652–67.

Conclusion

One is tempted to see in these native histories of civilization a rebuff to the rule of the conquerors, particularly in the case of the Iranians, who made them a part of the mythology underpinning their independent states in the tenth century AD. Yet surprisingly, all of our authors accepted the legitimacy of the conquests and the conquerors' rule. In the case of those who had long traditions of native rule and who wrote close to the time of the conquests, such as Berossus, Manetho, and Ibn al-Muqaffaʿ, there was a desire to pour the new rulers into the mold of past traditions of monarchy, the keepers of which were the native priestly classes or landed gentry. In the case of Artapanus and Philo of Byblos, whose peoples had not known native rule for centuries and who wrote at a time distant from the conquests, it was to separate the elite culture they had adopted from the ethnic identity of those who had brought it. In all cases, ethnic belonging was defined in terms of culture rather than or in addition to kinship, which facilitated both the adoption of the culture the conquerors brought and the conquerors' embrace of native custom and belief. But whereas the material culture and technology associated with the ancient kings was imminently adoptable—since it did not often challenge one's cherished beliefs—the sciences proved more difficult.

FIVE

"The Sciences of the Ancients": Speculation on the Origins of Philosophy, Medicine, and the Exact Sciences

> Extreme antiquity gives books authority.
>
> —Tertullian, *Apology*

> We have determined that all these nations, in spite of their differences and diversities of their convictions, form two categories. One category has cultivated science, given rise to the art of knowledge, and propagated the various aspects of scientific information; the other category did not contribute enough to science to deserve the honor of association or inclusion in the family of scientifically productive nations. Members of this group formulated no useful philosophy and generated no practical idea. The category that cultivated science is comprised of eight nations: the Indians, the Persians, the Chaldeans, the Greeks, the Romans, the people of Egypt, the Arabs, and the Hebrews.
>
> —Ṣāʿid al-Andalusī, *Book of the Categories of Nations*

IN ADDITION TO encouraging Iranians to record the history of their ancient kings, the move of the capital of the Islamic empire to Baghdad in the mid-eighth century AD had a second major consequence for the Muslim debate about the origins of culture: the translation of Greek scientific texts into Arabic. The new dynasty, the ʿAbbāsids, styled themselves as model Iranian kings, and since being a good Iranian king meant supporting the translation of scientific texts, they patronized the translation of Greek scientific texts into Arabic.[1] The choice of texts was guided by the practical considerations of the ruling elite—the translation of medical, astronomical, and mathematical treatises reflected the needs of the physicians, astrologers, secretaries, and engineers they patronized, who in turn patronized others.[2] The ruling elite and scholars were also interested in translating texts on philosophy (*falsafa*)—"a mixture of Aristote-

[1] Gutas, *Greek Thought*, 45. The first epigraph, from Tertullian's *Apology*, is on 19, translated by Glover. The second epigraph, from Ṣāʿid al-Andalusī's *Categories of Nations*, is on 6.

[2] Sabra, "Naturalization of Greek Science," 235, 657–58; Gutas, *Greek Thought*, 108–9, 112–15, 133–35.

lian and Neoplatonic doctrines and forms of argument"[3]—which could speak to the religious quandaries of the day, quandaries that had become acute in the cosmopolitan milieu of postcolonial Baghdad.[4]

The translation into Arabic of the rational sciences, or "sciences of the ancients" (*ʿulūm al-awāʾil*), as they were called,[5] aroused considerable interest in their origin[6] and sparked debate about their compatibility with Islam and the emerging "Arab sciences" (*ʿulūm al-ʿarab*) attending it.[7] The debate turned on how the sciences had originated and who had originated them. This was, in many ways, the continuation of a discussion that began in classical Greece and involved the entire Near East after Alexander's conquests.[8]

In classical Greece, medicine and philosophy were held to be Greek inventions, whereas the mathematical, or exact, sciences (*mathēmata*) were believed to have originated in the ancient Near East, usually Egypt or Babylon. In the Hellenistic and Roman periods, the "barbarian" nations also laid claim to medicine and philosophy, with some Greek and Roman agreement. Jews in particular focused on philosophy when advancing their claims to civilizational priority rather than laying claim to the other sciences or civilization in general.[9] This was for at least two reasons. First, soon after Alexander's conquests, Greeks promulgated the image of Jews as a philosophical race; when Greek and Roman authors later started to portray Jews as misanthropic outsiders, Jewish scholars sought to reinforce the earlier positive, transconfessional image. Second, once the Hebrew Bible was translated into Greek, Greek-speaking Jews could read their scriptures and note parallels with Greek philosophy.[10]

The trend of claiming priority for the Hebrew prophets in the realm of philosophy continued with the early Church Fathers and for much the same reason: criticized as cultural traitors for embracing a foreign religion, early Christian authors argued that biblical heroes had been responsible for creating the premier science of Rome—Greek philosophy. This was not a staid exercise in antiquarianism. Rather, describing the origins and development of a scientific tradition was meant to locate oneself in it[11] and, consequently, in elite society. It could also be used to legitimate a scientific discipline or a strand within it.

[3] Sabra, "Naturalization of Greek Science," 662.

[4] Gutas, *Greek Thought*, 120, 133–36.

[5] Sabra, "Naturalization of Greek Science," 230.

[6] Zhmud, *Origins*, 3–4.

[7] Joel Kraemer, *Humanism*, 10, 22, 110.

[8] See Van der Eijk, *Ancient Histories of Medicine*, 1, for a bibliography on recent studies of antique historiographies of the sciences.

[9] Jews also frequently claimed priority in law, which is outside the scope of this chapter but will be noted when it occurs.

[10] One exception might be Pseudo-Eupolemus, who probably lived before the Septuagint. See the next section.

[11] Van der Eijk, in *Ancient Histories of Medicine* (1–2), makes this point about Greek and Roman authors.

This dual function of scientific protography is also evident in early Muslim attempts to explain the origins of the sciences. Muslim scholars did not passively transmit the antique tradition but selected material that suited their social and scholarly agendas in ninth- and tenth-century Iraq. Significantly, these agendas did not include assimilating the sciences to an Arabo-Islamic orthodoxy, which did not exist at the time. Rather, some Muslim scholars sought to create an Islamic tradition of rational science in Arabic at a time when no single learned tradition held sway. Their explanations for how this new tradition emerged from the old tells us as much about the nature of Iraqi society at that time as it does about the survival of the antique historiography of the sciences in Islam.

The Eastern Origin of the Sciences

In earliest Greek myth, captured in verse by Homer and Pindar, medicine was said to be the gift of Chiron the Centaur to Asclepius, a son of the god Apollo.[12] Building on this tradition, Plato held that Asclepius's disciples were also his descendants, the so-called Asclepiadae,[13] one of whom was his contemporary Hippocrates of the island of Kos.[14] Hippocrates subscribed to a naturalistic explanation of science's origins (perhaps derived from his teacher Democritus—see chapter 3). The fifth-century BC Hippocratic text *On Ancient Medicine* holds that humans were once without medicine, but they discovered it by necessity and through rational thought and experimentation.[15] Those who discovered the method did so through the application of reason and were so amazed by the results, they attributed its origins to the gods.[16] Because of the discovery of a sound method of investigation, future discoveries will be made.[17]

In the first century BC Diodorus Siculus occupied the middle ground, writing that Asclepius had learned many things about medicine from his father, Apollo, and then went on to make his own discoveries due to his innate cleverness.[18] Aulus Cornelius Celsus (ca. 25 BC–ca. 50 AD), like the author of the Hippocratic *On Ancient Medicine*, portrayed Asclepius as a human who discov-

[12] Homer *Iliad* 4.217–19; Pindar, *Nemean Ode*, 3.51–55, and *Pythian Ode*, 3.5–7, 3.45–54f, in *Odes and Selected Fragments*.

[13] Plato *Republic* 599c.

[14] Plato *Protagoras* 311b, in *Plato in Twelve Volumes*.

[15] Hippocrates, *On Ancient Medicine*, 2, 3, 5, 7. See King, "Origins of Medicine," 248; Zhmud, *Origins*, 55, 58, 68; Cuomo, *Technology and Culture*, 17.

[16] Hippocrates, *On Ancient Medicine*, 14. Zhmud, *Origins*, 55, 58. Celsus's introduction to his *On Medicine* (1–2) has the same euhemeristic explanation for Asclepius's deification.

[17] Hippocrates, *On Ancient Medicine*, 2, 4. Zhmud, *Origins*, 58–59. In contrast, the Hippocratic *Places in Man* holds that "medicine in its present state is . . . by now completely discovered" (46). See Cuomo, *Technology and Culture*, 21.

[18] Diodorus Siculus *Library* 4.71.3, 5.74.6.

ered the rudiments of medicine, for which he was later deified. Hippocrates's main contribution was to separate it from the study of philosophy; for this and his advances in medicine, Celsus dubbed him the "father of all medical art."[19] Celsus's contemporary Pliny the Elder observed that medicine's practitioners traced its origins to the gods and that Hippocrates, according to Varro, copied Asclepius's prescriptions for cures on the walls of the god's temple in Kos and then burned it to the ground,[20] portending the avariciousness of the Greek medical profession that Pliny despised and wished to contrast negatively with Roman home remedies.[21] In the third century AD, Philostratus depicted an Indian sage arguing that Asclepius learned of the fundamentals of medicine through divination—fundamentals on which his later descendants built.[22] Galen's (d. ca. 216 AD) attitude was closer to that of the Indian sage: the god Asclepius (whose devotee Galen claimed to be) learned medicine from Apollo; before him, heroes such as Chiron the Centaur had limited experience with drugs and herbs. But despite Asclepius's achievements, his original teachings were corrupted once they passed beyond his family because people did not write them down.[23] That is why Galen set about preserving the works of the greatest of Asclepius's descendants, Hippocrates, whom he venerated as the founder of medicine.[24]

As for medicine's place of origin, Greek and Roman authors usually limited it to Greece. Thus, Herodotus praised Egyptian medicine but was unwilling to say the Egyptians invented it,[25] which is surprising given that he was ready to attribute so many other Greek sciences to them (see below). Isocrates (d. 338 BC), in *Busiris*, credited the development of medicine to the laws of the Egyptian king Busiris (a Greek fiction), since these laws gave the priestly class the leisure to invent medicine, philosophy, and the exact sciences.[26] But since Isocrates' *Busiris* is a paradoxical encomium, meant to prove something absurd,[27] we should be wary of reading the text as representative of his true views or those of his countrymen.[28] Indeed, in his *Pangyricus* Isocrates praises Athens for the same reasons he praises Busiris, one of which is originating or contributing to all of the arts.[29] In a similar vein, Pseudo-Galen, in the *Introduction to*

[19] Celsus, introduction to *On Medicine*, 1–2, 8, 7.2.

[20] Pliny *Natural History* 29.1–2.

[21] Wesley Smith, "Ancient Medical," 79–80. See also King, "Origins of Medicine," 246–48.

[22] Philostratus *Life of Apollonius of Tyana* 3.44.

[23] See Hart, *Asclepius*, 144, for translations of relevant passages.

[24] The veneration of Hippocrates, both as a divinity and as the founder of medicine, came about in the first century BC. See King, "Origins of Medicine," 250–56.

[25] Wesley Smith, "Ancient Medical," 82; Zhmud, *Origins*, 39.

[26] Isocrates *Busiris* 11.21–23.

[27] Vasunia, *Gift*, 183.

[28] Isocrates explains that he cannot prove the things he attributes to Busiris, since he bases them on conjecture about how someone as powerful as Busiris would have behaved (*Busiris* 11.32, 35).

[29] Isocrates *Pangyricus* 40.

Medicine, believes that Egyptians had a type of medicine, but it was not as good as that of the Greeks, who received it from Asclepius.[30]

There were some "barbarian" claimants to having originated medicine, but they intrude lightly on the Greek story, seeming to render native myths or speak to internal scientific disputes rather than challenging Greek claims to primacy in medicine. Hecataeus relates that Egyptians believed Horus revealed knowledge of medicine to humans after his mother, Isis, taught it to him,[31] which is perhaps where Pliny obtained the Egyptian claim to be the first to have invented the art.[32] The Egyptian priest Manetho related that Imhotep, a priest of Re and chancellor to Djoser, was esteemed by the Egyptians for his medical skills, on account of which they equated him with Asclepius.[33] However, Manetho placed the invention of medicine prior to Asclepius when he credited the second pharaoh Athothis with laying the foundations of the discipline. Philo of Byblos also evoked Asclepius and implicitly equated him with Eshmun, a Phoenician healing god, but he did not dwell at length on the origin of the healing arts; he wrote only that the descendants of Asclepius and his brothers "discovered herbs, a cure for venomous animal bites, and charms."[34] The anonymous Jewish authors of the Greek-language *Jubilees* (mid-second century BC) also treated the origin of healing herbs, explaining that God commanded angels to teach Noah their use to cure diseases—instructions that Noah wrote down into a book, which he then gave to his eldest son, Shem.[35]

As for the mathematical sciences, classical Greek authors after Aeschylus believed these originated in the Near East, mainly in Egypt.[36] Aristotle, echoing Isocrates, claimed all of them originated in Egypt because the priestly class there was allowed the leisure to pursue them.[37] Herodotus believed that geometry developed out of Egyptian land surveying;[38] later authors were split only on whether it was Thales or Pythagoras who had brought it to Greece.[39] Herodotus also claimed that the Babylonians were responsible for several as-

[30] Zhmud, *Origins*, 300n116.

[31] Diodorus Siculus *Library* 1.25. Burton notes that there is a basis for this in Egyptian mythology (*Commentary*, 109–10).

[32] Pliny *Natural History* 7.57.

[33] F2a (Verbrugghe and Wickersham, *Berossos and Manetho*, 134; F2 in Jacoby's *Fragmente*).

[34] Eusebius *Preparation for the Gospel* 10.38, 14. Philo makes Asclepius the eighth of Suduc's sons. In Phoenician mythology, the eighth son of the god Sadykos (Suduc in Philo) is Eshmun, a healing god. There are other texts that attest to Phoenicians' equating Eshmun and Asclepius. See Baumgarten, *Phoenician History*, 227–31.

[35] *Jubilees* 10.10–14. The Islamic-era Ibn Waḥshiyya also mentions Noah's medical books (Hämeen-Anttila, *Last Pagans*, 174).

[36] Zhmud, *Origins*, 298. Aeschylus had them originate with either Palamedes or Prometheus.

[37] Aristotle *Metaphysics* 1.981b.

[38] Herodotus *Histories* 2.109.

[39] See Zhmud, *Origins*, 101, for sources.

tronomical innovations.[40] Plato hinted at either an Egyptian or a Phoenician origin for arithmetic.[41]

Later Hellenistic writers did not dispute the fact that these innovations had come from the Near East, but if they lived in the region, they tended to argue for its local origin in the country they inhabited. Thus, Hecataeus related that Babylonians followed the example of Egyptian astronomy,[42] obviously in deference to his Ptolemaic patrons and at the expense of their Seleucid rivals. Pseudo-Eupolemus, probably a Samaritan who flourished in the early second century under the Seleucids,[43] equated the biblical Enoch with the titan Atlas[44] and claimed that he discovered astrology/astronomy (the words are used interchangeably) and that angels had revealed unspecified knowledge to his son Methuselah. After the Flood, Abraham, who had learned astronomy/astrology and other sciences in Chaldea, passed them along to the Phoenicians and then to the Egyptians.[45]

As with Hecataeus's account, Pseudo-Eupolemus's claims should be read against the backdrop of a local rivalry with other Mediterranean claimants to cultural genesis.[46] He subsumes a pagan myth in a biblical structure to confirm the biblical story,[47] validates the Hebrews' adoption of Babylonian sciences,[48] and affirms their precedence over rival cultural progenitors, the Phoenicians and Egyptians.[49] His preference of Phoenicia over Egypt reinforces the notion that Pseudo-Eupolemus was located in Phoenicia. It should also not escape our attention that Pseudo-Eupolemus's description of the origins of astrology came at the expense of Egypt and Phoenicia,[50] which in his account became intermediaries of culture rather than its points of origin. The biblical hero is its true originator.

[40] Herodotus *Histories* 2.109.

[41] Plato *Laws* 747a–c, in *Plato in Twelve Volumes* (see Zhmud, *Origins*, 298n104).

[42] Diodorus Siculus, *Antiquities of Egypt*, 28.

[43] Wacholder, "Pseudo-Eupolemus," 87; see Sterling, *Historiography*, 187–206, for a bibliography. There is inferential evidence that hints he may have been a priest who knew Hebrew. On his identity as a priest, see Wacholder, *Eupolemus*, 289. For his knowledge of Hebrew, see Sterling, *Historiography*, 200. For skepticism about his identity, see Gruen, *Heritage and Hellenism*, 148. Pseudo-Eupolemus should not be confused with Eupolemus, a Jew who lived in the second century BC and wrote on biblical culture heroes.

[44] The Greeks started crediting Atlas with the discovery of astrology in the fifth century BC (Wacholder, "Pseudo-Eupolemus," 96; Sterling, *Historiography*, 202).

[45] Eusebius *Preparation for the Gospel* 9.17, 9.18. See Wacholder's discussion of the fragments in "Pseudo-Eupolemus."

[46] Mendels, *Land of Israel*, 116.

[47] Sterling, *Historiography*, 190, 204.

[48] Reed, "Was There Science," 8.

[49] Sterling, *Historiography*, 205; Gruen, *Heritage and Hellenism*, 149–50; Reed, "Was There Science," 8.

[50] Sterling, in *Historiography* (190–91), notes that Pseudo-Eupolemus puts Egypt last in line and suggests that this may reflect Pseudo-Eupolemus's political ties to the Seleucids when they were vying with the Egyptian Ptolemies for control of Coele-Syria.

The most contentious debate about the origins of the sciences in the Hellenistic era concerned philosophy. Classical Greeks were less charitable to non-Greeks than they had been regarding mathematical sciences. Aristotle wrote in the *Metaphysics* that Thales was the founder of philosophy because he was the first to speculate on first principles.[51] Aristotle's student Theophrastus agreed,[52] but in his work *On Discoveries* he gave a nod to Greek mythology by crediting Prometheus with inventing it (see chapter 1). In *Busiris*, Isocrates credited Phythagoras with bringing philosophy to Greece from Egypt,[53] but in *Panegyricus* he credited the inhabitants of Athens. For reasons discussed above, the latter was probably his real view.[54]

After Alexander's conquests, Greeks and non-Greeks moved the origins of philosophy eastward, attributing it to one ancient sage or another.[55] Diogenes Laertius (fl. third century AD) recorded something of the welter of claimants.

> There are some who say that the study of philosophy had its beginning among the barbarians. They urge that the Persians have had their Magi, the Babylonians or Assyrians their Chaldaeans, and the Indians their Gymnosophists; and among the Celts and Gauls there are the people called Druids or Holy Ones. . . . Also they say that Mochus was a Phoenician, Zalmoxis a Thracian, and Atlas a Libyan. If we may believe the Egyptians, Hephaestus was the son of the Nile, and with him philosophy began, priests and prophets being its chief exponents. . . .
>
> . . . But the advocates of the theory that philosophy took its rise among the barbarians go on to explain the different forms it assumed in different countries. As to the Gymnosophists and Druids we are told that they uttered their philosophy in riddles, bidding men to reverence the gods, to abstain from wrongdoing, and to practise courage. That the Gymnosophists at all events despise even death itself is affirmed by Clitarchus in his twelfth book; he also says that the Chaldaeans apply themselves to astronomy and forecasting the future; while the Magi spend their time in the worship of the gods, in sacrifices and in prayers, implying that none but themselves have the ear of the gods. . . . Clearchus of Soli in his tract *On Education* further makes the Gymnosophists to be descended from the Magi; and some trace the Jews also to the same origin.. . . [Egyptians] also laid down laws on the subject of justice, which they ascribed to Hermes; and they deified those animals which are

[51] Aristotle *Metaphysics* 1.983b6; see Mansfeld, "Aristotle," 111. Plato mentions Thales first in his list of seven Greek sages (*Protagoras* 342e–343b), but that is not indicative of his role in developing philosophy.

[52] Mansfeld, "Aristotle," 122.

[53] Isocrates *Busiris* 11.28, in *Isocrates*.

[54] Isocrates *Panegyricus* 47, in *Isocrates*.

[55] See Momigliano, *Alien Wisdom*, passim.

> serviceable to man. They also claimed to have invented geometry, astronomy, and arithmetic. Thus much concerning the invention of philosophy.[56]

Diogenes, a Greek, responded to all of this with great indignation: "These authors forget that the achievements which they attribute to the barbarians belong to the Greeks, with whom not merely philosophy but the human race itself began."[57] He went on to write that "the first to use the term and to call himself a philosopher or lover of wisdom, was Pythagoras."[58]

As we saw in the last chapter, these claims were not just made by conquered natives; the conquerors also made them on their behalf. Take the case of the Jews, who were mentioned in Diogenes' list and were favored originators of philosophy in the first Hellenistic century. Megasthenes (d. 290 BC), a Seleucid ambassador to the court of an Indian king, was said to have written a book on the Indians in which he asserted that Jews and the Brahmans preceded the Greeks in developing natural philosophy,[59] clever propaganda for his master Seleucus I, who laid claim to Palestine and India. Peripatetic philosophers also got in the game, claiming a more ancient pedigree by associating philosophy with the Jews. Clearchus of Soli (fl. fourth and third centuries BC), mentioned by Diogenes, recounted a meeting between Aristotle and a Jew in Asia Minor who was Hellenized both in language and soul. Aristotle, Clearchus averred, learned more from the Jew than vice versa. But Clearchus made it clear that despite the intellectual ascendancy of the Hellenized Jew, his learning came from farther aast, asserting that Jews were descended from Indian philosophers.[60] Doxographers also joined in. Hermippus of Smyrna (fl. third century BC), a biographer of Greek philosophers, said, according to Josephus, that Pythagoras learned Jewish practices from the soul of one of his disciples.[61] The Christian apologist Origen (d. 254 AD) cited another work, in which Hermippus wrote that the Greek philosopher Pythagoras took his philosophy from the Jews.[62]

Whatever the veracity of these accounts or their true authorship, they are probably representative of early knowledge of Jews among literate Greeks in the century after Alexander's conquests (with the exception of Hecataeus, who had native interlocutors). All of them draw on two common tropes in classical Greek anthropology in order to fill gaps in their authors' knowledge: the idea

[56] Diogenes Laertius, *Lives*, prologue of bk. 1, 1–2, 6, 9, 11. Diogenes records Manetho and Hecataeus among his sources for these claims.

[57] Ibid., 3.

[58] Ibid., 12.

[59] Stern, *Greek and Latin Authors*, 1.46.

[60] Josephus *Apion* 1.176–82, in *The Works of Flavius Josephus*. Theophrastus also wrote that the Jews are "philosophers by race" (see Stern, *Greek and Latin Authors* 1:10).

[61] Josephus *Apion* 1:163–65, in *The Works of Flavius Josephus*.

[62] Origen *Contra Celsum* 1.15.

that antiquity equals cultural superiority and the notion that Greek culture had been derived from the East.[63]

Jews also contributed to this representation of themselves as a philosophical people, although we do not have a record of it until two centuries after the conquests. Eupolemus (d. mid-second century BC),[64] a Jewish historian and Maccabean ambassador, argued that Moses was the "first wise man" (i.e., philosopher) and credited him with giving the Jews written laws and the alphabet. The Phoenicians got the latter from the Jews, and from the Phoenicians it passed to the Greeks.[65] Eupolemus lived in Palestine and not Egypt, so his attempts to discredit a rival cultural claimant are directed at the Phoenicians—the nearest neighbor with a venerable history—rather than the Egyptians. Although the text establishes the cultural superiority of the Jews, it is much less polemical toward the Greeks than one might think given that its author lived in the immediate aftermath of the revolt against Greek rule.[66]

Aristobulus, a second-century Jewish author who lived in Egypt, adhered more closely to the theme of the prophets as purveyors of science and philosophy. In a book dedicated to Ptolemy VI Philometor,[67] he argued, on the basis of alleged conceptual similarities between the Hebrew Bible and Greek philosophy, that Homer, Hesiod, Pythagoras, Socrates, Plato, and others had all studied the Pentateuch in Greek.[68] He even asserted that Plato followed Mosaic law, which he read in Greek centuries before the Septuagint existed.[69] Aristobulus also hinted that Abraham had influenced the verse of Orpheus[70] and that Homer and Hesiod had relied on Jewish sources.[71] As with Artapanus (see chapter 4) and Eupolemus, Moses is the premier culture hero; however, his medium of influence is textual and aimed primarily at the Greeks.[72]

One reason why Jews, particularly those living in Alexandria, were reinforcing the earlier positive image of their people as philosophers is that the image was under attack. Whereas the earlier image of the Jews was as a completely Greek people, now they were being depicted as completely Other. Thus Agatharchides of Cnidus (fl. second century BC), a Hellenistic historian who lived in

[63] On the two tropes, see Momigliano, *Alien Wisdom*, 146–47. See Copenhaver, "Historiography of Discovery," 195–96, for the development of these tropes in Herodotus. For the impact of Herodotus on later historians, see Murray, "Herodotus."

[64] Sterling, *Historiography*, 208.

[65] Quoted in Eusebius *Preparation for the Gospel* 9.26. See Wacholder, *Eupolemus*, 71–96; Mendels, *Land of Israel*, 31; Sterling, *Historiography*, 218–19; Gruen, *Heritage and Hellenism*, 153–54.

[66] Contra Sterling, who sees a far more polemical edge (*Historiography*, 218–21).

[67] Momigliano, *Alien Wisdom*, 116; Gruen, *Heritage and Hellenism*, 246–47; Hengel, "Judaism and Hellenism," 21.

[68] Eusebius *Preparation for the Gospel* 13.12.

[69] Ibid.

[70] Ibid., 13.12.5. See Gruen, *Heritage and Hellenism*, 248–50.

[71] Eusebius *Preparation for the Gospel* 13.12.13–15; Gruen, *Heritage and Hellenism*, 50.

[72] Gruen, *Heritage and Hellenism*, 247–48.

Egypt, wrote that Jews who defended Jerusalem against the Ptolemies did not fight on the Sabbath because of their "superstition."[73] A Greek geographer, Mnaseas of Patara (probably lived in the second century BC), wrote in his *Periegesis* that the Jews worshiped the golden head of an ass.[74]

Although the charge that Jews worshiped a donkey was certainly meant as an insult, their worship of a single invisible god may have been worse in the eyes of some non-Jewish Hellenistic authors. In pagan societies, public worship of the local gods was linked to support of the state. Consequently, rejection of the local gods, or "atheism," could be dangerous to one's health, as Socrates had discovered. Such danger was implied when Apollonius Molon (fl. first century BC), the head of a school of rhetoric on the island of Rhodes, called the Jews atheists.[75] It was a charge that would be echoed with greater frequency after the Romans conquered Palestine and Jews fanned out across the empire.

The Theft of Philosophy

Philo and Josephus

In the final decades of the first century BC and throughout the first and second centuries AD, hostility toward the Jews escalated in areas where Jews were numerous.[76] One major reason for this hostility was the Jewish belief in a single god to the exclusion of all others. Such a notion threatened social stability in a republic, and later empire, that was built on tolerance for local deities. Even more, it was viewed as incredibly arrogant for foreigners to refuse to assimilate to the dominant culture; hence the charge of misanthropy that was repeatedly leveled at the Jews by pagans, possibly as early as Hecataeus and Manetho.[77] This may not have mattered when Jews remained in Palestine, but as the community grew in Alexandria and then in Rome, the heart of the empire, there was increasing discomfort with their unwillingness to assimilate, as evinced by the Roman historian Tacitus (d. 120 AD).

> The Egyptians worship many animals and images of monstrous form; the Jews have purely mental conceptions of Deity, as one in essence. They call those profane who make representations of God in human shape out of per-

[73] Josephus *Apion* 1:205–12, in *The Works of Flavius Josephus*; Diodorus Siculus *Library* 12:5–6.

[74] Josephus *Apion* 2:112–14, in *The Works of Flavius Josephus*.

[75] Ibid., 2.145–150.

[76] For a survey of the material, see Schäfer's *Judeophobia*.

[77] Diodorus Siculus *Library* 9.3.4 (trans. Stern, in *Greek and Latin Authors* 1:28); Verbrugghe and Wickersham, *Berossos and Manetho*, 116, F12. Manetho's negative characterization of the Jews may have been attributed to him by later Egyptian pagans (see chapter 4 and Verbrugghe and Wickersham, *Berossos and Manetho*, 116).

> ishable materials. They believe that Being to be supreme and eternal, neither capable of representation, nor of decay. They therefore do not allow any images to stand in their cities, much less in their temples. This flattery is not paid to their kings, nor this honour to our Emperors.[78]

The success of the Jews at converting Roman citizens to their religion served to heighten this discomfort.[79] Again, Tacitus: "Those who come over to their religion adopt the practice, and have this lesson first instilled into them, to despise all gods, to disown their country, and set at nought parents, children, and brethren."[80] Seneca the Younger (d. 65 AD), a Stoic philosopher, was even more alarmist: "The customs of that most accursed nation have gained such strength that they have been now received in all lands, the conquered have given laws to the conquerors."[81] Little wonder, then, that attacks on the Jews took the form of denigrating their cultural achievements. Thus, Apollonius remarked (in the words of Josephus) that the Jews were the "weakest of all the barbarians, and that this is the reason why [they] are the only people who have made no improvements in life."[82] Gone were the early postconquest days of depicting Jews as a philosophical race.

This negative depiction of the Jews was also fueled by the conflict between Jews and pagans in Alexandria. Thus Josephus notes that a certain Lysimachus of Alexandria reiterated various anti-Jewish tropes from Manetho, characterizing Jews as misanthropic lepers.[83] Apion (fl. first half of first century AD), an Alexandrian rhetorician who was probably of Egyptian origin, wrote a five-volume history of Egypt, which, like Manetho's work, had a section on the Jews. Furthermore, like Manetho, he characterized them as exiled, misanthropic lepers.[84] He also included the charge that the Jews worshiped a golden ass (see above).[85] All of this was meant to bolster his case that the Jews were foreign and seditious.[86]

Since their new overlords had adopted the cultural history and sensitivities of the Greeks, the response to these charges by Jews living under Roman rule was similar to that of their earlier coreligionists: stress the antiquity of biblical heroes; emphasize the dependence of the Greeks on these heroes for scientific and philosophical knowledge; and downplay the original cultural contributions

[78] Tacitus *History* 5.5, in *The Complete Works of Tacitus.*

[79] In the first century BC, Horace (d. 8 BC) alluded to the success of Jewish proselytizing in his *Satires*: "We are much more numerous, and like the Jews we shall force you to join our throng." Horace *Satires* 1:4, in *The Works of Horace.*

[80] Tacitus *History* 5:5, in *The Complete Works of Tacitus.*

[81] Augustine *City of God* 6:11.

[82] Josephus *Apion* 2.145–50, in *The Works of Flavius Josephus.*

[83] Ibid., 1.304–20.

[84] Ibid., 2.15, 2.121.

[85] Ibid., 2.80.

[86] Ibid., 2.65, 68.

of the Egyptians, their primary cultural competitors. But unlike the previous generation of Jewish authors, the rhetoric of those living under Roman rule was sharper because of the denigration of their cultural contribution to humanity, the depiction of them as outsiders, and the suspicion that their doctrines were undermining the state. Thus, the philosopher Philo (d. ca. 50 AD), the most prominent Alexandrian Jew of the time, wrote that the Greek philosopher Heraclitus (d. ca. 475 BC) took his theory of opposites from Moses "like a thief."[87] He also averred that Moses had preceded Plato in coming up with the idea of creation's coming from preexistent matter.[88] Elsewhere he asserted that Greek lawmakers "copied" some laws from the laws of Moses.[89] And even if Greeks had originated their own laws, they were not as good as the Mosaic laws, since the latter had remained unchanged.[90]

Even though Philo maintained that the Greeks had stolen some of their philosophical doctrines and laws from Moses, he did not go so far as to say that they had stolen all of their doctrines from him, as Josephus and later Christian apologists would do. Thus, in his life of Moses, Philo wrote that Moses had learned the wisdom of the Greeks, Egyptians, and neighboring nations during his time in Egypt.[91]

His contemporary Josephus (d. after 100 AD), a native of Jerusalem, was not so charitable to the Greeks or the Egyptians. Thus in his *Antiquities*, Josephus argued that it was Seth and his descendants who had invented astronomy, the secrets of which they inscribed on stelae before the Flood.[92] He also asserted that Abraham had discovered monotheism through astronomical observation[93] and had brought arithmetic and astronomy to Egypt from Mesopotamia.[94] Like Philo, Josephus also used the dependency theme to argue for the cultural inferiority of Hellenism. Thus in his *Against Apion*, a work written to rebut the charges of the Egyptian pagans from Manetho to Chaeremon, Josephus claimed that Greek knowledge was built on the teachings of Moses,[95] who was the first lawgiver.[96] The Greeks were just mimics: "Our earliest imitators were the Greek philosophers, who, though ostensibly observing the laws of their own coun-

[87] Philo *Questions and Answers on Genesis* 4:152. For similar references, see Roth, "Theft," 64–65.

[88] Philo *De Providentia* 2.111, in Hadas-Lebel's *De providentia*; cf. Justin Martyr *Apologia* 1:59.

[89] Philo *De Specialibus Legibus* 4:61, in *Works*.

[90] Philo *Vita Mosis* 2.3.12, ibid.

[91] Ibid., 1.5. Clemens of Alexandria alludes to this passage in his depiction of Moses as a culture hero in his *Stromata* 1.23.

[92] Josephus *Antiquities* 1.70–71, in *The Works of Flavius Josephus*. (For a parallel, see chapter 2, on Cainan in *Jubilees*.)

[93] Ibid., 1.127.

[94] Ibid., 1.167–68. See Reed's extended discussion in "Abraham as Chaldean Scientist."

[95] Josephus *Apion* 2.17, in *The Works of Flavius Josephus*; see Ginzberg, "Aristotle in Jewish Legend."

[96] Josephus *Apion* 2:154.

tries, yet in their conduct and philosophy were Moses's disciples."[97] Pythagoras, for example, was not only familiar with Jewish doctrines; he "was in very great measure a follower and admirer of them."[98] Moreover, Plato had copied Moses in writing that citizens must study law and take measures to prevent aliens from mixing with citizens.[99]

Who was the intended audience of Philo's and Josephus's polemics? Like any good apologia, they were meant to both bolster the home team and denigrate its opponents. Thus, Hellenized Jews had to be reassured of the compatibility of their cultural identity with the dominant culture but also convinced of its superior value lest they fully assimilate. By the same token, words such as *thief* and *imitators* were meant to remind Hellenes that their lauded culture was derivative and of foreign origin, thus blunting the characterization of Jews as foreigners and negating the charge of cultural betrayal leveled at Roman converts to Judaism. If Roman citizens were following the example of the great Greek thinkers of the past by following Jewish teachings, why should this be a cause for concern?

Not surprisingly, there is no evidence that the dependency argument was embraced by any pagan intellectual. Nevertheless, pagans associated Jews with two innovations: dream interpretation and the belief in a single, invisible god. Regarding the former, the Roman historian Pompeius Trogus (alive in 5 AD) wrote that Joseph was the first to interpret dreams.[100] Similarly, Strabo (d. after 21 AD) wrote that Moses allowed people who saw the future in their dreams to sleep in the temple so as to have visions that others could benefit from.[101] And sometime in the second century, Antonius Diogenes (fl. second century AD) wrote that Pythagoras had learned to interpret dreams from the Egyptians, Arabs, Chaldeans, and Hebrews after visiting them.[102]

As for the Jewish belief in a single, transcendent god, no early pagan author explicitly wrote that the Jews were the first to come up with the notion. Nevertheless, it does seem that some associated its genesis with the Jews. A few, like Strabo (d. after 21 AD), remarked on it neutrally. Strabo wrote in his *Geography* that Moses was an Egyptian priest who realized that the worship of divinity

[97] Ibid., 2:281.

[98] Ibid., 1.161. Josephus quotes Hermippus of Smyrna (fl. third century BC) as saying that Pythagoras learned some Jewish and Thracian practices from the soul of a departed disciple (*Apion* 1:163–65; see above). Origen cites a different work of Hermippus, *On Lawgivers*, in which he contends that Pythagoras took his philosophy from the Jews (*Contra Celsum* 1.15).

[99] Ibid., 2:257.

[100] Justin *Epitome of Pompeius Trogus* 36.2.8.

[101] Strabo, *Geography* 16.2.35–40. In addition to hearing Jewish legends (at least in the case of Trogus), the notion that Jews had specialized knowledge about dream interpretation was probably based on their occupation as soothsayers in Rome. Thus, in one of his satires, Juvenal (d. ca. 127 AD) makes fun of the poverty of Jews (*Satire* 3.12–16, 6.542–47, in Ramsay, *Juvenal*) and writes that Jews tell fortunes for gullible Romans for a small fee (*Satire* 6.542–47, in Ramsay, *Juvenal*).

[102] Porphyry *Life of Pythagoras* 11, in Guthrie, *Pythagorean Sourcebook*.

through images was wrong, for God was too great to be represented by an image: "God is this one thing alone that encompasses us all and encompasses land and sea—the thing which we call heaven, or universe, or the nature of all that exists."[103] Similarly, the Roman epic poet Lucan (d. 65 AD) remarked in his *Bellum Civile* that the Jews believed in an unseen God.[104] But others were more derisive. For example, the Roman satirist Juvenal (d. ca. 127 AD) quipped that the Jews worshiped clouds and a heavenly deity. Echoing Seneca (see above), he also expressed his annoyance with Romans who adopted the Jews' foreign laws and neglected their own.[105]

Even though pagan intellectuals associated Jews with the doctrine of monotheism, there is no indication that they believed this doctrine had had any impact on Greek philosophy or that Israelite culture heroes had influenced Greek culture. Admittedly, the neo-Pythagorean philosopher Numenius of Apamea (d. 200 AD) had referred to the Jewish doctrine in his lost work *On the Good* in support of his notion of God's incorporeality[106] and had remarked, "For what is Plato other than Moses in Attic Greek?"[107] But this only indicates his recognition of the similarity of Jewish and Platonic philosophy, not his endorsement of the dependency theme. Like other pagan philosophers of his time, he could accept monotheism as an integral part of his philosophical tradition without positing a dependence one way or the other.[108]

The Church Fathers

As detailed in chapter 4, early Christians were stigmatized as outsiders who had embraced an alien religious tradition of no account or achievement compared with the Greco-Roman civilization. One response was to claim that the Greco-Roman civilization had foreign origins. The second strategy, detailed below, was to follow Philo and Josephus in arguing that pagans had stolen philosophy from the Jews.[109] To make this argument, authors had to demonstrate the antiquity of Israelite heroes. If the Jews were older than the Greeks, the argument went, and the Greeks and Jews shared similar theological or legal doctrines, then the Greeks must have gotten their doctrines from the Jews.

Daniel Ridings has argued that this was not an argument addressed to fellow Christians to legitimate the use of Hellenistic philosophy but rather one addressed to sympathetic pagans who might be turned against the Christians by

[103] Strabo, *Geography*, 16.2.35. Strabo further reports that he persuaded many people of the truth of this doctrine and led them to Jerusalem (16.2.36).

[104] Lucan *Bellum Civile* 2.592–93.

[105] Juvenal *Satire* 14.96–106, in Ramsay, *Juvenal*.

[106] Numenius, *De Bono*, in Eusebius *Preparation for the Gospel* 9.7.

[107] Eusebius *Preparation for the Gospel* 9.6.

[108] On the rise of pagan monotheism in Late Antiquity, see Athanassiadi and Frede, *Pagan Monotheism*, 1–20.

[109] See Droge, *Homer or Moses?* passim.

the assertions of pagan intellectuals such as Celsus that Jewish civilization (and now its standard-bearer, the Christians) had contributed nothing to Hellenistic civilization.[110] But even if we accept that the primary goal of Christian authors was not to legitimate the use of Greek philosophy, their apologetics, like those of Josephus and Philo, must have also been directed toward Hellenized Christians who they feared would assimilate (or reassimilate if they were pagan converts) entirely to the dominant culture. Indeed, Ridings himself quotes one passage from Clement of Alexandria (d. ca. 215 AD) to this effect:

> But, it seems, most of those who register themselves under the name [as Christians] are like Odysseus' companions when they boorishly pursue the teaching, passing by, not the Sirens, but rhythm and melody, plugging up their ears with ignorance, since they know that once they have submitted their ears to the Hellenic studies they will never again return. But the one who plucks out that which is useful, for the benefit of the catechumens—especially when they are Hellenes—("The earth and its fullness belong to the Lord") should not refrain from polymathy like an irrational animal. He should gather as much help as he can for the listeners. But they should absolutely not waste any more time there than is enough to extract the valuable element from these aids, so that they, in possession of this, can come home to the true philosophy carrying with them security from all corners as solid confidence for the soul.[111]

One of the earliest Christian apologists to employ the dependence argument was Justin Martyr (d. ca. 165 AD), who claimed that the truths the Greeks discovered must have derived from the Hebrew prophets, since Moses predated all of the Greek philosophers.[112] His student Tatian (fl. latter half of second century AD) used the same tactic in his *Oratio ad Graecos*, arguing that the Greeks had unwittingly derived all of their true philosophical doctrines from Moses, but then they corrupted them.[113]

The first systematic elaboration of the dependency theme along the lines laid out by Philo and Josephus—citing specific instances of doctrinal theft—is found in the writings of the above-quoted Clement.[114] In his *Stromata*, Clement begins the first book with an argument for the antiquity of the Hebrews, seeing it as a necessary prelude to proving that the Hellenes stole from the Hebrews. "In a little while I will deal with the question of the philosophers' doctrines hav-

[110] Ridings, *Attic*, 132–39.

[111] Clement *Stromata* 6.11.89.1–3; see Ridings, *Attic*, 136.

[112] Justin Martyr, *2 Apologia*, 8–10; Copenhaver, "Historiography of Discovery," 198.

[113] Tatian *Address to the Greeks* 2.40.

[114] Origen, a later Christian apologist (d. ca. 254 AD), responded directly to Celsus. In contrast with Clement, he focused primarily on proving the antiquity of the Jews in order to rebut the pagan charges, criticizing Celsus for rejecting Jewish history as spurious while accepting that of the Egyptians, Persians, and other ancient civilizations as authentic. He pointed to the writings collected by Josephus as proof that the Jews were ancient (Origen, *Contra Celsum*, 1.16).

ing been stolen from the Hebrews. But first, in conformity with that, I must deal with the dates for Moses, by which it will be shown without a doubt that Hebrew philosophy is the most ancient of all wisdom."[115]

Having proven this to his satisfaction, Clement then goes on to point out various instances in which the Hellenes took philosophical doctrines from the Hebrews, stealing them, he writes, from the Hebrew Bible as Prometheus stole fire, and then garbling them, either through malice or misunderstanding.[116] His aim, he asserts, is to provide proof for the statement attributed to Jesus in John 10:8: "All those who were prior to the coming of the Lord were thieves and robbers."[117] Ridings has meticulously cataloged the various "thefts" Clement mentioned, so we need not survey them here.[118] Suffice it to say that they are all in the realm of philosophy and law and that Plato and Pythagoras are the primary offenders. Thus, Hellenes may have some part of the truth, but it is derivative and defective; pagans should abandon it, Clement argues, and become Christians, since Christ and his teachings are the fulfillment and completion of Jewish wisdom.[119]

Another author who stressed the theft of philosophy was Eusebius of Caesarea (b. ca. 260, d. 339 AD). Unlike Clement, Eusebius wrote at a time when Christianity was officially tolerated in the Roman Empire and was known to pagans. One might think, therefore, that Christians no longer had to worry about impressing educated pagans. Nevertheless, Eusebius followed the lead of Clement and portrayed Greek civilization, particularly philosophy, as a theft from foreigners. In particular, he claimed the Greeks stole the notion of monotheism and the fundamental philosophical doctrines from the Hebrews. "They [the Hellenes] found nothing in the others which was comparable to the good which some of them found in the Hebrews. That was the knowledge of the God of the Universe and a contemptuous opinion of their own gods, which will be demonstrated very shortly as the discussion continues."[120]

In contrast to Clement, Eusebius was willing to concede that the Hellenes may have come up with some of their own doctrines.[121] But whether they thought of things on their own or stole them, the point is that the Hebrews had thought of them first; thus, the criticism that the Christians had turned their

[115] Clement *Stromata* 1.21.101.1 (trans. Ridings, in *Attic*, 37).

[116] Ibid., 1.17.87.1–3. In *Stromata* 5.1.10.2–3, Clement also mentions that fallen angels revealed some "secrets" to the women they had intercourse with (although we are not told what, specifically, they imparted). Other angels withheld their knowledge of "providence" and "celestial bodies" until the coming of Christ. Clement avers that poets reworked the latter, which philosophers heard and garbled, since they did not understand the "prophetic allegory" (see Ridings, *Attic*, 46, 124–25).

[117] Clement *Stromata* 2.1.1.1 (see Ridings, *Attic*, 78).

[118] See the useful table in Ridings, *Attic*, 112–17.

[119] See, for example, Clement *Stromata* 5.13.87.1, 6.17.154.1–4.

[120] Eusebius *Preparation for the Gospel* 10.4.28–29 (trans. Ridings, in *Attic*, 157). See also Eusebius *Preparation for the Gospel* 10.1.3–4.

[121] Ibid., 10.1.5 (see Ridings, *Attic*, 153–54).

back on their own culture in favor of a foreign one is false[122]—if anyone is guilty of such an offense, it is the Hellenes, who stole from foreigners and, more to the point, from the Hebrews.

Eusebius's lengthy rebuttal of these charges—despite the growing ascendancy of Christianity at the time when he wrote them—shows how much the accusation of cultural betrayal still smarted and how much Christian etiological debates at this time were bound up with debates over identity. Even after the complete cultural and political triumph of Christianity in the fifth century, Christian intellectuals were still touchy on this count. Thus, Theodoret (d. 460 AD) bristled at pagan intellectuals who mocked Scripture as simplistic.[123] "Those who cling to the Hellenic mythology have often, in their contacts with me, made fun of our faith, saying that we recommend those who are being trained in Scripture nothing else other than faith. They criticized the lack of education in the apostles, calling them "barbarians," who do not possess the polish of fine speech."[124]

In defense, Theodoret wrote a book in which he repeated the earlier accusation of theft against the Hellenes,[125] echoing Eusebius's earlier rebuttal: if the paragons of Greek learning had borrowed from the Hebrews, then why do contemporary Hellenes turn up their noses at Hebrew Scripture?[126]

The political triumph of Christianity meant that its version of the history of the sciences dominated among people living around the Mediterranean and in the western half of the Near East. The dominance of the Christian narrative, however, meant that there was less interest in debating the origins of culture. The story was already known, and there was no longer any real challenge to it. Of course, the charge of cultural betrayal could still sting, as in the case of Theodoret, but he was one of the last Christian intellectuals who would have to hear it. By the end of the fifth century, pagan intellectuals had power in only one area, the teaching of the liberal arts, and even there they were fast fading.[127]

Revelation or Perspiration?

Like the early Church Fathers, a primary concern of early Muslims writing about the origins of philosophy, medicine, and the exact sciences was to explain the role of the Greeks in developing them. Muslims, however, were not writing as outsiders against a dominant pagan culture; rather, they were com-

[122] Eusebius mentions this criticism in Eusebius *Preparation for the Gospel* 1.5.10 (see Ridings, *Attic*, 154).

[123] Theodoret *Curatio* 1.17–18, in Pásztori-Kupán, *Theodoret* (see Ridings, *Attic*, 199).

[124] Ibid., 1, in Pásztori-Kupán, *Theodoret* (trans. Ridings, in *Attic*, 225). This recalls Augustine's own difficulties with the simplicity of the Bible and its language.

[125] See Ridings, *Attic*, 197–229.

[126] Ibid., 227.

[127] Chuvin, *Last Pagans*, 108.

peting with one another for the orientation of the Islamic empire's learned culture. Those who wished to see the "sciences of the ancients" dominate, or at least be accepted in polite society, split into two groups. The first made the argument that some pagan authors had made: the Greeks, unaided by revelation, had either invented the rational sciences or perfected them. Any people who valued reason could benefit from their learning and advance on their work. The second group argued that God had revealed the sciences to biblical heroes, from whom the Greeks and the rest of humanity derived them. The difference between the two groups was one of emphasis rather than of kind, and both groups were viewed with equal suspicion by those who wanted to keep Islam "pure."

Of the first group, al-Kindī (d. ca. 252 AH / 866 AD) was the earliest. An Arab polymath who was deeply involved in the translation work under the ʿAbbāsids and who tutored a son of the Caliph al-Muʿtaṣim,[128] Kindī wrote a treatise, *On First Philosophy,* for his patron. In it, he acknowledges the accomplishments of his non-Muslim predecessors in philosophy, which he defines as "knowledge of the true nature of things." Although these predecessors may have fallen short in some aspects, Muslims should be grateful to those who discovered true principles through research and toil, which accumulate over time. To punctuate his point, he quotes Aristotle as saying, "We ought to be grateful to the father of those who have contributed any truth."[129] These "human sciences," he writes in his *Introduction to the Study of Aristotle*, are distinct from the "divine science" because the former was the result of human research and ingenuity, whereas the latter required no effort, since it was given to humans through revelation.[130]

Kindī's project was to expose Arabic speakers to these sciences through translation, summary, and explanation.[131] In other words, he was endeavoring to establish a native Arab tradition of scientific inquiry. He even created a genealogy that linked the Arabs to the Greeks, contending that Arabs are related to the Greeks because their ancestor Qaḥṭān was the brother of the ancestor of the Greeks, who left Yemen for the West. Kindī's genealogy implies that by embracing the Greek sciences, Arabs were merely embracing their ancient heritage. [132]

A variation on this theme was offered a century later by Abū Naṣr al-Fārābī (d. 339 AH / 950 AD). In his *Taḥṣīl al-saʿāda* (Attainment of Happiness), he argues that philosophy first arose among the Chaldeans of Iraq. From there, it was transferred to the Egyptians, then to the Greeks, then back to the Syrians,

[128] Sabra, "Situating," 660–61.

[129] Kindī, *On First Philosophy* (trans. Ivry, in *Al-Kindī's Metaphysics*). See Sabra, "Situating," 660–61; Joel Kraemer, "Preliminary Study," 149.

[130] Joel Kraemer, "Preliminary Study," 149.

[131] Sabra, "Situating," 661.

[132] Masʿūdī, *Murūj*, §666 (Pellat edition); cited in Gutas, *Greek Thought*, 88.

and finally to the Arabs.[133] Fārābī is also said to have argued (erroneously) that the school of Aristotle had actually moved from Alexandria, via Antioch, Merv, and Ḥarrān, to Baghdad.[134] Of course, Fārābī studied philosophy in Baghdad, so his account of its origins places him and his teachers (one of whom was a Christian cleric) at the completion of the circle.[135] Like Kindī, Fārābī believed that the rational sciences were cumulative and the property of all humans; if the Greeks excelled others, it is only because they worked harder at it.[136]

Fārābī was not the only Muslim in tenth-century Iraq to boast of the ancient Babylonians' contribution to the sciences. Ibn Waḥshiyya (d. 318 AH / 930f AD), who claims to be a Chaldean,[137] also boasts of the contribution of his ancient ancestors to the sciences. Unlike Fārābī, however, he is much more defensive. The learning of his people, Ibn Waḥshiyya writes, had ebbed with their power and been appropriated by unlearned invaders, who now looked down on its originators and claimed that his countrymen had made no contribution to civilization. This is why he has undertaken the task of preserving the native sciences of his people, as he explains in prefaces to his Arabic translations of Syriac books on agriculture and poison.[138] To make his point, he attributes the books' contents to ancient native authors, enhancing their authority and ties to the land.[139]

Just as Ibn Waḥshiyya reminds the Arabs that they took their sciences from the people they conquered, he reminds the Persians that they took their sciences from Babylon.[140] That is not to say that they did not make improvements upon what they took; Ibn Waḥshiyya praises both Arabs and Persians for their scientific advances.[141] But they should not grow proud and forget they took the sciences from others by force.

[133] Al-Fārābī, *Taḥṣīl,* in *Alfarabi's Philosophy of Plato and Aristotle*, 43, 49–50; see Joel Kraemer, *Humanism*, 3.

[134] Ibn Abī Uṣaybiʿa, *ʿUyūn*, 204–5; see Lameer, "From Alexandria"; Gutas, *Greek Thought*, 90; Joel Kraemer, *Humanism*, 77n156. Others were not so eager to subsume Greek science into the Arab past. Ibn Qutayba, for example, chose to dismiss the Greek sciences altogether, or at least astronomy. In his *Anwāʿ*, he claimed that it was inferior to the Arab knowledge of astronomy (see Gutas, *Greek Thought*, 164–65).

[135] For details on Fārābī's life, see Gutas's entry "Fārābī, Abū Naṣr" in *EIr*. This is echoed by Fārābī's Nabatean contemporary Ibn Waḥshiyya, who writes in the preface to his translation of *The Book of Poisons* that "perhaps nine tenths of sciences belong to the Nabateans [the indigenous people of Iraq] and one tenth to all other nations together" (Hämeen-Anttila, *Last Pagans*, 41).

[136] Joel Kraemer, "Preliminary Study," 150–51. Al-Jāḥiẓ expresses the same sentiment in his *Book of Animals*, for which he owed a great deal to Aristotle (Sabra, "Situating," 660).

[137] Hämeen-Anttila, *Last Pagans*, 16, 43.

[138] Ibn Waḥshiyya, *Book of Poisons*, 20–23 (trans. Levey, in "Book of Poisons"); Ibn Waḥshiyya, *Nabatean Agriculture*, text 2–3 (in Hämeen-Anttila's *Last Pagans*).

[139] Ibn Waḥshiyya, *Book of Poisons*, 20 (trans. Levey, in "Book of Poisons"); Ibn Waḥshiyya, *Nabatean Agriculture*, text 2 (in Hämeen-Anttila's *Last Pagans*). See Hämeen-Anttila's thoughts on Ibn Waḥshiyya's use of pseudo-"Nabatean" names (Hämeen-Anttila, *Last Pagans*, 19).

[140] Ibn Waḥshiyya, *Book of Poisons*, 23 (trans. Levey, in "Book of Poisons").

[141] Ibid., 20–23.

> Should I praise those others who attempted to be chief, achieving mastery over cities and their dwellers, striking the people with the sword, subduing them to their power, compelling and oppressing the peoples to accept their lies, gathering a mob of inferior people and then enticing them to attack noblemen, the rich, and kings? Noblemen, the rich, and kings obeyed them and entered under their flag as a prerequisite for release from punishment. Then they said to us, "Pray for us and always remember use with praise and panegyric." In this way, they wish to keep us from remembering those who benefit us, those who constitute the legatees of the useful sciences by which means we are living in this world, the home of wretchedness and grievousness.[142]

Because the Persians first did this to his forefathers, Ibn Waḥshiyya cannot help gloating that it has been done to them by the Arabs: "The Arabs have done to the Persians what they did to the Nabateans [the Syriac-speaking rural inhabitants of Iraq], quite exactly and have revenged the Nabateans against the Persians."[143]

Severus Sebokht (d. 666/67 AD), a Syriac-speaking Christian from Iraq who died more than a decade after the Arabs conquered the Persians, sounds a similar note of wounded pride. But in this instance, it is directed against Greek speakers who held that Greeks are superior in the sciences and that there is no scientific knowledge among the "Syrians." After demonstrating that Ptolemy depended on Babylonian astronomy, he quips, "Nobody I think will dispute that the Babylonians are Syrians."[144] Elsewhere, he observes that Greeks would not make this assertion if they bothered to learn other languages and thus expose themselves to foreign scholarship.[145]

Although Severus lived at the dawn of the Islamic empire and Ibn Waḥshiyya at its setting, both men worried less about denigrating the scientific achievements of those who currently ruled Iraq, the Arabs, and more about the achievements of those who had conquered Iraq in the past and who still claimed cultural preeminence in their day—the Greeks for Severus and the Persians for Ibn Waḥshiyya. The Arabs did not merit prolonged polemic.

As in antiquity, the discussion of the ethnic origins of the sciences was intertwined with epistemology. Determining whether a human mind could invent the sciences bore on the question of which people originated it. Take, for example, the *History of Physicians* by the Christian translator Isḥāq b. Ḥunayn (d. 289 AH / 910f AD), the son of the famous Christian translator of Greek texts, Ḥunayn b. Isḥāq. In 290 AH / 902 AD, Ibn Ḥunayn listened to a debate between two men about the origins of medicine in the presence of the vizier, Abū al-Ḥusayn Walī al-Dawla. One of the men contended that Hippocrates was the first

[142] Ibid., 23.
[143] Ibn Waḥshiyya, *Nabatean Agriculture*, text 3, in Hameen-Anttila.
[144] Brock, "Syriac Attitudes," 23–24.
[145] See Saliba, "Science," 42n35.

physician, and the other retorted that there were many more before him. The vizier then turned to Ibn Ḥunayn and asked him to judge between them. Ibn Ḥunayn sided with the latter, whereupon the vizier asked him to write a book about the chronology of medicine. His *History of Physicians* was the result.

Most of Ibn Ḥunayn's history of medicine is based on a chronology of medicine written by John the Grammarian (Yaḥyā al-Naḥwī), an obscure Alexandrian commentator on medical texts who lived before the Arab conquest of Egypt (Muslim historians mistakenly equated him with John Philoponos).[146] John held that Asclepius I, from the island of Kos, had invented medicine through empirical methods. A chain of disciples transmitted the knowledge down the generations, who continued to enlarge the corpus of knowledge. Seven physicians in particular, including Hippocrates and Galen, the last great physician, made significant contributions.[147]

This is a thoroughly Greek and thoroughly profane explanation of the origins of medicine. In fact, Ibn Ḥunayn makes it a point at the very end of his history to write that medicine appeared 3,378 years before Abraham, and he makes no attempt to attribute its origins to Adam or a biblical prophet.[148] However, he does relate in his preface to John's chronology that there are competing explanations regarding the origins of medicine. Ibn Ḥunayn remarks that the proponents of these theories can be divided into two groups: those who believe that medicine existed from the beginning of humankind's existence and others who hold that it developed over time. Of the latter, there are those who believe that medicine is so complex that only God could have taught it to humans through inspiration (either through dreams or by guiding their experiences) and those who believe that humans invented it on their own. Various originators are put forward by the latter group, including the Egyptians, the people of Kos, Indians, and Persian sorcerers. Ibn Ḥunayn also relates that some say that Hermes invented (*istakhraja*) it, as he "invented all of the crafts and philosophy."[149]

Ibn Ḥunayn's arguments for the primacy of experiments in medicine resonate with those of his freethinking contemporary Abū Bakr al-Rāzī (d. 313 or 323 AH / 925 or 935 AD), a non-Muslim physician who believed humans could discern the nature of spiritual and material reality themselves and did not need the help of revelation.[150] In his *Spiritual Physick*, he writes about the human invention of medicine and astronomy.

> The Creator (Exalted be His Name) gave and bestowed upon us Reason to the end that we might thereby attain and achieve every advantage, that lies

[146] Swain, "Galen," 399.

[147] Isḥāq, *Ta'rīkh*, 75–79 (trans. Rosenthal, in "Isḥâq b. Ḥunayn's Ta'rîh al-Aṭibba'").

[148] Ibid., 80.

[149] Ibid., 73–74. Cf. a similar disagreement over the origin of Adam's scientific knowledge. The disagreement is between Yanbūshād and Qūthāmā, two of the Nabatean authors cited by Ibn Waḥshiyya in his *Nabatean Agriculture* (see Hämeen-Anttila, *Last Pagans*, 178).

[150] The third/eighth-century freethinker Abū ʿĪsā al-Warrāq and his pupil Ibn al-Rāwandī had made similar arguments before him. For a sampling, see Stroumsa, "Barāhima."

> within the nature of such as us to attain and achieve, in this world and the next. It is God's greatest blessing to us, and there is nothing that surpasses it in procuring our advantage and profit. By Reason we are preferred above the irrational beasts, so that we rule over them and manage them, subjecting and controlling them in ways profitable alike to us and them. By Reason we reach all that raises us up, and sweetens and beautifies our life, and through it we obtain our purpose and desire. For by Reason we have comprehended the manufacture and use of ships, so that we have reached into distant lands divided from us by the seas; by it we have achieved medicine with its many uses to the body, and all the other arts that yield us profit. By Reason we have comprehended matters obscure and remote, things that were secret and hidden from us; by it we have learned the shape of the earth and the sky, the dimension of the sun, moon and other stars, their distances and motions; by it we have achieved even the knowledge of the Almighty, our Creator, the most majestic of all that we have sought to reach and our most profitable attainment. In short, Reason is the thing without which our state would be the state of wild beasts.[151]

Like the empiricists, those advancing the dependency argument focused on medicine and astronomy; however, they attributed it to either the ingeniousness of the prophets or their receipt of revelation. The Iranian astrologer Abū Maʿshar al-Balkhī (d. 272 AH / 886 AD) wrote that most of the sciences had been invented by the first Hermes, who had lived before the Flood in Egypt (there were two more who lived after the Flood).[152] He was the first to speculate on medicine and the movements of celestial bodies. He was also the first to build temples (i.e., pyramids) in which God was glorified. Persians, Abū Maʿshar relates, identify this Hermes with Hōshang (see chapter 4). For his part, Abū Maʿshar identifies Hermes with Enoch—an equation favored by Hellenized Jews (see chapter 2)—and also the Qur'anic Idrīs.[153]

One problem remained, however: Abū Maʿshar had placed Hermes before the time of the Flood (a necessity, given his identity with Enoch). This would mean that his cultural inventions were destroyed by the deluge. To solve this problem, Abū Maʿshar employed the antique solution of buried knowledge.[154] As with the antique use of the motif, it not only solved a chronological problem but also legitimated whatever "rediscovered" knowledge was put forward in the discoverer's name.[155] Thus, when Hermes saw that a universal deluge was com-

[151] Rāzī, *Spiritual Physick*, 20.

[152] Ibn Juljul, *Ṭabaqāt al-aṭibbā'*, 5–10.

[153] The identification of Enoch with the Qur'anic Idrīs occurred very early in Muslim history (see chapter 3). This identification was also quite common among Abū Maʿshar's contemporaries. See Ṭabarī (*Jāmiʿ al-bayān* 17:73).

[154] He may have been directly inspired by a similar depiction of Hermes in Pseudo-Manetho's *Book of Sothis* (see Van Bladel, *Arabic Hermes*, 134–63).

[155] For example, in the introduction to the *Dhakhīrat al-Iskandar*, an Islamic-era book on alchemy and medicine, we read that Aristotle received the book from Apollonius of Tyana, who had

ing, he inscribed his knowledge of all the sciences and crafts inside the temples so that they would not be destroyed by the Flood. Sometime after the Flood, the second Hermes, who lived in Babylon, renewed these sciences.[156]

Later Muslim authors also attributed the origins of astronomy and medicine to antediluvian heroes. For example, Abū Ḥātim al-Rāzī (d. 322 AH / 933f AD), an Ismāʿīlī (i.e., Shīʿī Gnostic) propagandist, attributed the origins of astronomy to Hermes and the origins of medicine to Adam.[157] But whereas Abū Maʿshar had remained silent on the question of how these sciences were derived, Abū Ḥātim al-Rāzī held that God had revealed it to them.

Abū Ḥātim mentions these two etiologies in the course of his refutation of Abū Bakr al-Rāzī (see above), who had argued that humans had invented astronomy and medicine, which were of far greater use than the worthless words of prophets.[158] In keeping with his Ismāʿīlī belief that true knowledge could come only from one of God's chosen mouthpieces (which included infallible imams),[159] Abū Ḥātim retorts that "no one is able to know the nature of a thing with his mind and his innate capacity. This is not possible with respect to [human] minds."[160] To bolster his point, he observes that the contemporary knowledge of astronomy or medicine is simply too sophisticated and complicated for humans to have come up with themselves—an argument from complexity similar to that used by modern proponents of intelligent design. If humans had tried to come up with medicine, he avers, they would have poisoned themselves. But since medicine is so essential to human survival, it must have been given to humans by Adam.[161]

Another author who attributed the origin of some of the sciences to the prophets was al-ʿĀmirī (d. 381 AH / 992 AD), a Sunni theologian. Like Abū Ḥātim, ʿĀmirī credits Hermes with being the founder of astronomy. Drawing on some version of the Enoch story in the *Astronomical Book*, ʿĀmirī maintains that Hermes gained this knowledge after he ascended to the heavens and observed the motions of celestial bodies.[162] ʿĀmirī also relates that medicine, ac-

---

recovered the book from a tomb where Hermes had buried it (Ruska, *Tabula Smaragdina*, 72, 79; see Brown, "Hermes," 167n75).

[156] Abū Maʿshar relates a similar account about the Iranian kings in his *Ikhtilāf al-zījāt* (preserved in Ibn Nadīm's *Fihrist* 2:576 and Shahrazūrī's *Nuzhat al-arwāḥ*, 115–16). In it, he writes that to preserve their sciences from decay, the Persian kings wrote them down on a type of exceptionally durable paper called *tūz* and placed them in a fortress for safekeeping. Many years later, this fortress crumbled, and people discovered these documents, which contained the sciences of the ancients (*ʿulūm al-awāʾil*) in ancient Persian script.

[157] Rāzī, *Aʿlām*, 278–80.

[158] Ibid., 273–75.

[159] Rowson, "Futility." For a general overview of Ismāʿīlī skepticism toward sources of knowledge other than an imam or a prophet, see Joel Kraemer, *Humanism*, 29.

[160] Rāzī, *Aʿlām*, 291 (see Rowson, "Futility").

[161] Rāzī, *Aʿlām*, 293–313.

[162] ʿĀmirī, *Amad*, 145 (see Rowson, "Futility"). Similarly, the Ikhwān al-Ṣafāʾ also held that astrology was revealed to various figures who ascended to heaven, including Hermes/Idrīs and Ptolemy (see Joel Kraemer, *Humanism*, 160).

cording to physicians, was derived in the same way when Asclepius ascended to heaven and learned it there.[163] Both of these sciences, he argues elsewhere, are too subtle and complicated for humans to have derived themselves, although he allows that some of the more theoretical sciences, such as geometry, could have been derived by humans.[164]

In his *Amad*, ʿĀmirī advances an argument for the prophetic origin of the sciences in a form that is very familiar to us from the writings of Jewish and Christian apologists. In chapter 3, he writes that Empedocles learned his wisdom from the mysterious Qur'anic sage Luqmān, who lived at the time of David and to whom God had given wisdom (Qur'an 31:12). Empedocles then returned to Greece and conveyed his knowledge to his fellow countrymen. On account of this, he is considered the first Greek sage.[165]

Another Greek philosopher, Pythagoras, learned from the prophets more indirectly. While he was in Egypt, he associated with the companions of Solomon after they migrated there from Syria. From them he learned the natural and divine/metaphysical (*ilāhiyya*) sciences, having already learned geometry from the Egyptians (he also derived the science of melodies on his own). This prophetic wisdom was later passed on to the rest of the Greek philosophers through Socrates, who derived his wisdom from Pythagoras.[166]

This story was a staple in later Islamic histories of the Hellenistic sciences, which derive it, directly or indirectly, from ʿĀmirī 's *Amad*.[167] As for ʿĀmirī's source for the account, it is unclear. The general notion that Pythagoras studied with Jews can be found in pre-Islamic pagan, Jewish, and Christian sources (see above), and the story of him studying with Jews in Egypt can be found in Christian sources.[168] The latter leads Evrett Rowson to posit that ʿĀmirī derived this portion of the story from Christian sources.[169] In contrast, ʿĀmirī 's assertion that Empedocles was the first philosopher is found nowhere else—Greek and early Muslim sources say it was Thales or Pythagoras.[170] Moreover, the depiction of Empedocles as a student of Luqmān or any other prophetic source of wisdom is also not found in earlier literature.[171] This is not to say that ʿĀmirī

[163] ʿĀmirī, *Iʿlām*, 106 (see Rowson, "Futility").

[164] Rowson, "Futility," citing an unpublished manuscript of ʿĀmirī's "Taqrīr li-awjuh al-taqdīr."

[165] ʿĀmirī, *Amad*, 71.

[166] Ibid.

[167] For the transmission history, see Rowson's commentary in his edition of ʿĀmirī's *Amad*, 203–4.

[168] See Rowson in ʿĀmirī's *Amad*, 204–5, for references. The pagan philosopher Porphyry wrote that it was common knowledge that Pythagoras had learned geometry from the Egyptians (he also related that Pythagoras learned astronomy from the Chaldeans, arithmetic from the Phoenicians, and religious rites from the Magians; see Porphyry *Life of Pythagoras* 6). Porphyry's student Iamblichus wrote that Pythagoras had invented harmonics on his own (Iamblichus *Life of Pythagoras* 26, in Guthrie, *Pythagorean Sourcebook*; Rowson cites both in his commentary on ʿĀmirī, in *Amad*, 208n3).

[169] ʿĀmirī, *Amad*, 204.

[170] See Ibn Nadīm, *Fihrist*, 400.

[171] The point regarding Luqmān is Rowson's (206), commenting on ʿĀmirī's *Amad*. The conten-

made up the story; rather, it probably originated with a group of Ismāʿīlīs who, ʿĀmirī writes, "claim to be followers of his [Empedocles's] wisdom and speak of him with high esteem."[172] As Rowson points out, linking Empedocles with Luqmān would have been a good way to legitimate the writings ascribed to their teacher.[173] But one could also argue that ʿĀmirī made the link as a retort to these Ismāʿīlīs, who may have thought Empedocles received his knowledge through direct divine revelation.

Conclusion

The dependency argument put forward by ʿĀmirī, Abū Maʿshar, and others became the standard explanation for the origins of philosophy, medicine, and the exact sciences (or at least astronomy) among the decreasing number of Muslims who cared about such matters.[174] It is not that later Muslim authors failed to recognize the role of human ingenuity; rather, complex sciences such as medicine and astronomy were deemed too difficult for humans to have initiated on their own. As we have seen, this was not a perspective exclusive to Muslims. Pagans had made similar arguments. Moreover, it was not the only argument to be made, as the examples of Kindī, Fārābī, and Abū Bakr al-Rāzī demonstrate.

We have also seen that speculation on the origins of the sciences is not just about epistemology. It is also about identity and legitimacy. Authors delineate the origins of a tradition and its development over time to explain what it is and where they, the authors, are located in its transmission. Fārābī claims that philosophy began in Iraq and was reborn in Iraq in his day, where he studied at the feet of its guardians. Eusebius claims it came from the revelation of Moses and the Christians of his day were its true heirs, not the Jews or the pagans.

If histories of science serve many of the same functions across time, their shifting content can indicate social changes as well. One of the most important is the end of Greek learning as the intellectual coin of the realm in the Near East, which it had been since Alexander's conquests. The revival of the Greek sciences under the ʿAbbāsids obscures this somewhat, but by the twelfth century AD, the religious sciences had won the day and become the standard for intellectual discourse. This was not because "the sciences of the ancients" were repudiated so much as their useful parts were absorbed and their roots forgotten or ignored.[175]

---

tion that there is no instance of Empedocles studying with an Israelite prophet in early Islamic or antique literature is mine.

[172] ʿĀmirī, *Amad,* 71.

[173] Rowson, commenting on ʿĀmirī's *Amad*, 206.

[174] For example, Ṣāʿid al-Andalusī's *Categories of Nations.*

[175] See Sabra, "Appropriation," for some of the reasons.

Conclusion

THE GREEK, ROMAN, and Arab conquests of the complex civilizations of the Near East created social and political dilemmas for both the conquerors and the conquered because they brought together and destabilized the hierarchies of competing elites and their learned high cultures, which were tied to their status and legitimacy. Various groups addressed these dilemmas by writing culture myths in the language of the conquerors that encoded their visions of the cultural orientation of the empire and their place in it. This impulse often lies behind three kinds of protographical literature we surveyed: catalogs of firsts, native histories of civilization, and histories of the sciences. That their authors employed culture myths from ancient authorities is as much due to the time-tested social utility of these myths as it is to the authors' veneration of antiquity.

Despite the similar literary outcomes resulting from parallel political and social circumstances after the Greek, Roman, and Arab conquests, there is a major difference between the three that is reflected in the culture myths that followed: the conquering Arabs lacked a learned high culture. This meant that despite a shared intellectual interest in the origins of civilization after the three conquests, the scholarly contest in the Islamic period was as much about the content of the conqueror's culture as it was about the position and privilege of particular ethnicities in relation to that culture. This provided an opportunity for native elites like the Iranian scholar Ibn Qutayba to enhance their standing by cataloging the conquering Arabs' cultural geneaology and defending it against competing genealogies, including that of their own forefathers: more Arab than the Arabs, to modify a modern phrase.[1] Others, by contrast, invited the conquerors to become more like their native kings, an invitation that grew more appealing (or dangerous, in Ibn Qutayba's view) when the metropole was relocated near that of the previous Iranian empire.

Early Iranian Muslims preserved their culture myths in an Islamic framework to assimilate to the new order or to encourage the new order to assimilate to them. Some later authors jettisoned the Islamic framework altogether and reworked the material into national epics that justified the creation of new

[1] "More English than the English." See Ashcroft, Griffiths, and Tiffin, *Empire Writes Back*, 4.

Iranian kingdoms. No matter what the framework, the culture myths were generally the same, underscoring the ambiguity of boasting about ancient cultural achievements. Such boasting could be intended to draw conquerors closer as well as push them away.

Later premodern conquests of the region did not lead to the same level of interest in culture myths. This is probably because the various conquerors who swept in from Central Asia had either already accepted the dominant culture before they came (the Seljuqs and Ottomans) or adopted it when they arrived (the Mongols). Furthermore, the elite, learned culture of the lands they conquered had already been homogenized by the eleventh century AD, so there were no competing cultural visions.

We have to come all the way up to the modern period of European colonialism to find a parallel. Even then it is not entirely analogous, since no single European power conquered the entire Near East but rather two (the British and the French) colonized parts of it, which meant that there was not a single language of discourse. Nevertheless, the Europeans' conquest of other lands with civilizations of antiquity comparable with that of the Near East, such as India, created a historiographical competition for civilizational preeminence on a global scale between native elites and their European partisans similar to what took place at the regional level after the Greek, Roman, and Arab conquests.[2] Like its ancient antecedents, the resulting modern historiography of civilization's origins is not a product of the conqueror or of the conquered but a mixture of both.

European colonialism has also given rise to native accounts of Western science that ratify its content while distancing it from its originators, similar to native mythologizing about the origins of the Greek sciences after Alexander's conquests. The Jewish tradition of the "theft of philosophy" has a strong parallel today in claims that ancient scriptures anticipate modern Western scientific achievements, as attested by the numerous Muslim "scientific interpretations" (*tafāsīr ʿilmiyya*) of the Qur'an and similar glosses on the Vedas.[3]

Throughout the millennia of culture myths surveyed in this book, the most contentious and frequently mentioned innovation has been ironsmithing, and attitudes toward it were indicative of attitudes toward civilization in general, since it was usually implicated in civilization's rise. But despite the pro- or anticivilization sentiment of the authors of these myths, their attitudes toward technological development did not necessarily dictate the attitudes of those who venerated their texts. Hesiod and the Yahwist wrote myths that decried civilization's dark side, particularly the violence wrought by iron weapons. But the

[2] For examples, see Sreedharan, *Textbook of Historiography*, 398, 400–405, 424–29; and Majumdar, "Nationalist Historians," 416–22.

[3] For a brief analysis and comparison of Muslim and Hindu scientific interpretations of scripture, see Jansen, *Islamic Fundamentalism*, 163 and n. 17.

nations that venerated their stories also celebrated civilization's benefits and strove to add to them and claim them as their own. They did so by altering their culture myths in the retelling, emphasizing some myths more than others, or by inventing new ones to complement the old. Muḥammad, drawing on more positive scriptural assessments of civilization that grew out of this process, ignored negative culture myths, even crediting God with giving iron and ironsmithing to humans. But Muḥammad's followers later reintroduced negative culture myths in stories meant to supplement his account. Thus, regardless of the content of a nation's core culture myths, an equilibrium between pro- and anticivilization sentiment followed once the nation became part of an empire.

The supernatural never disappeared from human thinking about the origins of civilization. Although some early Greek thinkers downplayed or dismissed the influence of the divine on human innovation, many of their contemporaries continued to assert it. From that time on, one or the other position had its advocates, and neither position necessarily led to or discouraged scientific innovation. Romans could believe in Democritus's profane schema of culture's prehistory but not advance the exact sciences much beyond the Greeks. Muslims could believe in the divine origins of the sciences and still acknowledge that later humans, including their contempories, had advanced upon them.

Emblematic of the interplay between conquest and culture myths and the resulting ironies and shifting identities is Abū Maʿshar's story of Hermes mentioned in the last chapter and in the introduction. The Iranian astronomer associated the pagan Greek god Hermes and civilization's origins with Egypt and Babylon, drawing on lore that preceded (some would say produced)[4] Alexander's conquest of the Near East. In the aftermath, both Greeks and natives argued for the Eastern origins of civilization to address the intellectual, political, and social dilemmas posed by empire.

Abū Maʿshar's pastiche of this postconquest lore also speaks to the intellectual, political, and social dilemmas of his own day in ninth-century Iraq. The Arab character of the empire was fast fading, and the learned traditions of previous empires, Greek and Iranian, were reasserting themselves at the same time that the Islamic religious sciences were coming into their own. Which tradition deserved priority once the Arabs were gone, and how would they mesh with the religious culture the Arabs had left behind? Abū Maʿshar's solution is elegant because it addresses the multiple ethnic and intellectual problems posed by the Greek sciences and Iranian ascendancy in the ninth century AD: Hermes, equated with an antediluvian prophet named in the Qur'an and associated with ancient Egypt, Babylon, and Iran, had brought the arts and sciences to all of humankind. He was, at once, the scribal prophet of the Muslim traditionists, the founding king of the Iranians, and the sage of the scientists, a patchwork symbol of Iraqi pluralism.

[4] Vasunia, *Gift*, 249.

Bibliography

Reference Works

EI[2] = *Encyclopedia of Islam*. 2nd edition. Edited by P. J. Bearman, Th. Bianquis, C. E. Bosworth, E. van Donzel, and W. P. Heinrichs et al. Leiden: E. J. Brill: 1960–2005.

EIr = *Encyclopedia Iranica*. Online edition. Edited by Ehsan Yarshater et al. Columbia University. Available at www.iranica.com.

Primary and Secondary Sources

Abū al-Faraj al-Iṣfahānī. *Kitāb al-aghānī*. 25 vols. Edited by ʿAbd al-Sattār Aḥmad al-Farrāj. Beirut: Dār al-Thaqāfa, 1990.

Adams, Geoff W. *The Roman Emperor Gaius "Caligula" and His Hellenistic Aspirations*. Boca Raton, Fla.: Brown Walker Press, 2007.

Adler, William. *Time Immemorial: Archaic History and Its Sources in Christian Chronography from Julius Africanus to George Syncellus*. Washington, D.C.: Dumbarton Oaks Research Library and Collection, 1989.

Aeschylus. *Works*. Translated by Herbert Weir Smyth. Cambridge, Mass.: Harvard University Press, 1926.

Afsaruddin, Asma. *Excellence and Precedence: Medieval Islamic Discourse on Legitimate Leadership*. Leiden: E. J. Brill, 2002.

Agard, Walter R. "Athens' Choice of Athena." *Classical Weekly* 38, no. 2 (1944): 14–15.

Ahmad, Barakat. *Muhammad and the Jews: A Re-examination*. New Delhi: Vikas Publishing House, 1979.

ʿĀmirī (al-). *Al-Amad*. Translated in *A Muslim Philosopher on the Soul and Its Fate: Al-ʿĀmirī's Kitāb al-Amad ʿalā al-abad*, edited and translated by Everett K. Rowson. New Haven, Conn.: American Oriental Society, 1988.

———. *Kitāb al-iʿlām bi-manāqib al-Islām*. Edited by Aḥmad ʿAbd al-Ḥamīd Ghurāb. Cairo: Dār al-Kitāb al-ʿArabī, 1967.

Anderson, Gary A., and Michael E. Stone. *A Synopsis of the Books of Adam and Eve*. Atlanta: Scholars Press, 1994.

Anon. *Book of the Cave of Treasures*. Translated by E. A. Wallis Budge. London: Religious Tract Society, 1927.

Anon. *The Dinkard*. Volumes 1–13, 17, 19, edited by Peshotan Dastur Behramjee Sanjana. English translation by Ratanshah E. Kohiyar. Bombay: Duftur Ashkara Press, 1874–1928.

Anon. *The Zend-Avesta*, Parts 1–3, translated by James Darmesteter and L. H. Mills, edited by F. Max Müller. Oxford: Clarendon Press, 1887.

Arberry, A. J., trans. *The Koran Interpreted*. New York: Macmillan, 1955.

Aristotle. *Metaphysics*. Books 1–9, translated by Hugh Tredennick. Loeb Classical Library. Cambridge, Mass.: Harvard University Press, 1996.

Arjomand, Said. "ʿAbd Allah Ibn al-Muqaffaʿ and the ʿAbbasid Revolution." *Iranian Studies* 27, nos. 1–4 (1994): 9–36.
Armayor, Kimball. "Herodotus' Influence on Manethon and the Implications for Egyptology." *Classical Bulletin* 61, no. 1 (1985): 7–11.
Ashcroft, Bill, Gareth Griffiths, and Helen Tiffin. *The Empire Writes Back: Theory and Practice in Post-colonial Literatures*. London: Routledge, 2002.
Asheri, David, Alan Lloyd, Aldo Corcella, Oswyn Murray, and Alfonso Moreno. *A Commentary on Herodotus Books I–IV*. Oxford: Oxford University Press, 2007.
Ashtiany, Julia, ed. *Abbasid Belles-Lettres: Cambridge History of Arabic Literature*. Vol. 2. Cambridge: Cambridge University Press, 1990.
ʿAskarī (al-), Abū Hilāl. *Kitāb al-awāʾil*. 2 vols. Edited by Walīd Qassāb and Muhammad al-Misrī. Riyadh: Dār al-ʿUlūm lil-Tibāʿa waʾl-Nashr, 1980–81.
Athanassakis, Apostolos. *The Homeric Hymns*. Baltimore: Johns Hopkins University Press, 2004.
Athanassiadi, Polymnia, and Michael Frede, eds. *Pagan Monotheism in Late Antiquity*. Oxford: Clarendon Press, 1999.
Augustine. *City of God*. Translated by Marcus Dodds. In *Nicene and Post-Nicene Fathers*, ser. 1, vol. 2, edited by Philip Schaff. New York: Christian Literature, 1887.
Aws b. Ḥajar. *Dīwān*. Edited by Muḥammad Yūsuf Najm. Beirut: Dār Ṣādir, 1960.
Azraqī (al-). *Akhbār Makka*. 2 vols. Edited by Alī ʿUmar. Cairo: Maktabat al-Thaqāfa al-Dīniyya, 2004.
Bagnall, Roger S. "Decolonizing Ptolemaic Egypt." In *Hellenistic Constructs: Essays in Culture, History, and Historiography*, edited by Paul Cartledge, Peter Garnsey, and Erich Gruen, 225–41. Berkeley: University of California Press, 1997.
Bakrī (al-), Abū ʿUbayd. *Muʿjam mā istaʿjama min asmāʾ al-bilād*. Edited by Jamāl Ṭulba. 5 vols. Beirut: Dār al-Kutub al-ʿIlmiyya, 1998.
Balādhūrī (al-). *Ansāb al-ashrāf*. Edited by Maḥmūd al-Fardūs al-ʿAẓm. Damascus: Dār al-Yaqẓa, 1996.
———. *Futūḥ al-buldān*. Edited by M. J. de Goeje. Leiden: E. J. Brill, 1866.
Balʿamī. *Tarīkh-i Balʿamī*. Idarih-yi Kull-i Nigārish-i Vizārat-i Farhang, 1962 or 1963.
Barclay, John. "The Empire Writes Back: Josephan Rhetoric in Flavian Rome." In *Flavius Josephus and Flavian Rome*, edited by Jonathan Edmondson, Steve Mason, and James Rives, 315–32. Oxford: Oxford University Press, 2005.
Bar-Kochva, Bezalel. *Pseudo-Hecataeus, "On the Jews": Legitimizing the Jewish Diaspora*. Berkeley: University of California Press, 1996.
Barr, James. "Philo of Byblos and His 'Phoenician History.'" *Bulletin of the John Rylands Library* 57 (1974): 17–68.
Bashear, Suliman. *Arabs and Others in Early Islam*. Princeton, N.J.: Darwin Press, 1997.
Bashshār b. Burd. *Dīwān*. Edited by Muhammad al-Tāhir b. ʿĀshūr et al. Cairo: Maṭbaʿat Lajnat al-Taʾlīf waʾl-Tarjama, 1950–66.
Bastian, Dawn E., and Judy K. Mitchell. *Handbook of Native American Mythology*. Santa Barbara, Calif.: ABC-CLIO, 2004.
Baumgarten, Albert. *The* Phoenician History *of Philo of Byblos*. Leiden: E. J. Brill, 1981.
Bayhaqī (al-), Ibrāhīm b. Muḥammad. *Kitāb al-maḥāsin waʾl-masāwī*. Edited by Friedrich Schwally. Giessen: J. Ricker, 1902.
Beagon, Mary. *The Elder Pliny on the Human Animal: Natural History Book 7*. Translated with an introduction and commentary. Oxford: Oxford University Press, 2005.

Beeston, A.F.L., ed. and trans. *Selections from the Poetry of Baššār*. Cambridge: Cambridge University Press, 1977.
Bezold, C. *Die Schatzhöhle (Meʿárath Gazzé)*. Leipzig: Hinrichs, 1883–88. Reprint, Amsterdam: Philo Press, 1981.
Bhabha, Homi. *The Location of Culture*. London: Routledge, 1994.
Bīrūnī (al-), Abū Rayḥān. *The Chronology of Ancient Nations*. Translated by C. E. Sachau. London: W. H. Allen, 1879.
Black, J. A., et al. *The Electronic Text Corpus of Sumerian Literature*. Oxford, 1998–2006. http://etcsl.orinst.ox.ac.uk/.
Bleeker, C. J. *Hathor and Thoth: Two Key Figures of the Ancient Egyptian Religion*. Leiden: E. J. Brill, 1973.
Blundell, Sue. *The Origins of Civilization in Greek and Roman Thought*. London: Croom Helm, 1986.
Bohak, Gideon. "Recent Trends in the Study of Greco-Roman Jews." *Classical Journal* 99, no. 2 (December 2003–January 2004): 195–202.
Borgeaud, P., and Y. Volokhine. "La formation de la légende de Sarapis: Une approche transculturelle." *Archiv für Religionsgeschichte* 2 (2000): 37–76.
Bosworth, C. E. "The Heritage of Rulership in Early Islamic Iran and the Search for Dynastic Connections with the Past." *Iranian Studies* 11 (1978): 51–62.
Bowersock, G. W. "Herodotus, Alexander, and Rome." *American Scholar* 58 (1989): 407–14.
Boyce, Mary. "Middle Persian Literature." In *Iranistik II, Literatur I*, 31–66. Leiden: E. J. Brill, 1968.
Boylan, Patrick. *Thoth, the Hermes of Egypt: A Study of Some Aspects of Theological Thought in Ancient Egypt*. London: Oxford University Press, 1922.
Brock, Sebastian. "From Antagonism to Assimilation: Syriac Attitudes to Greek Learning." In *East of Byzantium: Syria and Armenia in the Formative Period*, edited by Nina G. Garsoian, 17–34. Washington, D.C.: Dumbarton Oaks, Center for Byzantine Studies, 1982.
———. "Jewish Traditions in Syriac Sources." *Journal of Jewish Studies* 30 (1979): 212–32.
Brown, Kevin. "Hermes Trismegistus and Apollonius of Tyana in the Writings of Bahá'u'lláh." In *Revisioning the Sacred: New Perspectives on a Bahá'í Theology*, edited by Jack McLean, 153–87. Los Angeles: Kalimát Press, 1997.
Burstein, Stanley. "The Babyloniaca of Berossus." In *Sources from the Ancient Near East*. Vol. 1, fasc. 5. Malibu: Udena Publication, 1978.
———. "Hecataeus of Abdera's History of Egypt." In *Life in a Multi-cultural Society: Egypt from Cambyses to Constantine*, edited by Janet H. Johnson, 45–49, SAOC no. 51. Chicago: University of Chicago Press, 1992.
Burton, Anne. *Diodorus Siculus*. Book 1, *A Commentary*. Leiden: E. J. Brill, 1972.
Carnoy, Albert J. *Mythology of All Races: Iranian Mythology*. London: Marshall Jones, 1917.
Cartledge, Paul. Introduction to *Hellenistic Constructs: Essays in Culture, History, and Historiography*, edited by Paul Cartledge, Peter Garnsey, and Erich Gruen, 1–19. Berkeley: University of California Press, 1997.
Castellino, G. "The Origins of Civilization According to Biblical and Cuneiform Texts." Translated by David Baker. In *"I Studied Inscriptions from before the Flood": Ancient*

Near Eastern, Literary, and Linguistic Approaches to Genesis 1–11, edited by Richard Hess and David Toshio Tsumura. 1956. Reprint, Winona Lake: Eisenbrauns, 1994.

Celsus. *On Medicine.* Translated by W. G. Spencer. Loeb Classical Library. Cambridge, Mass.: Harvard University Press, 1938.

Charles, R. H., ed. *The Apocrypha and Pseudepigrapha of the Old Testament.* 2 vols. Oxford: Clarendon Press, 1913.

———, trans. *The Chronicle of John, Bishop of Nikiu.* London: Oxford University Press, 1916.

Charlesworth, James. *The Pseudepigrapha and Modern Research.* Missoula, Mont.: Scholars Press for the Society of Biblical Literature, 1976.

Childs, Brevard S. "The Etiological Tale Re-examined." *Vetus Testamentum* 24, fasc. 4 (October 1974): 387–97.

Choksy, Jamsheed K. *Conflict and Cooperation: Zoroastrian Subalterns and Muslim Elites in Medieval Iranian Society.* New York: Columbia University Press, 1997.

Chuvin, Peter. *A Chronicle of the Last Pagans.* Translated by B. A. Archer. Cambridge, Mass.: Harvard University Press, 1990.

Cicero. *De natura deorum.* Translated by H. Rackham. Loeb Classical Library. Cambridge, Mass.: Harvard University Press, 1933.

Clay, Jenny Strauss. *Hesiod's Cosmos.* Cambridge: Cambridge University Press, 2003.

Clement of Alexandria. *Stromata.* Translated by William Wilson. From *Ante-Nicene Fathers.* Vol. 2, edited by Alexander Roberts et al. Buffalo, N.Y.: Christian Literature Publishing, 1885.

Cole, Thomas. *Democritus and the Sources of Greek Anthropology.* Cleveland: American Philological Association by the Press of Western Reserve University, 1967.

Copenhaver, Brian P. "The Historiography of Discovery in the Renaissance: The Sources and Composition of Polydore Vergil's *De inventoribus rerum,* I–III." *Journal of the Warburg and Courtauld Institutes* 41 (1978): 192–214.

Crone, Patricia. "*The Book of Watchers* in the Qur'an." In *Exchange and Transmission across Cultural Boundaries: Philosophy, Mysticism and Science in the Mediterranean.* Proceeding of a workshop in memory of Professor Shlomo Pines, Institute for Advanced Studies, Jerusalem, 28 February–2 March 2005, edited by H. Ben-Shammai, S. Shaked, and S. Stroumsa. Jerusalem: Israel Academy of Sciences and Humanities, forthcoming.

———. "How Did the Quranic Pagans Make a Living?" *Bulletin of the School of Oriental and African Studies* 68, no. 3 (2005): 387–99.

———. "Imperial Trauma: The Case of the Arabs." *Common Knowledge* 12, no. 1 (2006): 107–16.

———. "Jāhilī and Jewish Law: The Qasāma." *Jerusalem Studies in Arabic and Islam* 4 (1984): 153–201.

———. *Meccan Trade and the Rise of Islam.* Princeton, N.J.: Princeton University Press, 1987.

———. "Post-Colonialism in Tenth-Century Islam." *Der Islam* 83 (2006): 2–38.

———. *Slaves on Horses: The Evolution of the Islamic Polity.* Cambridge: Cambridge University Press, 1980.

Cuomo, S. *Technology and Culture in Greek and Roman Antiquity.* Cambridge: Cambridge University Press, 2007.

Dabiri, Ghazzal. "The Origins and Development of Persian Epics." PhD diss., UCLA, 2007.

Dalley, Stephanie, trans. and ed. *Myths from Mesopotamia: Creation, the Flood, Gilgamesh, and Others*. Oxford: Oxford University Press, 2000.

———. "Near Eastern Myths and Legends." In *The Biblical World*, edited by John Barton, 1:41–64. London: Routledge, 2002.

———. "Semiramis in History and Legend: A Case Study in Interpretation of an Assyrian Historical Tradition, with Observations on Archetypes in Ancient Historiography, on Euhemerism before Euhemerus, and on the So-Called Greek Ethnographic Style." In *Cultural Borrowings and Ethnic Appropriations in Antiquity*, edited by Erich Gruen, 11–22. Stuttgart: Franz Steiner Verlag, 2005.

Davidson, Olga. *Poet and Hero in the Persian Book of Kings*. Ithaca, N.Y.: Cornell University Press, 1994.

Davies, Philip. "Judaeans in Egypt: Hebrew and Greek Stories." In *Did Moses Speak Attic? Jewish Historiography and Scripture in the Hellenistic Period*, edited by Lester Grabbe, 108–28. Sheffield, UK: Sheffield Academic Press, 2001.

Dawlatshāh Samarqandī. *Tadhkirat al-shuʿarāʾ*. Edited by E. G. Browne. Leiden: E. J. Brill, 1901.

Déclais, Jean-Louis. *David raconté par les musulmans*. Paris: Cerf, 1999.

De Jonge, Marinus, and Johannes Tromp. *The Life of Adam and Eve and Related Literature*. Sheffield, UK: Sheffield Academic Press, 1997.

Derrida, Jacques. "From 'Plato's Pharmacy' in *Dissemination*." In *A Derrida Reader: Between the Blinds*, edited by Peggy Kamuf, 112–42. New York: Columbia University Press, 1991.

Dillery, John. "The First Egyptian Narrative History: Manetho and Greek Historiography." *Zeitschrift für Papyrologie und Epigraphik* 127 (1999): 93–116.

———. "Quintus Fabius Pictor and Greco-Roman Historiography at Rome." In *Vertis in Usum: Studies in Honor of Edward Courtney*, edited by John Miller, Cynthia Damon, and K. Sara Myers, 1–24. Leipzig: K. G. Saur, 2002.

Dillon, John. "Providence." In *Anchor Bible Dictionary–21*, edited by David N. Freedman, 5:520. New York: Doubleday, 1992.

Diodorus Siculus. *The Antiquities of Egypt: A Translation, with Notes, of Book I of the* Library of History *of Diodorus Siculus*. Translated by Edwin Murphy. New Brunswick, N.J.: Transaction Publishers, 1990.

———. *Library of History*. Vol. 3. Translated by C. H. Oldfather. Loeb Classical Library. Cambridge, Mass.: Harvard University Press, 1939.

———. *Library of History*. Fragments of Books XXXIII–XL. Vol. 12. Translated by Russel M. Greer and Francis R. Walton. Loeb Classical Library. Cambridge, Mass.: Harvard University Press, 1984.

Diogenes Laertius. *Lives of Eminent Philosophers*. Translated by R. D. Hicks. Loeb Classical Library. Cambridge, Mass.: Harvard University Press, 1925.

Dodds, E. R. *The Ancient Concept of Progress and Other Essays on Greek Literature and Beliefs*. Oxford: Clarendon Press, 1973.

Drews, Robert. "The Babylonian Chronicles and Berossus." *Iraq* 37, no. 1 (Spring 1975): 39–55.

Droge, Arthur J. *Homer or Moses? Early Christian Interpretations of the History of Culture*. Tübingen: J.C.B. Mohr, 1989.

Dziekan, Marek M. "Searching for the Origins of Things: On the ʿIlm al-Awāʾil in the Culture of the Arabic Middle Ages." *Studia Arabistyczne i Islamistyczne* 4 (1996): 13–27.

Edelstein, Ludwig. *The Idea of Progress in Classical Antiquity.* Baltimore: Johns Hopkins University Press, 1967.

Edwards, M. J. "Philo or Sanchuniathon? A Phoenicean Cosmogony." *Classical Quarterly* 41, no. 1 (1991): 213–20.

Ellis, P. *The Yahwist: The Bible's First Theologian.* Notre Dame, Ind.: University of Notre Dame, 1968.

Espín, Orlando O., and James B. Nickoloff. *An Introductory Dictionary of Theology and Religious Studies.* Collegeville, Minn.: Liturgical Press, 2007.

Eusebius. *Preparation for the Gospel.* 2 vols. Translated by Edwin Hamilton Gifford. Eugene, Ore.: Wipf and Stock, 2002.

Evelyn-White, Hugh G., trans. *Hesiod: The Homeric Hymns and Homerica.* Loeb Classical Library. Cambridge, Mass.: Harvard University Press, 1914.

Fārābī (al-), Abū Naṣr. *Alfarabi's Philosophy of Plato and Aristotle.* Translated by Muhsin Mahdi. New York: Free Press of Glencoe, 1962.

Firdawsī. *Shāhnāma.* Published as *Šach-nāme.* 9 vols. Edited by E. E. Bertels. Moscow: Izdvo Nauka, 1960–71.

———. *The Shahnama of Firdausi.* 5 vols. Translated by Arthur George Warner and Edmond Warner. London: Kegan Paul, Trench, Truebner, 1909.

Fortenbaugh, W. W., P. M. Huby, R. W. Sharples, and D. Gutas, eds. *Theophrastus of Eresus: Sources for His Life, Writings, Thought, and Influence.* Parts 1–2. Leiden: E. J. Brill, 1992.

Frick, Peter. *Divine Providence in Philo of Alexandria.* Tübingen: J.C.B. Mohr, 1999.

Gerson, Lloyd P. *God and Greek Philosophy: Studies in the Early History of Natural Theology.* New York: Routledge, 1990.

Gibb, H.A.R. "The Social Significance of Shu'ubiyya." *Studies on the Civilization of Islam.* Edited by Stanford Shaw and William Polk. Princeton, N.J.: Princeton University Press, 1962.

Ginzberg, Louis. "Aristotle in Jewish Legend." In *The Jewish Encyclopedia* 1:98–99. New York: Funk and Wagnalls, 1901.

———. *The Legends of the Jews.* 7 vols. Translated by Henrietta Szold. Philadelphia: Jewish Publication Society of America, 1936–1942.

Gmirkin, Russell. *Berossus and Genesis, Manetho and Exodus: Hellenistic Histories and the Date of the Pentateuch.* New York: T&T Clark, 2006.

Goitein, S. D. "Between Hellenism and Renaissance: Islam, the Intermediate Civilization." *Islamic Studies* 2 (1963): 217–33.

Goldziher, Ignaz. *Muslim Studies.* Vol. 1, translated by S. M. Stern. Albany: State University of New York Press, 1977.

Goodblatt, David. *Elements of Ancient Jewish Nationalism.* Cambridge: Cambridge University Press, 2006.

Goodrum, Matthew R. "Biblical Anthropology and the Idea of Human Prehistory in Late Antiquity." *History and Anthropology* 13, no. 2 (2002): 69–78.

———. "Prolegomenon to a History of Paleoanthropology: The Study of Human Origins as a Scientific Enterprise." Part 1, "Antiquity to the Eighteenth Century." *Evolutionary Anthropology* 13 (2004): 172–80.

Goshe, R. "Das kitāb al-awā'il: Eine literarhistorische Studie." In *Festgabe zur 25. Versammlung deutscher Philologen und Schulmänner*, 2–38. Halle, 1867.
Götze, A. "Die Nachwirking der Schatzhöhle." *Zeitschrift für Semitistik und verwandte Gebiete* 2 (1924): 51–94.
Grabbe, Lester L. "Hellenistic Judaism." In *Judaism in Late Antiquity*, edited by J. Neusner, 2:53–83. Leiden: E. J. Brill, 1995.
Graf, Fritz. "Mythical Production: Aspects of Myth and Technology in Antiquity." In *From Myth to Reason?* edited by Richard Buxton, 317–28. Oxford: Oxford University Press, 1999.
Greenfield, Johnas. "Apkallu." In *Dictionary of Deities and Demons in the Bible*, edited by K. van der Toorn, Bob Becking, and Pieter Willem van der Horst. Leiden: E. J. Brill, 1999.
———. "The Seven Pillars of Wisdom (Prov. 9:1): A Mistranslation." *Jewish Quarterly Review* 76, no. 1 (1985): 13–20.
Grimal, Nicolas-Christophe. *A History of Ancient Egypt*. Oxford: Blackwell, 1992.
Gruen, Erich S. *Heritage and Hellenism: The Reinvention of Jewish Tradition*. Berkeley: University of California Press, 1998.
———. "The Use and Abuse of the Exodus Story." *Jewish History* 12, no. 1 (1998): 93–122.
Grünbaum, Max. *Neue beiträge zur semitischen sagenkunde*. Leiden: E. J. Brill, 1893.
Gunkel, Hermann. *Genesis: Translated and Interpreted by Hermann Gunkel*. Translated by Mark E. Biddle. Macon, Ga.: Mercer University Press, 1997.
Gutas, Dimitri. *Greek Thought, Arabic Culture: The Graeco-Arabic Translation Movement in Baghdad and Early ʿAbbāsid Society (2nd–4th / 8th–10th centuries)*. London: Routledge, 1998.
Guthrie, W.K.C. *In The Beginning: Some Greek Views on the Origins of Life and the Early State of Man*. Ithaca, N.Y.: Cornell University Press, 1957.
———, trans. *The Pythagorean Sourcebook and Library*. Edited and introduced by Fideler. Grand Rapids, Mich.: Phanes Press, 1987.
Hadas-Lebel, M. *De providentia I et II: Les oeuvres de Philon d'Alexandrie*. Vol. 35. Paris, 1973.
Hallo, William. "Antediluvian Cities." *Journal of Cuneiform Studies* 23 (1970): 57–67.
———. "On the Antiquity of Sumerian Literature." *JAOS* 83, no. 2 (1963): 167–76.
Hamdānī (al-). *Al-Iklīl*. Translated by Nabih Faris. Princeton, N.J.: Princeton University Press, 1938.
Hämeen-Anttila, Jaakko. *The Last Pagans of Iraq: Ibn Waḥshiyya and His Nabatean Agriculture*. Leiden: E. J. Brill, 2006.
Hansen, William F. *Classical Mythology: A Guide to the Mythical World of the Greeks and Romans*. New York: Oxford University Press, 2005.
Hanson, Paul D. "Rebellion in Heaven, Azazel, and Euhemeristic Heroes in 1 Enoch 6–11." *Journal of Biblical Literature* 96 (1997): 195–233.
Hart, Gerald David. *Asclepius: The God of Medicine*. London: Royal Society of Medicine Press, 2000.
Hartman, Sven S. *Gayōmart: Étude sur le syncretisme dans l'ancien Iran*. Uppsala: Almqvist & Wiksells, 1953.
Hawting, Gerald. *The Idea of Idolatry and the Emergence of Islam: From Polemic to History*. Cambridge: Cambridge University Press, 1999.

Heck, Gene W. "'Arabia without Spices': An Alternative Hypothesis." *Journal of the American Oriental Society* 123 (2003): 547–76.
Heidel, Alexander. *The Babylonian Genesis*. Chicago: University of Chicago Press, 1951.
Hendel, Ronald. "Genesis 1–11 and Its Mesopotamian Problem." *Cultural Borrowings and Ethnic Appropriations in Antiquity*, edited by Erich Gruen, 23–26. Stuttgart: Franz Steiner Verlag, 2005.
Hengel, Martin. "Judaism and Hellenism Revisited." *Hellenism in the Land of Israel*. Edited by John Collins and Gregory Sterling, 6–37. Notre Dame: University of Notre Dame Press, 2001.
Henrichs, Albert. "The Sophists and Hellenistic Religion: Prodicus as the Spiritual Father of the ISIS Aretalogies." *Harvard Studies in Classical Philology* 88 (1984): 139–58.
Herodotus. *The Histories*. Translated by A. D. Godley. Loeb Classical Library. Cambridge, Mass.: Harvard University Press, 1920.
Hiebert, Theodore. *The Yahwist's Landscape: Nature and Religion in Early Israel*. New York: Oxford University Press, 1996.
Hippocrates. *On Ancient Medicine*. Translated by Mark Schiefsky. Leiden: E. J. Brill, 2005.
———. *Places in Man. Glands. Fleshes. Prorrhetic 1–2. Physician. Use of Liquids. Ulcers. Haemorrhoids and Fistulas*. Translated by Paul Potter. Loeb Classical Library. Cambridge, Mass.: Harvard University Press, 1995.
Hoffner, Harry. *Hittite Myths*. Atlanta: Scholars Press, 1990.
Homer. *The Iliad*. Translated by Richmond Lattimore. Chicago: University of Chicago Press, 1961.
———. *Odyssey*. Translated by Samuel Butler and edited by Louise Ropes Loomis. New York: W. J. Black, 1944.
Horace. *The Works of Horace*. Translated by Christopher Smart and Theodore Alois Buckley. New York: Harper & Brothers, 1863.
Horovitz, J. *Koranische Untersuchungen*. Berlin: Walter de Gruyter, 1926.
Ibn Abī Shayba. *Muṣannaf*. 9 vols. Edited by Saʿīd al-Laḥḥām. Beirut: Dār al-Fikr, 1989.
Ibn Abī Uṣaybiʿa. *ʿUyūn al-anbāʾ fī ṭabaqāt al-aṭibbāʾ*. Edited by Nizār Riḍā. Beirut: Dār Maktabat al-Ḥayā, 1965.
Ibn Durayd, Muḥammad b. al-Ḥasan. *Jamharat al-lugha*. 3 vols. Edited by Ramzī Munīr Baʿlabakkī. Beirut: Dār al-ʿIlm lil-Malāyīn, 1987–88.
Ibn Ḥabīb, Muḥammad. *Kitāb al-muḥabbar*. Edited by I. Lichtenstädter. Hayderabad, India: Maṭbaʿat Jamʿiyyat Dāʾirat al-Maʿārif al-ʿUthmāniyya, 1942.
Ibn Hishām. *Kitāb al-tījān fī mulūk Ḥimyar*. Sanʿaʾ: Markaz al-Dirāsāt waʾl-Abḥath al-Yamaniyya, 1979.
———. *Al-Sīra al-nabawiyya*. 5 vols. Edited by Jamāl Thābit et al. Cairo: Dār al-Ḥadīth, 1996.
Ibn Juljul. *Ṭabaqāt al-aṭibbāʾ waʾl-ḥukamāʾ*. Edited by Fuʾād Sayyid. Cairo: Maṭbaʿat al-Maʿhad al-ʿIlmī, 1955.
Ibn al-Kalbī. *Kitāb al-aṣnām*. Edited by Aḥmad Zakī. Cairo: al-Dār al-Qawmiyya lil-Ṭibāʿa waʾl-Nashr, 1965.
———. *Nasab al-khayl*. In *Kitābān fī al-khayl*, edited by Ibn al-Aʿrābī. Beirut: ʿĀlam al-Kutub, 1987.
———. *Nasab Maʿadd waʾl-Yaman al-kabīr*. 2 vols. Edited by Nājī Ḥasan. Beirut: ʿĀlam al-Kutub, 1988.

Ibn Manẓūr. *Lisān al-ʿarab.* 15 vols. Beirut: Dār Sādir, 1955–56.
Ibn Nadīm. *Fihrist.* 2 vols. Translated by Bayard Dodge. New York: Columbia University Press, 1970.
Ibn Qutayba. *Al-Maʿārif.* Edited by T. ʿUkāsha. Cairo: Dār al-Maʿārif, 1969.
Ibn Rusta. *Al-Aʿlāq al-nafīsa* Vol. 7 Leiden: E. J. Brill, 1967.
Ibn Saʿd. *Kitāb al-ṭabaqāt al-kabīr.* Edited by ʿAlī Muḥammad ʿUmar. Cairo: Maktabat al-Khānjī, 2001.
Ikhwān al-Ṣafā'. *Rasā'il ikhwān aṣ-ṣafā' wa-khillān al-wafā'.* 4 vols. Qom, Iran: Maktab al-Iʿlām al-Islāmī, 1985.
Isaac, Benjamin. *The Invention of Racism in Classical Antiquity.* Princeton, N.J.: Princeton University Press, 2004.
Iṣfahānī (al-), Ḥamza. *Ta'rīkh sinī mulūk al-arḍ wa'l-anbiyā'.* Beirut: Dār Maktabat al-Ḥayā, 1961.
Isocrates. *Isocrates.* Vol. 3, translated by La Rue Van Hook. Loeb Classical Library. Cambridge, Mass.: Harvard University Press, 1945.
Ivry, Alfred L. *Al-Kindi's Metaphysics.* Albany: State University of New York Press, 1978.
Jacobsen, Thorkild. "The Eridu Genesis." *Journal of Biblical Literature* 100 (1981): 529.
———. *The Treasures of Darkness: A History of Mesopotamian Religion.* New Haven, Conn.: Yale University Press, 1976.
Jacoby, Felix. *Die Fragmente der griechischen Historiker.* Leiden: E. J. Brill, 1958.
Jāḥiẓ. *Al-Bayān wa'l-tibyān.* 4 vols. Edited by ʿAbd al-Salām Hārūn. Cairo: Maktabat al-Khānjī, 1948–50.
———. *Al-Ḥayawān.* Edited by ʿAbd al-Salām Muḥammad Hārūn. Egypt: Muṣṭafā al-Bābī al-Ḥalabī, 1966.
Jansen, Johannes J. G. *The Dual Nature of Islamic Fundamentalism.* Ithaca, N.Y.: Cornell University Press, 1997.
Jawharī (al-). *Al-Siḥāḥ.* Edited by Imīl Badīʿ Yaʿqūb and Muhammad Nabīl Tarīfī. Beirut: Dār al-Kutub al-ʿIlmiyya, 1999.
Jeffery, Arthur. *The Foreign Vocabulary of the Qur'an.* Baroda, India: Oriental Institute, 1938.
John of Nikiu. *The Chronology of John, Bishop of Nikiu.* Translated by R. H. Charles. London: Oxford University Press, 1916.
Johnson, Aaron P. "Identity, Descent, and Polemic: Ethnic Argumentation in Eusebius' *Praeparatio Evangelica.*" *Journal of Early Christian Studies* 12, no. 1 (2004): 23–56.
Josephus. *The Works of Flavius Josephus.* Translated by William Whiston. Auburn, N.Y.: John E. Beardsley, 1895.
Junge, F. "Zur Fehldatierung des sog: Denkmals memphitischer Theologie oder der Beitrag der ägyptischen Theologie zur Geistesgeschichte der Spätzeit." *Mitteilungen des deutschen Instituts für ägyptische Altertumskunde in Kairo* 29 (1973): 195–204.
Justin. *Epitome of the Philippic History of Pompeius Trogus.* Translated by John Selby Watson. London: Henry G. Bohn, 1853.
Justin Martyr. *Apologia.* In *The Ante-Nicene Fathers,* edited by Alexander Roberts and James Donaldson. Grand Rapids, Mich.: W. B. Eerdmanns, 1986.
Kawashima, Robert S. "Homo Faber in J's Primeval History." *Zeitschrift für die Alttestamentliche Wissenschaft* 116, no. 4 (2004): 483–501.
Kennedy, Hugh. *When Baghdad Ruled the Muslim World.* Cambridge, Mass.: Da Capo Press, 2005.

Khalidi, Tarif. *Arabic Historical Thought in the Classical Period*. Cambridge: Cambridge University Press, 1994.

———. "The Idea of Progress in Classical Islam." *Journal of Near Eastern Studies* 40, no. 4 (1981): 277–89.

———. *The Muslim Jesus*. Cambridge, Mass.: Harvard University Press, 2001.

Khalīl b. Aḥmad. *Kitāb al-ʿayn*. Edited by ʿAbd al-Ḥamīd Hindāwī. Beirut: Dār al-Kutub al-ʿIlmiyya, 2003.

Khāliqī Muṭlaq, Jalāl. "Az Shāhnāmih tā Khudāynāmih." http://www.noufe.com/persish/Khaleghi/pdf/azshahnametakhodayname.pdf.

Khanbaghi, Aptin. "De-Zoroastrianization and Islamization: The Two Phases of Iran's Religious Transition, 747–837 CE." *Comparative Studies of South Asia, Africa and the Middle East* 29, no. 2 (2009): 210–12.

King, Helen. "The Origins of Medicine in the Second Century AD." In *Rethinking Revolutions through Ancient Greece*, edited by Simon Goldhill and Robin Osborne, 246–63. Cambridge: Cambridge University Press, 2006.

Kirk, G. S., and J. E. Raven. *The Presocratic Philosophers: A Critical History with a Selection of Texts*. Cambridge: Cambridge University Press, 1971.

Kister, M. J. "Ādam: A Study of Some Legends in Tafsīr and Ḥadīth Literature." In *Israel Oriental Studies*, vol. 13, edited by Joel L. Kraemer, 113–74. Leiden: E. J. Brill, 1993.

Kleingunther, Adolf. *Protos Heuretes: Untersuchungen zur Geschichte einer Fragestellung*. Philologus suppl. 26, no. 1. Leipzig: Dieterich, 1933.

Komoróczy, G. "Berosos and the Mesopotamian Literature." *Acta Antiqua* 21 (1973): 127–52.

König, Jason, and Tim Whitmarsh. "Ordering Knowledge." In *Ordering Knowledge in the Roman Empire*, edited by Jason König and Tim Whitmarsh, 3–42. Cambridge; New York: Cambridge University Press, 2007.

Kraemer, Joel L. *Humanism in the Renaissance of Islam: The Cultural Revival during the Buyid Age*. Leiden: E. J. Brill, 1986.

———. "Humanism in the Renaissance of Islam: A Preliminary Study." *Journal of the American Oriental Society* 104, no. 1 (January–March 1984): 135–64.

Kraemer, Samuel, and John Maier. *Myths of Enki, the Crafty God*. Oxford: Oxford University Press, 1989.

Kramer, Samuel. *Sumerian Mythology: A Study of Spiritual and Literary Achievement in the Third Millennium B.C.* New York: Harper & Brothers, 1961.

Kuhrt, A. "Berossus' Babyloniaka and Seleucid Rule in Babylonia." In *Hellenism in the East: The Interaction of Greek and Non-Greek Civilizations from Syria to Central Asia after Alexander*, edited by A. Kuhrt and S. M. Sherwin-White, 32–56. London: Duckworth, 1987.

Kuhrt, A., and S. M. Sherwin-White, eds. *Hellenism in the East*. London: Duckworth, 1987.

Kulaynī (al-). *Al-Kāfī*. 8 vols. Qom, Iran: Dar al-Kutub al-Islamiyyah, 1985.

Kvanvig, Helge. *Roots of Apocalyptic: The Mesopotamian Background of the Enoch Figure and of the Son of Man*. Neukirchen-Vluyn: Neukirchener Verlag, 1988.

Laërtius, Diogenes. *Lives of the Eminent Philosophers*. 2 vols. Translated by Robert Drew Hicks. Loeb Classical Library. Cambridge, Mass.: Harvard University Press; London: W. Heinemann, 1925.

Lambden, Stephen. "From Fig Leaves to Fingernails: Some Notes on the Garments of

Adam and Eve in the Hebrew Bible and Select Early Postbiblical Jewish Writings." In *A Walk in the Garden: Biblical, Iconographical and Literary Images of Eden,* edited by Paul Morris and Deborah Sawyer, 79–82. Sheffield, UK: JSOT Press, 1992.

Lambert, W. G. "The Twenty-one 'Poultices.'" *Anatolian Studies* 30 (1980): 77–83.

Lameer, Joep. "From Alexandria to Baghdad: Reflections on the Genesis of a Problematical Tradition." In *The Ancient Tradition in Christian and Islamic Hellenism: Studies on the Transmission of Greek Philosophy and Sciences,* edited by Gerhard Endress and Remke Kruk, 181–91. Leiden: Research School CNWS, School of Asian, African, and Amerindian Studies, 1997.

Lane, Edward William. *Arabic-English Lexicon.* Cambridge: Islamic Texts Society, 1984.

Lang, Katherine. "Awā'il in Arabic Historiography: Beginnings and Identities in the Middle Abbasid Empire." PhD diss., University of Chicago, 1997.

Leeming, David Adams. *Storytelling Encyclopedia: Historical, Cultural, and Multiethnic Approaches to Oral Traditions around the World.* Phoenix, Ariz.: Oryx Press, 1997.

Lefkowitz, Mary. *Not Out of Africa: How Afrocentrism Became an Excuse to Teach Myth as History.* New York: Basic Books, 1997.

Lenzi, Alan. "The Uruk List of Kings and Sages and Late Mesopotamian Scholarship." *Journal of Ancient Near Eastern Religions* 8, no. 2. (2008): 137–69.

Lesko, Leonard. "Ancient Egyptian Cosmogonies and Cosmology." In *Religion in Ancient Egypt,* edited by Byron Shafer, 88–122. Ithaca, N.Y.: Cornell University Press, 1991.

Leslau, Wolf. *Comparative Dictionary of Geʿez.* Wiesbaden: O. Harrassowitz, 1987.

Levey, Martin. "Ibn al-Wahshiya's 'Book of Poisons,' *Kitāb al-Sumūm*: Studies in the History of Arabic Pharmacology II." *Journal of the History of Medicine and Allied Sciences* 4 (1963): 370–77.

Lewis, Bernard. *Islam from the Prophet Muhammad to the Capture of Constantinople.* 2 vols. Oxford: Oxford University Press, 1987.

Lucan. *Pharsalia* [aka *Bellum Civile*]. Translated by Edward Ridley. London: Longmans, Green, 1905.

Lyman, Rebecca. "Justin and Hellenism: Some Postcolonial Perspectives." In *Justin Martyr and His Worlds,* edited by Sara Parvis and Paul Foster, 160–68. Minneapolis: Fortress Press, 2007.

Maccoby, Hyam. *The Sacred Executioner: Human Sacrifice and the Legacy of Guilt.* London: Thames and Hudson, 1982.

Majumdar, R. C. "Nationalist Historians." In *Historians of India, Pakistan and Ceylon,* 416–28. London: Oxford University Press, 1961.

Malkin, Irad. "Postcolonial Concepts and Ancient Greek Colonization." *Modern Language Quarterly* 65, no. 3 (September 2004): 341–64.

Mānīʿ (al-), ʿAbd al-ʿAzīz. "An Edition of *Ghāyat al-wasā'il ilā maʿrifat al-awā'il.*" PhD diss., University of Exeter, 1976.

Mansfeld, Jaap. "Aristotle and Others on Thales, or The Beginnings of Natural Philosophy." *Mnemosyne* 38, fasc. 1–2 (1985): 109–29.

Markiewicz, T. "Bocchoris the Lawgiver—or Was He Really?" *Journal of Egyptian History* 1 (2008): 309–30.

Masʿūdī (al-). *Murūj al-dhahab.* Edited by Yūsuf Asʿad Dāghir. Beirut: Dār al-Andalus, 1973.

———. *Murūj al-dhahab.* Edited by C. Pellat. 7 vols. Beirut: Université Libanaise, 1965–79.

Meisami, J. S. "The Past in Service of the Present: Two Views of History in Medieval Persia." *Poetics Today* 14, no. 2 (1993): 247–75.

———. *Persian Historiography to the End of the Twelfth Century.* Edinburgh: Edinburgh University Press, 1999.

Mellor, Ronald. "*Graecia Capta*: The Confrontation between Greek and Roman Identity." In *Hellenisms: Culture, Identity, and Ethnicity from Antiquity to Modernity,* edited by Katerina Zacharia, 79–128. Aldershot, UK: Ashgate, 2008.

Mendels, D. *The Land of Israel as a Political Concept in Hasmonean Literature: Recourse to History in Second Century B.C. Claims to the Holy Land.* Tübingen: J.C.B. Mohr, 1987.

———. "The Polemical Character of Manetho's *Aegyptiaca*." In *Purposes of History: Studies in Greek Historiography from the 4th to the 2nd Centuries B.C.*, edited by H. Verdin, G. Schepens, and E. De Keyser, 91–110. Louvain, Belgium: Universitas catholica Lovaniensis, 1990.

Michalowski, Piotr. "Commemoration, Writing, and Genre in Ancient Mesopotamia." In *The Limits of Historiography: Genre and Narrative in Ancient Historical Texts,* edited by Christina S. Kraus, 69–90. Leiden: E. J. Brill, 1999.

Milik, J. T. *The Books of Enoch: Aramaic Fragments of Qumran Cave 4.* Oxford: Clarendon Press, 1976.

Minorsky, V. "The Older Preface to the Shāh-nāmeh." In *Iranica: Twenty Articles,* 260–73. Tehran: University of Tehran, 1964.

Momigliano, A. *Alien Wisdom: The Limits of Hellenization.* Cambridge: Cambridge University Press, 1975.

———. "Greek Historiography." *History and Theory* 17, no. 1 (February 1978): 1–28.

———. "J. G. Droysen between Greeks and Jews." In *A. D. Momigliano: Studies on Modern Scholarship,* edited by Glen Bowersock and Tim Cornell, 147–61. Berkeley: University of California Press, 1994.

Morony, Michael. *Iraq after the Muslim Conquest.* Princeton, N.J.: Princeton University Press, 1984.

Moyer, Ian. "At the Limits of Hellenism: Egyptian Priests and the Greek World." PhD diss., University of Chicago, 2004.

Muqātil b. Sulaymān. *Tafsīr.* Edited by ʿAbd Allāh Maḥmūd Shiḥāta. 5 vols. Cairo: al-Hayʾa al-Miṣriyya al-ʿĀmma lil-Kitāb, 1979–89.

Murray, Oswyn. "Herodotus and Hellenistic Culture." *Classical Quarterly* 22, no. 2 (November 1972): 200–213.

Nelson, Stephanie Anne, and David Grene. *God and the Land: The Metaphysics of Farming in Hesiod and Vergil.* New York: Oxford University Press, 1998.

Nickelsburg, George W. E. *1 Enoch 1: A Commentary on the Book of 1 Enoch, Chapters 1–36; 81–108.* Minneapolis: Fortress Press, 2001.

Niesiołowski-Spanò, Łukasz. "Two Aetiological Narratives in Genesis and Their Dates." *Studia Judaica* 9 (2006): 367–81.

Nimis, Stephen. "Egypt in Greco-Roman History and Fiction." *Alif: Journal of Comparative Poetics* 24 (2004): 34–67.

Nöldeke, Theodor. *The Iranian National Epic, or, The Shahnamah.* Translated by L. Bogdanov. Philadelphia: Porcupine Press, 1979.

Norris, H. T. "*Shuʿūbiyyah* in Arabic Literature." In *The Cambridge History of Arabic*

Literature: ʿAbbasid Belles-Lettres, edited by Julia Ashtiany et al., 31–47. Cambridge: Cambridge University Press, 1990.

Noth, Albrecht, with Lawrence Conrad. *The Early Arabic Historical Tradition: A Source-Critical Study.* Translated by Michael Bonner. Princeton, N.J.: Darwin Press, 1994.

Noy, Dov. "Motif-Index of Talmudic-Midrashic Literature." PhD diss., Indiana University, 1954.

Oden, Robert. "Philo of Byblos and Hellenistic Historiography." *Palestine Exploration Quarterly* (1978): 115–26.

Omidsalar, Mahmoud. "Could al-Thaʿalibi Have Used the *Shâhnâma* as a Source?" *Der Islam* 75 (1998): 338–46.

Origen. *Contra Celsum.* Translated by Henry Chadwick. Cambridge: Cambridge University Press, 1980.

Pásztori-Kupán, István. *Theodoret of Cyrus.* New York: Routledge, 2006.

Philo. *Complete Works.* Translated by Charles Yonge. Peabody, Mass.: Hendrickson Publishers, 1993.

———. *Questions and Answers on Genesis.* Translated by Ralph Marcus. Loeb Classical Library. Cambridge, Mass.: Harvard University Press, 1953.

Philostratus. *Life of Apollonius of Tyana.* Vol 1, translated by Christopher Jones. Loeb Classical Library. Cambridge, Mass.: Harvard University Press, 2005.

Pindar. *The Odes and Selected Fragments.* Translated by G. S. Conway and Richard Stoneman. London: J. M. Dent, 1997.

Plato. *Plato in Twelve Volumes.* Vol. 9, translated by Harold N. Fowler. Loeb Classical Library. Cambridge, Mass.: Harvard University Press, 1925.

———. *The Republic.* Loeb Classical Library. Cambridge, Mass.: Harvard University Press, 1935.

Pliny. *Natural History.* Book 7, translated by Mary Beagon. Oxford: Oxford University Press, 2005.

———. *Natural History.* Book 7, translated by John Bostock. London: H. G. Bohn, 1855–57.

———. *Natural History.* Books 28–32, translated by W.H.S. Jones. Loeb Classical Library. Cambridge, Mass.: Harvard University Press, 1963.

Plutarch. *Moralia.* 14 vols. Translated by Frank Cole Babbit et al. Loeb Classical Library. Cambridge, Mass.: Harvard University Press, 1927–69.

Preuschen, Erwin. *Die Apokryphen Gnostischen Adamschriften.* Giessen: J. Rickerʿsche Verlagsbuchhandlung, 1900.

Pritchard, James, ed. *Ancient Near Eastern Texts Relating to the Old Testament.* 3rd ed. Princeton, N.J.: Princeton University Press, 1971.

Pucci ben Zeev, M. "The Reliability of Josephus Flavius: The Case of Hecataeus' and Manetho's Accounts of Jews and Judaism; Fifteen Years of Contemporary Research (1974–1990)." *Journal for the Study of Judaism* 24 (1993): 215–34.

Pythagoras. *The Life of Pythagoras.* Translated by Kenneth S. Guthrie. Alpine, N. J.: Platonist Press, 1919.

Ramsay, G. G., trans. *Juvenal and Persius.* Loeb Classical Library. Cambridge, Mass.: Harvard University Press, 1918.

Rāzī (al-), Abū Bakr. *The Spiritual Physick of Rhazes.* Translated by A. J. Arberry. London: John Murray, 1950.

Rāzī (al-), Abū Ḥātim. *Aʿlām al-nubuwwa.* Edited by Ṣalāḥ al-Ṣāvī et al. Tehran: Anjuman-i Shāhanshāhī-i Falsafah-i Īrān, 1977.
Redford, Donald B. *Pharaonic King-Lists, Annals and Day-Books.* Mississauga, Ontario: Benben Publications, 1986.
———. "Review of *Imhotep and Amenhotep* by Dietrich Wildung." *Journal of the American Oriental Society* 102, no. 1 (January–March 1982): 172–73.
Reed, Annette Yoshiko. "Abraham as Chaldean Scientist and Father of the Jews: Josephus, Ant. 1.154–168, and the Greco-Roman Discourse about Astronomy/Astrology." *Journal for the Study of Judaism* 35, no. 2 (2004): 119–58.
———. "Was There Science in Ancient Judaism? Historical and Cross-Cultural Perspectives on Religion and Science." *Studies in Religion/Sciences Religieuses* 36, nos. 3–4 (2007): 461–96.
———. "What the Fallen Angels Taught: The Reception-History of the Book of the Watchers in Judaism and Christianty." PhD diss., Princeton University, 2002.
Reiner, Erica. "The Etiological Myth of the Seven Sages." *Orientalia* 30, fasc. 1 (1961): 1–11
Ridings, Daniel. *The Attic Moses: The Dependency Theme in Some Early Christian Writers.* Göteborg, Sweden: Acta Universitatis Gothoburgensis, 1995.
Robinson, Neil. *Discovering the Qur'an: A Contemporary Approach to a Veiled Text.* London: SCM Press, 1996.
Rosenthal, Franz. "Isḥâq b. Ḥunayn's Ta'rîḫ al-Aṭibbâ'." *Oriens* 7 (1954): 55–71.
Roth, Norman. "The 'Theft of Philosophy' by the Greeks from the Jews." *Classical Folia: Studies in the Christian Perpetuation of the Classics* 32 (1978): 53–67.
Rotroff, Susan I. "The Greeks and the Other in the Age of Alexander." *Greeks and Barbarians: Essays on the Interactions between Greeks and Non-Greeks in Antiquity and the Consequences for Eurocentrism,* edited by John E. Coleman and Clark A. Walz, 221–35. Bethesda, Md.: Capital Decisions, 1997.
Rowson, Everett. "The Futility of Empiricism: Muslim Arguments for the Prophetic Origin of the Sciences." Unpublished ms.
Rubin, Zeev. "Ibn al-Muqaffaʿ and the Account of Sasanian History in the Arabic Codex Sprenger 30." *Jerusalem Studies in Arabic and Islam* 30 (2005): 52–93.
Rüpke, Jörg. *Religion of the Romans.* Translated and edited by Richard Gordon. Cambridge: Polity Press, 2007.
Ruska, Julius. *Tabula Smaragdina: Ein Beitrag zur Geschichte der hermetischen Literatur.* Heidelberg: Carl Winters Universitätsbuchhandlung, 1926.
Sabra, A. I. "The Appropriation and Subsequent Naturalization of Greek Science in Medieval Islam: A Preliminary Statement." *History of Science* 25 (1987): 223–43.
———. "Situating Arabic Science: Locality versus Essence." *Isis* 87, no. 4 (1996): 654–70.
Ṣāʿid al-Andalusī. *Book of the Categories of Nations.* Translated by Semaʿan Salem and Alok Kumar. Austin: University of Texas Press, 1991.
Said, Edward. *Culture and Imperialism.* New York: Vintage, 1994.
Saliba, George A. "Science before Islam." In *Science and Technology in Islam: The Exact and Natural Sciences,* vol. 4, edited by Aḥmad Yūsuf al-Ḥassan et al., 27–49. Paris: UNESCO, 2001.
Samuel, Alan E. *The Shifting Sands of History: Interpretations of Ptolemaic Egypt.* Lanham, Md.: University Press of America, 1989.

Sanders, Seth L. "Writing, Ritual, and Apocalypse: Studies in the Theme of Ascent to Heaven in Ancient Mesopotamia and Second Temple Judaism." PhD diss., Johns Hopkins University, 1999.

Savant, Sara. "Finding Our Place in the Past: Genealogy and Ethnicity in Islam." PhD diss., Harvard University, 2006.

Sawyer, John. "Cain and Hephaestus: Possible Relics of Metalworking Traditions in Genesis 4." *Abr-Nahrain* 24 (1986): 155–66.

Schäfer, Peter. *Judeophobia: Attitudes toward the Jews in the Ancient World.* Cambridge, Mass.: Harvard University Press, 1997.

Seal, Graham. *Encyclopedia of Folk Heroes.* Santa Barbara, Calif.: ABC-CLIO, 2001.

Seesengood, Robert. "Hybridity and the Rhetoric of Endurance: Reading Paul's Athletic Metaphors in a Context of Postcolonial Self-Construction." *The Bible and Critical Theory* 1, no. 3 (2005): 1–14.

Senner, Wayne M. *The Origins of Writing.* Lincoln: University of Nebraska Press, 1991.

Sethe, Kurt. *Imhotep, der Asklepios der Aegypter: Ein Vergötterter Mensch aus der Zeit des Königs Doser.* Leipzig: J. C. Hinrichs, 1902.

Shahbazi, A. *Ferdowsī: A Critical Biography.* Cambridge, Mass.: Harvard University Center for Middle Eastern Studies, 1991.

Shahrazūrī, Shams al-Dīn. *Kitāb nuzhat al-arwāḥ wa-rawḍat al-afrāḥ.* Edited by Muḥammad ʿAlī Abū Rayyān. Alexandria, Egypt: Manshūrāt Markaz al-Turāth al-Qawmī, 1993.

Sharon, Diane. *Patterns of Destiny: Narrative Structures of Foundation and Doom in the Hebrew Bible.* Winona Lake, Ind.: Eisenbrauns, 2002.

Shiblī, Muḥammad b. ʿAbd Allāh. *Maḥāsin al-wasāʾil fī maʿrifat al-awāʾil.* Edited by Muḥammad al-Tūnjī. Beirut: Dār al-Nafāʾis, 1992.

Sijistānī, Abū Ḥātim Sahl ibn Muḥammad. *Al-Muʿammarūn.* Edited by ʿAbd al-Munʿim ʿĀmir. Cairo: ʿĪsā al-Bābī al-Ḥalabī, 1961.

Smith, R. Scott, and Stephen Trzaskoma. *Apollodorus'* Library *and Hyginus'* Fabulae*: Two Handbooks of Greek Mythology.* Indianapolis, Ind.: Hackett Publishing, 2007.

Smith, Sidney. "Events in Arabia in the 6th Century A.D." *Bulletin of the School of Oriental and African Studies* 16, no. 3 (1954): 425–68.

Smith, Wesley. "Notes on Ancient Medical Historiography." *Bulletin of the History of Medicine* 63, no. 1 (1989): 73–109.

Sophocles. *Antigone.* Translated by Richard Jebb. Cambridge: Cambridge University Press, 1891.

Sozomen. *Ecclesiastical History.* Translated by Chester D. Hartranft. From *Nicene and Post-Nicene Fathers.* 2nd ser., vol. 2, edited by Philip Schaff and Henry Wace. Buffalo, N.Y.: Christian Literature Publishing, 1890.

Spence, Lewis. *An Introduction to Mythology.* 1921. Reprint, New York: Cosimo Classics, 2005.

Speyer, Heinrich. *Die biblischen Erzählungen im Qoran.* Gräfenhainichen, Germany: Schultze, 1931.

Spivak, Gayatri. "Can the Subaltern Speak?" In *Marxism and the Interpretation of Culture,* edited by Cary Nelson and Lawrence Grossberg, 271–313. Urbana: University of Illinois Press, 1988.

Sreedharan, E. *A Textbook of Historiography, 500 B.C. to A.D. 2000.* New Delhi: Orient Blackswan, 2004.

Stambaugh, J. E. *Sarapis under the Early Ptolemies*. Leiden: E. J. Brill, 1972.
Sterling, Gregory. *Historiography and Self-Definition: Josephos, Luke-Acts and Apologetic Historiography*. Leiden: E. J. Brill, 1992.
Stern, Menahem, ed. and trans. *Greek and Latin Authors on Jews and Judaism*. Vols. 1–2. Jerusalem: Academic Press, 1974.
Stern, S. M. "Yaʿqub the Coppersmith and Persian National Sentiment." In *Iran and Islam*, edited by C. E. Bosworth, 535–55. Edinburgh: Edinburgh University Press, 1971.
Stone, Michael E. "The Book of Enoch and Judaism in the Third Century B.C.E." *Catholic Biblical Quarterly* 40 (1978): 479–92.
———. *A History of the Literature of Adam and Eve*. Atlanta: Scholars Press, 1992.
Strabo. *Geography*. 8 vols. Translated by H. L. Jones. Cambridge, Mass.: Harvard University Press, 1917–32.
Stroumsa, S. "The Barāhima in Early Kalām." *Jerusalem Studies in Arabic and Islam* 6 (1985): 229–41.
Suter, David. "Fallen Angel, Fallen Priest: The Problem of Family Purity in *1 Enoch* 6–16." *HUCA* 50 (1979): 115–35.
Suyūṭī (al-). *Al-Muzhir fī ʿulūm al-lugha wa-anwāʿihā*. Edited by Muḥammad Aḥmad Jād al-Mawlā et al. 2 vols. Cairo: Dār Ihyāʾ al-Kutub al-ʿArabiyya, 1971.
———. *Wasāʾil ilā maʿrifat al-awāʾil*. Edited by ʿAbd al-Qādir Aḥmad ʿAbd al-Qādir. Kuwait: Maktabat Dār Ibn Qutayba, 1990.
Swain, Simon. "Beyond the Limits of Greek Biography: Galen from Alexandria to the Arabs." In *The Limits of Ancient Biography*, edited by B. McGing and J. Mossman, 395–434. Swansea: Classical Press of Wales, 2006.
Synkellos, George. *The Chronography of George Synkellos: A Byzantine Chronicle of Universal History from Creation*. Translated by William Adler and Paul Tuffin. Oxford: Oxford University Press, 2002.
Ṭabarī (al-). *Jāmiʿ al-bayān*. 30 vol. Egypt: Mustafā al-Bābī al-Halabī, 1954–68.
———. *Taʾrīkh al-rusul waʾl-mulūk*. Vol. 1, *From Creation to the Flood*. Translated by Franz Rosenthal. Albany: State University of New York Press, 1989.
———. *Taʾrīkh al-rusul waʾl-mulūk*. Vol. 5, *The Sāsānids, the Byzantines, the Lakmids, and Yemen*. Translated by C. E. Bosworth. Albany: State University of New York Press, 1999.
———. *Taʾrīkh al-rusul waʾl-mulūk*. Vol. 7, *The Foundation of the Community*. Translated by M. V. McDonald. New York: State University of New York Press, 1987.
Tacitus. *Complete Works of Tacitus*. Translated by Alfred John Church, William Jackson Brodribb, and Moses Hadas. New York: Random House, 1942.
Tatian. *Tatian's Address to the Greeks*. Translated by J. E. Ryland. Hila, Mont.: Kessinger, 2004.
Tavakoli-Targhi, Mohamad. "Contested Memories: Narrative Structures and Allegorical Meaning of Iran's Pre-Islamic History." *Iranian Studies* 29, nos. 1–2 (1996): 149–75.
Tawḥīdī, Abū Ḥayyān. *Al-Baṣāʾir waʾl-dhakhāʾir*. Edited by Wadād al-Qāḍī. 6 vols. Beirut: Dār Ṣādir, 1988.
Tertullian. *Apology and De Spectaculis*. Translated by Terrot R. Glover et al. Loeb Classical Library. Cambridge, Mass.: Harvard University Press, 1931.
Theodoret. *On Divine Providence*. Translated by Thomas Halton. New York: Newman Press, 1988.

Thraede, Klaus. "Erfinder II." *Reallexikon für Antike und Christentum* 5 (1962): 1191–1278.

———. "Das Lob des Erfinders: Bemerkungen zur Analyse der Heuremata-Kataloge." *Rheinisches Museum zur Vorgeschichte* 105 (1961): 158–86.

Van Bladel, Kevin. *The Arabic Hermes: From Pagan Sage to Prophet of Science*. New York: Oxford University Press, 2009.

Van der Eijk, Philip J. "Historical Awareness, Historiography and Doxography in Greek and Roman Medicine." In *Ancient Histories of Medicine: Essays in Medical Doxography and Historiography in Classical Antiquity*, edited by Philip J. van der Eijk, 1–32. Leiden: E. J. Brill, 1999.

VanderKam, James C. "The Angel Story in the Book of Jubilees." In *Pseudepigraphic Pespectives: The Apocrypha and Pseudepigrapha in Light of the Dead Sea Scrolls*, edited by Esther G. Chazon and Michael Stone, 151–70. Leiden: E. J. Brill, 1999.

———. *Enoch and the Growth of an Apocalyptic Tradition*. Washington, D.C.: Catholic Biblical Association of America, 1984.

Van Groningen, B. A. *In the Grip of the Past: Essay on an Aspect of Greek Thought*. Leiden: E. J. Brill, 1953.

Van Seters, John. *Prologue to History: The Yahwist as Historian in Genesis*. Louisville, Ky.: Westminster / John Knox Press, 1992.

Vasunia, Phiroze. *The Gift of the Nile: Hellenizing Egypt from Aeschylus to Alexander*. Berkeley: University of California Press, 2001.

Verbrugghe, Gerald P., and John M. Wickersham. *Berossos and Manetho, Introduced and Translated: Native Traditions in Ancient Mesopotamia and Egypt*. Ann Arbor: University of Michigan Press, 1996.

Vergil, Polydore. *On Discovery*. Edited and Translated by Brian Copenhaver. Cambridge, Mass.: Harvard University Press, 2002.

Wacholder, Ben Zion. *Eupolemus: A Study of Judaeo-Greek Literature*. Cincinnati: Hebrew Union College, 1974.

———. "Pseudo-Eupolemus' Two Greek Fragments on the Life of Abraham." *Hebrew Union College Annual* 34 (1963): 83–113.

Wallace-Hadrill, Andrew. "Pliny the Elder and Man's Unnatural History." *Greece and Rome* 37, no. 1 (1990): 80–96.

Wansbrough, John. *The Sectarian Milieu: Content and Composition of Islamic Salvation History*. Oxford: Oxford University Press, 1978.

Wāqidī (al-). *Kitāb al-maghāzī*. Edited by Marsden Jones. 3 vols. London: Oxford University Press, 1966.

Waxman, M. *A History of Jewish Literature: From the Close of the Canon to the End of the Twelfth Century*. Vol. 1. New York: Thomas Yoseloff, 1960.

Wensinck, A. *Muhammad and the Jews of Medina*. Translated and edited by Wolfgang Behn. 1908. Reprint, Freiburg im Breisgau: K. Schwarz, 1975.

West, Edward William, trans. *Pahlavi Texts*. Parts 4–5, edited by F. Max Müller. Oxford: Clarendon Press, 1897.

Westermann, Claus. *Genesis 1–11: A Commentary*. Translated by John J. Scullion. 1974. Reprint, Minneapolis: Augsburg Publishing House, 1984.

Wildung, Dietrich. *Imhotep und Amenhotep: Gottwerdung im alten Ägypten*. Munich: Deutscher Kunstverlag, 1977.

Wright, Benjamin G. "History, Fiction, and the Construction of Ancient Jewish Identities." *Prooftexts* 26 (2006): 449–68.

Yang, Lihui, Deming An, and Jessica Anderson Turner. *Handbook of Chinese Mythology*. Santa Barbara, Calif.: ABC-CLIO, 2005.

Yāqūt b. ʿAbd Allāh. *Muʿjam al-buldān*. 5 vols. Beirut: Dār Ṣādir lil-Ṭibāʿa wa'l-Nashr, 1955–57.

Zabīdī (al-). *Tāj al-ʿarūs min jawāhir al-Qāmūs*. Edited by ʿAlī Shīrī. 20 vols. Beirut: Dār al-Fikr, 1994.

Zamakhsharī (al-). *Al-Jibāl wa'l-amkina wa'l-miyāh*. Edited by Aḥmad ʿAbd al-Tawwāb ʿAwaḍ. Cairo: Dār al-Faḍīla, 1999.

——. *Rabīʿ al-abrār wa-nuṣūṣ al-akhbār*. Edited by Salīm al-Nuʿaymī. 4 vols. Baghdad: al-Jumhūriyya al-ʿIrāqiyya, Wizārat al-Awqāf wa'l-Shu'ūn al-Dīniyya, 1989.

Zhmud, Leonid. *The Origins of the History of Science in Classical Antiquity*. Translated by Alexander Chernoglazov. Berlin: Walter de Gruyter, 2006.

Ziriklī, Khayr al-Dīn. *Al-Aʿlām*. 8 vols. Beirut: Dār al-ʿIlm lil-Malāyīn, 1986.

Zubayrī, Muṣʿab b. ʿAbd Allāh. *Nasab Quraysh*. Edited by Levi Provencal. Cairo: Dar al-Maʿarif, 1953.

Index